SOLOMONIC JUDGEMENTS

SOLOMONIC JUDGEMENTS

Studies in the limitations
of rationality

JON ELSTER

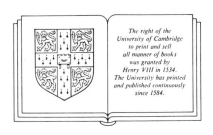

The right of the
University of Cambridge
to print and sell
all manner of books
was granted by
Henry VIII in 1534.
The University has printed
and published continuously
since 1584.

CAMBRIDGE UNIVERSITY PRESS

Cambridge
New York   Port Chester   Melbourne   Sydney

EDITIONS DE LA MAISON DES SCIENCES
DE L'HOMME

Paris

Published by the Press Syndicate of the University of Cambridge
The Pitt Building, Trumpington Street, Cambridge CB2 1RP
32 East 57th Street, New York, NY 10022, USA
10 Stamford Road, Oakleigh, Melbourne 3166, Australia
and
Editions de la Maison des Sciences de l'Homme
54 Boulevard Raspail, 75270 Paris, Cedex 06, France

First published 1989

Printed in the United States of America

Library of Congress Cataloging-in-Publication Data
Elster, Jon, 1940–
Solomonic judgements : studies in the limitations of rationality /
by Jon Elster.

p. cm.
Bibliography: p.
ISBN 0-521-37457-X – ISBN 0-521-37608-4 (pbk.)
1. Social choice. 2. Reasoning. 3. Decision-making. 4. Custody
of children. I. Title.
HB846.8.E47 1989
302'.13 – dc 19   88-33997
                                                    CIP

British Library Cataloguing in Publication Data
Elster, Jon, *1940–*
Solomonic judgements: studies in the limitations of
rationality.

1. Rationality
I. Title
153.4'3

ISBN 2-7351-0298-X hard covers (France only)
ISBN 2-7351-02971 paperback (France only)
ISBN 0-521-37457-X hard covers
ISBN 0-521-37608-4 paperback

CONTENTS

vi *Contents*

PREFACE AND ACKNOWLEDGEMENTS

The essays collected here form a sequel to *Ulysses and the Sirens* (1979) and *Sour Grapes* (1983). As in these earlier books, the topic is rationality: its scope, limits and failures. A common premise of all three books is the normative privilege of rationality in the study of human behaviour. Chapter I of *Ulysses and the Sirens* and chapter I of *Sour Grapes* attempted to define and defend this ideal of rationality. In the first chapter of this volume I discuss how the ideal breaks down when it fails to tell people what to do or when people fail to do what it tells them to do. The latter failure, that of irrational behaviour, was extensively examined in both earlier works and is more briefly discussed here, in I.4 and IV.4. The former failure, which arises when the notion of rationality is indeterminate, is the main topic of the present volume. The central argument is that rationality itself requires us to recognize this limitation of our rational powers, and that the belief in the omnipotence of reason is just another form of irrationality. To illustrate this proposition I consider both individual choice (mainly in chapters I and III) and social decisions (mainly in chapters II and IV).

The book is bound to convey a certain disillusionment with instrumental rationality. The emphasis is not wholly negative, however. On the more constructive side, I consider several non-instrumental grounds for action. With respect to political choices, I argue in chapter IV that *justice* offers a guide to reform which is more robust than outcome-oriented considerations could ever be. With respect to individual choice, I mention briefly in chapter I that *social norms* can supplement or replace rationality in the explanation of action. I develop the latter argument at much greater length in *The Cement of Society,* a companion volume to the present book in which I attempt to fill in some of the blanks left by the partial self-immolation of rationality.

Chapter I has not been previously published. Chapter II is a revised and much expanded version of the Tanner Lectures given at Brasenose College, Oxford, in May 1987. Chapter III first appeared, in largely the same form, in the *University of Chicago Law Review*, 1987. Chapter IV is an extensively rewritten version of an article that appeared in *Archives Européennes de Sociologie*, 1987.

The common origin of chapters II and III was a seminar at the Institute for Social Research in Oslo when, in a discussion of child custody legislation, Karl Ove Moene suggested that custody disputes might be resolved by the flip of a coin. The proposal seemed intriguing, not only as a way of resolving custody disputes but as a way of making up one's mind in many different contexts. In collecting examples and thinking about them, I was constantly helped and prompted by Fredrik Engelstad and Aanund Hylland. Together with Akhil Amar, Robert Bartlett, John Broome, G. A. Cohen, Jonathan Cole, J. Gregory Dees, Gerald Dworkin, Torstein Eckhoff, Ed Green, Stephen Holmes, Mark Kishlansky, William Kruskal, Isaac Levi, Karl Ove Moene, Maurice Pope, Kirsten Sandberg, Stephen Stigler and Cass Sunstein, they also gave extremely valuable suggestions and comments on earlier drafts of chapter II. I am also grateful for comments by the participants in seminars at the University of California, Davis, Yale Law School, and the University of Miami Law School.

Chapter III is part of a project on distributive justice in child custody and child placement, financed by the Norwegian Social Science Research Council. I am indebted to my colleague in this project, Kirsten Sandberg, for useful discussions and invaluable guidance, and to Robert Mnookin for helpful advice and criticism. I am also grateful for comments by Kirsti Strøm Bull, G. A. Cohen, Tove Stang Dahl, Torstein Eckhoff, Fredrik Engelstad, Helga Hernes, Aanund Hylland, Karl Ove Moene, Lucy Smith and Cass Sunstein, as well as the participants in the Seminar on Ethics and Public Policy at the University of Chicago and in the Legal Theory Workshop at Columbia University.

Several chapters, especially II and III, make ventures into legal theory, a field about which I knew nothing and still know next to nothing. Most of what I have learned, especially about American law, I owe to Cass Sunstein. Over the past years he has been an unfailing source of guidance, criticism and constructive suggestions. I could not have done without his help. I am also grateful to Tove Stang Dahl and Kirsten Sandberg for helping me to understand that the concerns of legal scholars are much closer to those of philosophers and social scientists than I used to think.

I

WHEN RATIONALITY FAILS

I.1 INTRODUCTION

There are two ways in which theories can fail to explain: through indeterminacy and through inadequacy. A theory is indeterminate when and to the extent that it fails to yield unique predictions. It is inadequate when its predictions fail. Of these, the second is the more serious problem. A theory may be less than fully determinate and yet have explanatory power if it excludes at least one abstractly possible event or state of affairs. To yield a determinate prediction, it must then be supplemented by other considerations. The theory is weak, but not useless. It is in more serious trouble if an event or state of affairs that actually materializes is among those excluded by the theory. In saying this, I am not espousing naïve falsificationism, but simply making the common-sense observation that it is worse for a theory to predict wrongly than to predict weakly but truthfully.[1] In the former case it must be replaced or modified, not supplemented.

My concern here is not with scientific theories in general, but with failures of rational-choice theory. As argued below, rational-choice theory is first and foremost a normative theory and only secondarily an explanatory approach. It tells people how to act and predicts that they will act in the way it tells them to. To the extent that it fails to give unambiguous prescriptions, it is indeterminate. To the extent that people fail to follow its prescriptions – to the extent, that is, that they behave irrationally – the theory is

---

[1] The Popperian view that it is better to predict strongly than weakly, because strong predictions are more likely to be falsified and therefore more surprising if not falsified, is quite consistent with this assertion. Popper was concerned with the ex ante choice of research strategy, whereas I am here discussing ex post properties of predictions.

inadequate. In this book as a whole, the emphasis is on the indeterminacy of rational-choice theory.[2] The inadequacy of the theory is also a constant theme, closely intertwined with that of indeterminacy. I argue, in fact, that *failure to recognize the indeterminacy of rational-choice theory can lead to irrational behaviour.*

Let me sketch, as a foil to the later discussion, how the problems of indeterminacy and inadequacy arise in another normative domain – the theory of distributive justice. My point of departure will be John Rawls's view that theories of distributive justice are constrained by data, namely people's intuitions about particular moral problems.[3] Any theory of justice can be judged, therefore, by the criteria of determinacy and adequacy. A theory of justice is determinate if it allows us to tell, at least in principle, how a given allocation problem should be resolved.[4] It is adequate if its prescriptions about particular cases correspond to our considered intuitions about these cases. In addition, of course, the theory must be independently plausible – that is, correspond to some general moral principle that can be defended in abstraction from particular cases.

Among the major theories of justice, utilitarianism and Robert Nozick's theory are intended to be determinate. Rawls's theory is explicitly not advanced with this intention. It is concerned only with the justice of the basic structure of society,[5] not with justice in particular contexts such as the allocation of scarce medical resources or the selection of soldiers for military service. For such problems, the theory has to be supplemented by local principles (II.5). I believe, although the argument cannot be made here,[6] that none of the major theories is adequate. Each yields consequences that are strongly counterintuitive,[7] even when we allow intuitions to be refined and modified pari passu with the construction of the theory. They stand in need of being replaced rather than supplemented.

---

[2] In Elster (1983a, 1984), the emphasis is mainly on cases of inadequacy.

[3] Rawls (1971), pp. 19–20.

[4] In practice, there are many obstacles to determinacy. Some theories require information about preferences and productive capacities that may be impossible to collect, if only because people may not find it in their interest to reveal them. Others require irretrievable information about events in the distant past or about hypothetical events that would have ensued if these past events had been different.

[5] Rawls (1971), p. 8.

[6] This is largely a euphemism for 'I don't yet have it'.

[7] Yaari and Bar-Hillel (1984); Frohlich, Oppenheimer and Eavey (1987).

These remarks are also relevant to the methodology of rational choice. Like the theory of justice, the theory of rational choice is constrained at both ends. On the one hand, the notion of rationality has to be independently plausible as a normative account of human behaviour. On the other hand, it has to yield prescriptions about particular cases that fit our preanalytical notions about what is rational in such cases. As in the case of justice, these notions are somewhat elastic. As we construct a theory of what is rational, some intuitions about what is rational in particular contexts may change. In particular, theory may force determinacy on our intuitions in situations where initially they were indeterminate. The theoretical notion of an equilibrium, for instance, can serve as a guide to intuition and action when otherwise we would not know what to think or to do. Other, more recalcitrant intuitions can force us to modify the theory.[8]

In what follows, I first set out the bare bones of rational-choice theory (I.2), including a discussion of whether desires can be rational. I then consider failures of rationality that are due to a lack of determinacy (I.3) and go on to discuss failures due to a lack of adequacy (I.4). In the final section (I.5), I briefly discuss how rationality can be supplemented or replaced by other guides to action. In chapter IV, the same issues are examined with respect to political choices.

I.2   RATIONAL ACTION

As I said, rational-choice theory is first and foremost normative.[9] It tells us what we ought to do in order to achieve our aims as well as possible. It does not, in the standard version, tell us what our aims ought to be. (Some nonstandard comments on this problem are offered later.) From the normative account, we can derive an explanatory theory by assuming that people are rational in the normatively appropriate sense. The privileged, but not exclusive status of this assumption is discussed in I.5

The central explananda of rational-choice theory are *actions*. To explain an action, we must first verify that it stands in an optimizing

---

[8] For an example, see Elster (1984), p. 121, n.17. A recent debate of similar issues is Binmore (1987).

[9] The following draws heavily on Elster (1983a), ch. 1, and Elster (1986a).

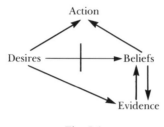

Fig. I.1

relationship to the desires and beliefs of the agent. The action should be the best way of satisfying the agent's desires, given his beliefs. Moreover, we must demand that these desires and beliefs be themselves rational. At the very least, they must be internally consistent. With respect to beliefs, we must also impose a more substantive requirement of rationality: they should be optimally related to the evidence available to the agent. (The substantive rationality of desires is discussed later.) In forming their beliefs, the agents should consider all and only the relevant evidence, with no element being unduly weighted. As a logical extension of this requirement, we also demand that the collection of evidence itself be subject to the canons of rationality. The efficacy of action may be destroyed both by the gathering of too little evidence and by the gathering of too much. The optimal amount of evidence is determined partly by our desires: more important decisions make it rational to collect more evidence. It is determined partly by our prior beliefs about the likely cost, quality and relevance of various types of evidence. Schematically, these relations can be represented as in Fig. I.1.

Rational action, then, involves three optimizing operations: finding the best action, for given beliefs and desires; forming the best-grounded belief, for given evidence; and collecting the right amount of evidence, for given desires and prior beliefs. Here, desires are the unmoved movers, reflecting Hume's dictum that 'reason is, and ought only to be the slave of the passions'.[10] Hume did not mean that reason ought to obey every whim and fancy of the passions. In particular, he would not have endorsed the direct shaping of reason by passion found in wishful thinking, illustrated

[10] Hume (1739), p. 415.

by the blocked arrow in the diagram. To serve his master well, a slave must have some independence of execution: beliefs born of passion serve passion badly.[11]

It follows from this sketch that rational-choice theory can go wrong at three levels, and that in each case the failure may be due either to indeterminacy or to irrationality. There may not exist a uniquely optimal action, belief or amount of evidence. Or people may fail to carry out the action, form the belief or collect the evidence as rationality requires them to do. Such failures of rationality are discussed in I.3 and I.4. Here I want to consider whether one can impose substantive rationality conditions on the desires of the agent.[12] The first idea that comes to mind is that it is rational to have the desires and emotions having which tends to make one happy. The proposal, however, turns out to be flawed.

To have a strong desire for something that is manifestly out of reach can make one desperately unhappy. Sometimes it seems natural to say that desires such as this are irrational. A person with moderate means who is tormented by desires for expensive luxury goods might well be called irrational. But we would not usually say that a person who lives in a totalitarian regime is irrational if he does not get rid of the desire for freedom that makes him deeply miserable.[13] Human beings are more than happiness machines:

Example 1. Psychiatric treatment of Soviet dissidents. The Serbsky Institute for Forensic Psychiatry in Moscow has become notorious for its treatment of political dissidents as mentally ill. 'Some psychiatrists have buttressed their argument about the dissenter's poor adaptation by pointing to the tenacity with which he acts out his beliefs despite the odds. . . . The dissenter does indeed operate in dangerous territory; the reaction of the regime is often harsh. But he is fully aware of the risks inherent in his non-conformist behaviour; his moral integrity compels him to take them. Some dissenters have parried the psychiatrists on this point by asking whether Lenin and his colleagues were "poorly adapted" when, in their struggle against

[11] Veyne (1976), p. 667.

[12] I discuss this question in Elster (1983a, secs. I.4 and III.4). For the closely related question of whether it makes sense to assess emotional reactions as rational or irrational, see Elster (1985a).

[13] We might want to say that, however, if his desire for freedom is caused by the fact that he does not have it. For a brief discussion of such 'counteradaptive preferences' see Elster (1983a), pp. 111–12.

the tsarist régime, they were constantly subject to harassment and arrest'.[14]

If anything, it is the conformist – the happy slave – rather than the dissident who appears to be irrational. Unconscious adaptation to the inevitable is a heteronomous mechanism, while rational desires must be autonomous.[15] One cannot be rational if one is the plaything of psychic processes that, unbeknownst to oneself, shape one's desires and values. This preanalytical idea is at least as strong as the intuition that rational desires are desires having which one is happy. Sometimes the two ideas point in the same direction. People who always most want what they cannot get are neither autonomous nor happy. People who adapt to their environment by a process of conscious character planning are both autonomous and happy.[16] At other times, as with the unconscious conformist and the autonomous dissident, the two ideas diverge. Tocqueville captures this ambiguity of conformism when he asks, 'Should I call it a blessing of God, or a last malediction of His anger, this disposition of the soul that makes men insensible to extreme misery and often even gives them a sort of depraved taste for the cause of their afflictions?'[17]

Could one entertain a similar proposal with respect to belief rationality? Could one argue, that is, that it is rational to have the beliefs having which one tends to be happy? In general, we would expect that one's happiness is best promoted by having beliefs which are well grounded in the evidence, since these are by definition the beliefs most likely to be true. Successful action requires correct factual beliefs. Yet in special cases this connection fails. To keep away from dangerous substances it may be necessary to have an exaggerated notion about the dangers of drug abuse.[18] High levels of motivation and achievement often require an unrealistically positive self-image, whereas people with more accurate self-perceptions tend to lose the motivations to go on with the business of living. They are sadder, but wiser:[19]

[14] Bloch and Reddaway (1978), p. 255.
[15] Elster (1983a), ch. 3.
[16] Ibid., pp. 117–19.
[17] Tocqueville (1969), p. 317.
[18] Winston (1980).
[19] Lewinsohn et al. (1980); see also Alloy and Abrahamson (1979) and, for a discussion of their findings, Elster (1985a).

Example 2. Stability of marriage. 'Expectations about divorce are partly self-fulfilling because a higher expected probability of divorce reduces investments in specific capital and thereby raises the actual probability'.[20] 'It is far from clear that a bride and a groom would be well advised to believe, on their wedding day, that the probability of their divorce is as high as .40'.[21] The low-probability expectations of divorce are only partly self-fulfilling. Our misplaced confidence in ourselves motivates us to achievements that make it somewhat less misplaced, but still less than fully justified.

A belief which is unjustified and indeed false may well be instrumentally useful, but it seems odd to call it rational. Rationality, as usually understood, is a variety of intentionality. For something to be rational, it has to be within the scope of conscious, deliberate action or reflection. Useful false beliefs obtain by fluke, not by conscious reflection upon the evidence. Although one cannot in the short run choose one's desires or one's emotional patterns, one can over time shape and bend them to some extent. Beliefs, by contrast, resist manipulation for instrumental purposes. Believing at will, for the sake of the good consequences of having the belief, is a self-defeating enterprise because one cannot – conceptually cannot – at one and the same time believe something and believe that the belief has been adopted on noncognitive grounds.[22] It is easy, therefore, to understand why exhortations to self-esteem, propagated by manuals on self-help therapy, have very limited success.[23]

I.3 INDETERMINACY

To explain and predict events or states of affairs, a theory must have determinate implications about what will happen under given initial conditions. Ideally, the implications should be not only determinate, but unique. Among all possible events or states, exactly one should be singled out by the theory. Outside quantum

---

[20] Becker (1981), p. 224.
[21] Nisbett and Ross (1981), p. 271.
[22] For this argument, see Williams (1973) and Elster (1984), sec. II.3. A recent challenge by Cook (1987) places too much weight on a (hypothetical) example in which the belief adopted at will is also the one that is better grounded in the evidence. A nonhypothetical example of a decision to adopt an unfounded belief would have been more convincing.
[23] Quattrone and Tversky (1986), p. 48.

mechanics, this is the explanatory ideal of science. A theory which does not yield unique predictions is incomplete. It may still, of course, be vastly superior to there being no theory at all. It can be very valuable to know that certain things will *not* happen. Also, for practical purposes it may not matter much which of the events consistent with the theory is actually realized. This said, the prospect of unique prediction dominates and guides scientific work.

In economics, and increasingly in the other social sciences, the neoclassical theory of choice holds out the promise of uniqueness. By its relentless insistence that all behavior is maximizing, it can draw on a basic mathematical theorem which says that every well-behaved function has exactly one maximum in a well-behaved set.[24] Moreover, in economic contexts many functions and sets are well behaved in the relevant sense. For the consumer, there is usually exactly one consumption bundle that maximizes utility within the set of purchases that satisfy his budget constraint. For the producer, there is exactly one combination of the factors of production which maximizes profit per unit of output.

Here I discuss a variety of circumstances under which rational-choice theory fails to yield unique predictions. There may be *several* options which are equally and maximally good. More important, there may be *no* option with the property that it is at least as good as any other.

The problem of multiple optima is, with one notable exception, relatively trivial. It arises when the agent is indifferent between two or more alternatives, each of which is deemed superior to all others. In such cases, rational-choice theory must be supplemented by other approaches to predict which of the equi-optimal alternatives will actually be chosen or 'picked'.[25] If they are very similar to one another, it is not important to be able to make this prediction. Nobody cares which of two apparently identical soup cans on the supermarket shelf is chosen. If the options differ from one another in offsetting ways, as when a consumer is indifferent between two cars with different strengths and weaknesses, the choice is more consequential. The car dealers will certainly care about the choice. I believe, however, that most

---

[24] Technically, the function must be continuous and the set be compact and convex.
[25] Ullmann-Margalit and Morgenbesser (1977).

cases of this kind are better described by saying that the consumer is unable to rank and compare the options (as discussed later). If he really were indifferent, a reduction of one dollar in the price of one car should induce a clear preference, but I do not believe it usually would.

The exception referred to is game theory, in which multiple optima abound. In noncooperative games with solutions in mixed strategies, it can be shown that an agent will always be indifferent between the strategy prescribed to him by the solution and any other linear combination of the pure strategies that enter into the solution, always assuming that the other players stick to their solution behaviour. John Harsanyi argues that the lack of a good reason for the agent to conform to the solution in such cases is a flaw in game theory as traditionally conceived. In his substitute solution concept, only 'centroid' or equiprobabilistic mixed strategies are allowed. This proposal reflects the idea that when there are several optima, one is chosen at random by 'what amounts to an unconscious chance mechanism inside [the agent's] nervous system'.[26] Here rational choice is supplemented by a purely causal mechanism. I have more to say about randomized strategies in II.3.

Nonexistence of rational choice is a more serious difficulty than nonunicity. The problem arises at all three levels distinguished earlier: when gathering evidence, when deriving beliefs from the given evidence, and when deriving an action from the given beliefs and desires. I shall consider them in the reverse order.

If the agent has an incomplete preference ordering, that is, is unable to compare and rank all the options in his feasible set, there may be no action which is optimal.[27] It would be misleading to say that the agent is irrational: having complete preferences is no part of what it means to be rational. On the contrary, to insist that preferences must be complete and all pairs of alternatives be comparable can be a form of hyperrationality – that is, of irrationality. Other forms of hyperrationality are considered in I.4.

Example 3. Choice of career. 'Life is not long, and too much of it must not pass in idle deliberation how it shall be spent: deliberation,

---

[26] Harsanyi (1977a), p. 114.
[27] A special and important case is that of moral conflict, discussed in Levi (1986).

which those who begin it by prudence, and continue it with subtlety, must, after long expence of thought, conclude by chance. To prefer one future mode of life to another, upon just reasons, requires faculties which it has not pleased our Creator to give to us'.[28] Suppose that I am about to choose between going to law school or to a school of forestry – a choice not simply of career but of lifestyle. I am attracted to both professions, but I cannot rank and compare them.[29] If I had tried both for a lifetime, I might be able to make an informed choice between them. As it is, I know too little about them to make a rational decision. What often happens in such cases is that peripheral considerations move to the center. In my ignorance about the first decimal – whether my life will go better as a lawyer or as a forester – I look to the second decimal. Perhaps I opt for law school because that will make it easier for me to visit my parents on weekends. This way of deciding is as good as any – but it is not one that can be underwritten by rational choice as superior to, say, just tossing a coin.

The nonexistence of an optimal action can also arise because of peculiar features of the feasible set. In planning models with infinite horizons and no time discounting, one can run into the paradox that 'there is always an incentive to postpone consumption: on the other hand postponing consumption for ever is clearly not optimal'.[30] While a theoretical possibility, this problem is not central to actual decision making. By contrast, the difficulties stemming from incomplete preferences are real and important. In addition to the problem of intrapersonal comparisons of welfare referred to in Example 3, the difficulty of making interpersonal comparisons can prevent us from ranking the options, if the ranking takes account of the welfare others derive from them.[31]

At the next level, nonexistence of an optimal belief can arise in two ways: because of uncertainty and because of strategic interaction. 'Uncertainty' here means radical ignorance, the lack of ability to assign numerical probabilities to the possible outcomes associ-

---

[28] J. Boswell, *The Life of Samuel Johnson,* A.D. 1766 (Aetat 57), a letter from Johnson to Boswell dated 21 August 1766. I owe this reference to John Broome.
[29] If I know myself well, I may be able to predict that whatever I do I shall end up preferring the occupation I choose, or perhaps the one that I do not choose, but this is not to know which choice will make me more happy.
[30] Heal (1973), p. 300.
[31] Sen and Williams (1982), p. 17.

ated with the various options. If such assignments are possible, we face a problem of decision making under risk, in which the rational decision rule – to maximize expected utility – can be counted on to yield an optimal choice. Farmers deciding on a crop mix or doctors deciding whether to operate act under risk. They can rely on well-defined probabilities derived from past frequencies. Stock market speculators, soldiers and others who have to act in novel situations cannot rely on frequencies. If they have sufficient information and good judgement, they may be able to make good probability estimates to feed into the expected utility calculus. If they have little information or poor judgement, rationality requires them to abstain from forming and acting upon such estimates. To attempt to do so would, for them, be a form of hyperrationality.

Example 4. Nuclear waste. 'Different geological mechanisms may be capable of generating the release of radioactive waste in the environment. Among these are groundwater flow, faulting, diapirism, erosion, fall of meteorites, magma intrusion, and modification of the drainage level of water. An approach to geological confinement is often sought by trying to quantify the probability of occurrence of any of these events and their nuisance value to man. Then, by combining these probabilities and nuisance values, one tries to assess the safety coefficient of the repository and to compare it to the accepted safety coefficients for present risks. This approach does not seem realistic to us *because basically the earth's development has not been a random phenomenon* (possibly apart from the fall of meteorites) and no geologist can seriously give reasonable figures for these probabilities'.[32] Here is a case in which objective probabilities and judgemental, subjective probabilities are equally out of reach.

When the situation is recognized as one of uncertainty, rational-choice theory is limited, but not powerless. Sometimes we are able to dismiss an option in the presence of another that, regardless of which state of the world obtains, has better consequences. Having done this, however, we are often left with several options for each of which there is some state in which it has better consequences than one of the others. Decision theory tells us that in choosing among these we are allowed to take account only of the best and

---

[32] De Marsily et al. (1977), p. 521. Italics added.

the worst consequences of each action.[33] This may also narrow the field a bit, but often more than one option will be left. In choosing among these, one may adopt the rule of thumb to choose the option with the best worst-consequences (maximin), but there are no grounds for saying that this is more rational than to choose the option with best best-consequences (maximax). To illustrate, consider the following matrix of outcomes as dependent on actions and states:

	S_1	S_2	S_3
A_1	3	4	5
A_2	1	2	8
A_3	2	0	7
A_4	0	0	6

Outcome A_4 can be excluded from consideration since under any state of affairs it yields worse consequences than A_2. Among the remaining, A_3 can also be excluded since both its best consequence and its worst consequence are worse than those of A_2. Of the remaining, maximin reasoning would make us prefer A_1 over A_2, while maximax would lead to the opposite choice. Psychological theories may be able to explain which choice will be made, but rational-choice theory, by itself, is indeterminate.

A special case arises when we have to choose among several scientific theories. Let us assume that each theory assigns numerical probabilities to the events that can occur, but that the choice of one theory rather than another is a matter of uncertainty. Controversies about the effect of CO_2 release in the atmosphere are of this kind. As shown by Jørgen Aasness and Aanund Hylland in unpublished work, this kind of theoretical uncertainty is less devastating than total ignorance, since we can use the content of the theories even if we do not know which of them is correct. If we can assume that one of them is correct, many abstractly possible states of affairs can be excluded and the optimal decision may differ from what it would have been had there been no restrictions on what could happen.

---

[33] Luce and Raiffa (1957), p. 296; Arrow and Hurwicz (1971). Other proposals are discussed in I.5.

To illustrate the point, assume that we have to choose between acts A_1 and A_2. There are two theories T_1 and T_2. According to T_1, state S_1 occurs with probability 1/3 and state S_2 with probability 2/3. According to T_3, state S_3 is certain to occur. The act–state matrix is the following:

	S_1	S_2	S_3
A_1	12	0	6
A_2	3	15	5

The best and worst outcomes of A_1 are, respectively, 12 and 0; those of A_2, 15 and 3. Define now X as the set of all triples $(\frac{2}{3} \cdot b, \frac{1}{3} \cdot b, 1 - b)$, where b ranges from 0 to 1. X is a subset of the set Y of all triples $(p_1, p_2, 1 - p_1 - p_2)$, with p_1 and p_2 ranging from 0 to 1. Y can be understood as the set of all abstractly possible probability vectors for the states S_i, whereas X is the restricted set that incorporates the information provided by the two theories. The standard theory of choice under uncertainty, defined over the full set Y, says that A_2 should be chosen, since it has a better best-consequence and a better worst-consequence than A_1. On the restricted set, however, A_1 is the best choice. It has a utility of $2b + 6$, whereas A_2 yields only $2b + 5$.

Later chapters provide several illustrations of choice under uncertainty. Chapter II, in particular, surveys a wide range of cases in which one might as well toss a coin to make up one's mind. Chapters III and IV consider in more detail the choice of custodial parent and political reform as examples of decision making under uncertainty.

Consider next strategic interaction as an obstacle to rational-belief formation. Often, rational choice requires beliefs about choices to be made by other people. These beliefs, to be rational, must take account of the fact that these others are similarly forming beliefs about oneself and about each other. Sometimes, these beliefs are indeterminate, when the situation has multiple equilibria with different winners and losers. The games of Chicken and Battle of the Sexes are well-known examples. Each of these games has two equilibria, each of which is better for both players than the worst outcome and preferred by one party to the other equilibrium. In the absence of enforcement or commitment devices, there is no way in which a player can form a rational belief about what the other will do.[34]

> *Example 5. Rational expectations.* To make decisions about consumption and investment, economic agents must form expectations about the future state of the economy. According to an earlier view, these are 'adaptive expectations', or extrapolations from current and past states. This view is unsatisfactory, because it assumes that people react mechanically without using all the information available to them. For instance, following the quadrupling of oil prices in 1973, we would expect expectations to change more radically and rapidly than what would be predicted by the theory of adaptive expectations. The theory of rational expectations, which emerged as a dominant paradigm in the 1970s, assumes that people are forward looking, not backward looking, when forming their expectations and that, moreover, they make the best use of the information available to them. Essentially, people predict the future development of the economy using a correct economic model. Since expectations are part of the model, rational expectations must be self-fulfilling. The problem[35] is that often there are several sets of expectations about the economy that, if held by everybody, would be self-fulfilling. In the absence of government intervention to eliminate some of the equilibria, rational agents will not be able to form mutually supporting, self-fulfilling expectations.

Uncertainty and strategic interaction, taken separately, create problems for rational belief formation. When both are present, they wreak havoc. In planning for war, generals are hindered both by uncertainty about whether their sophisticated systems will work and by strategic complexities. The old dictum – Don't base your plans on the enemy's intentions but on his capabilities – no longer applies, if it ever did, since generals are equally uncertain about the effectiveness of the weapons of the enemy (and about the degree of uncertainty among the generals on the other side).

[34] At least this holds for the symmetric version of these games. With asymmetries, tacit bargaining may lead the parties to converge to the equilibrium that favours the party who is least worried by the prospect of the worst outcome. The weak may accept a legal regime that favours the strong because, unlike the strong, they cannot survive in the state of nature.

[35] Actually, one of the many problems that beset rational-expectations theory. For a survey, see Begg (1982), pp. 61–70.

Example 6. Explaining investment. 'The outstanding fact is the extreme precariousness of the basis of knowledge on which our estimates of prospective yield will have to be made. Our knowledge of the factors which will govern the yield of an investment some years hence is usually very slight and often negligible. If we speak frankly, we have to admit that our basis of knowledge for estimating the yield ten years hence of a railway, a copper mine, a textile factor, the goodwill of a patent medicine, an Atlantic liner, a building in the city of London amounts to little and sometimes to nothing; or even five years hence'.[36] For the special case of investment in research and innovation, this lack of foreknowledge decomposes into the elements of uncertainty and strategic interaction. On the one hand, the outcome of innovative activities is inherently uncertain. One may strike gold, or find nothing. As Humphrey Lyttelton is reported to have said, 'If I knew where jazz was going I'd be there already'. But suppose one could know how the chance of finding gold is related to the amount one has invested. Under the 'winner-take-all' system of modern industry, it also matters whether one finds it before others do. If other firms invest massively, the chances that a given firm will be first past the post may be too small to make the investment worth while. If other firms do not invest, the chances are much higher. But if it is true of each firm that it should invest if and only if others do not, it has no basis for anticipating what others will do.[37] Entrepreneurs might as well follow Keynes's advice and be guided by their 'animal spirits'.

Finally, determinacy problems arise with respect to the optimal amount of information one should collect before forming an opinion. Information is useful, but costly to acquire. Ideally, the rational agent would strike a balance between these two considerations: he would acquire information up to the point at which the marginal cost of acquiring information equaled its expected marginal value. In some areas of decision making these calculations can be carried out with great accuracy. Thus 'To detect intestinal cancer, it has become common to perform a series of six inexpensive tests ('guaiacs') on a person's stool. The benefits of the first two tests are significant. However, when calculations are done for each of the last four tests to determine the costs of detecting a case of cancer (not even curing it), the costs are discovered to be

---

[36] Keynes (1936), pp. 149–50.
[37] Dasgupta and Stiglitz (1980).

$49 150, $469 534, $4 724 695 and $47 107 214, respectively. To some these calculations suggest that the routine should be reduced, say to a three-guaiac test'.[38]

Sometimes it is impossible to estimate the marginal cost and benefit of information. Consider a general in the midst of battle who does not know the exact disposition of the enemy troops. The value of more information, while potentially great, cannot be ascertained. Determining the expected value would require a highly implausible ability to form numerical probability estimates concerning the possible enemy positions. (Indeterminacy of rational belief due to strategic interaction is important here.) The costs of acquiring information are equally elusive. The opportunity costs might be enormous, if the time spent gathering information offered the enemy a chance to attack or to prepare his defence, or they might be quite trivial. Under such circumstances, one might as well follow Napoleon's maxim 'On s'engage et puis on voit'.

In between these extremes – medical diagnosis and the conduct of battle – fall most everyday situations. The observations that a rational person should make 'greater investment in information when undertaking major than minor decisions',[39] while true, does not help him to decide *how* much to invest. That decision requires estimates about the probable costs and benefits of the search for information. Search theories of unemployment, for instance, assume that the unemployed worker knows the distribution of job offers or at least the general shape of the distribution. Using this knowledge, he can calculate the optimal time spent searching for well-paid jobs. This argument is of dubious value. The doctor carrying out a medical diagnosis finds himself *many* times in the *same situation*. Most persons are unemployed only once or, if more than once, under widely diverging circumstances. They have no way of learning by experience what the job distribution looks like. To be sure, they know something about the job market, but there is no reason to think that they can piece together their bits of information to a reliable subjective distribution.[40] Similar argu-

---

[38] Menzel (1983), p. 6. The marginal value of the information is controversial, since it depends on an assessment of the value of life.

[39] Becker (1976), p. 7.

[40] On the general point, see Tversky and Kahneman (1974); Lichtenstein, Fischhoff and Phillips (1982). For a devastating criticism of optimal search theories, see Hey (1981).

ments apply to many consumer decisions, like the purchase of a car or an apartment. People know that it makes sense to spend some time searching and that it would be pointless to search forever, but between these lower and upper limits there is usually an interval of indeterminacy.

I.4 IRRATIONALITY

In this section I survey some main varieties of irrationality, including, as a special case, hyperrationality. The latter notion is defined as *the failure to recognize the failure* of rational-choice theory to yield unique prescriptions or predictions. As in Kant's critique, the first task of reason is to recognize its own limitations and draw the boundaries within which it can operate. The irrational belief in the omnipotence of reason is what I call hyperrationality. Later chapters provide numerous illustrations.

Failures to conform to well-defined prescriptions of rational-choice theory arise at all three levels distinguished in Fig. I.1. Consider first how actions can fail to relate optimally to given desires and beliefs. The paradigm case is weakness of will, characterized by the following features. (a) There is a prima facie judgement that X is good. (b) There is a prima facie judgement that Y is good. (c) There is an all-things-considered judgement that X is better than Y. (d) There is the fact that Y is chosen. Often, X is an act that is in the long-term interest of a person or corresponds to his moral will, whereas Y is a short-term impulse or a self-interested desire. There is no conceptual link, however, between weakness of will, myopia and selfishness.[41]

Example 7. Neo-Freudianism. Freud depicted two forms of human irrationality: being under the sway of the pleasure-seeking id and being dominated by the rigid, compulsive superego. As bearer of the rational will, the ego is engaged in a two-front war against these two enemies. The nature of the id, ego and superego in Freud's theory is somewhat unclear. Are they separate homunculi, each with a will of its own and capable of engaging in strategic interaction with the others?[42] Or, more soberly, are they conflicting tendencies

---

[41] Elster (1985b).
[42] Kolm (1980), pp. 302–11.

of one and the same subject? In his recent reinterpretation of Freud's trichotomy, George Ainslie has clarified the matter.[43] The ego's struggle with the id is interpreted in terms of time preference functions with the peculiar feature that a larger delayed reward which is preferred to a small early reward when they are both in the distant future becomes less preferred when the time for choice approaches. (Think of a person who makes an appointment with his dentist and then cancels it the day before.) To avoid such weak-willed behaviour, the ego can ally itself with the future, for if the situation can be expected to recur, *bunching* of all the small rewards and of all the large rewards makes it easier to choose the latter. By its rigid, uncompromising character, however, bunching may be as crippling to rationality as the problem it was supposed to resolve. If the ego abdicates its will to get rid of the id, it substitutes one form of weakness of will for another. Even when the person sees that it makes sense to give himself a break, he cannot bring himself to do so.

There is another set of cases in which desires and beliefs can fail to bring about the end for which they provide reasons. They have been referred to as 'excess of will',[44] although they are not in any sense the contrary of weakness of will. Assume that if I do X, I shall bring about Y, which is what I most desire. Moreover, I am able to do X, in the straightforward sense in which I am able to raise my arm. The snag, however, is that X will bring about Y only if I do X without the intention to bring about Y. Doing X for the purpose of bringing about Y will not succeed. Examples of X and Y could be: drinking hot tea at bedtime and falling asleep; working hard and forgetting a humiliating experience; looking at erotic pictures and becoming sexually aroused; joining a political movement and achieving self-respect.[45] Further examples are discussed at more length below and in chapter IV.

It might appear that someone who does X to achieve Y acts rationally. He is doing what he believes is (let us assume) the best way of getting what he most desires. This would be true if the situation conformed to the standard scheme of action, depicted in Fig. I.2.

The scheme goes from beliefs and desires through the intention

[43] Ainslie (1982, 1984, 1986).
[44] Farber (1976).
[45] These examples and many others are extensively discussed in Elster (1983a), ch. 2.

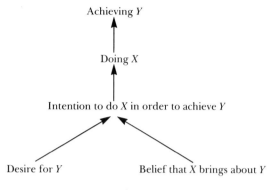

Fig. I.2

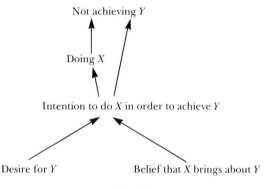

Fig. I.3

to the action and finally to the outcome of the action. There is no guarantee, of course, that the intended outcome will occur. The belief that *X* brings about *Y* could be mistaken. Extraneous factors might intervene. Actions that fail to bring about their intended outcomes for such reasons are not irrational. They fail, as it were, honourably. Matters stand differently when the failure is intrinsic to the action, as when the very intention to do *X* for the sake of *Y* interferes with the efficacy of *X* to bring about *Y*. This nonstandard scheme is shown in Fig. I.3.

Example 8. Don't wait for return of husband. This was the heading of a column in the *Miami Herald* (April 1987), in which Howard Halpern, a psychologist in private practice in New York City, answered the following question: 'I am a 57-year-old woman whose husband of 36 years has decided to live alone. We've sold our house and are living in separate dwellings. He speaks of "hope" and "working things out", while happily living the single life. I am unable to get on with my life in such an independent manner. We've had a great deal of joint and individual therapy, but it has not restored our relationship. We've lived together for a few months in the past two years. Each time I thought we would get back together, but then he would leave again. Is there something I should be doing besides waiting?' Mr Halpern answered, 'When you use the word "waiting", I get the impression that you have put your life on hold until your husband's hoped-for return. It is time to stop waiting. By that I don't mean you should make your separation legal – I'm not suggesting any action in particular. I think you must accept your situation as real, understand that your husband may not return and refuse to let your life be dependent on his decision. You have already made efforts to get him to return. Now you must pay attention to your own life and outline your own goals. Focusing on yourself may make you more appealing to him, but that is not the reason to do it. You must do it for yourself'. It is hard to think of advice that would be more misguided. The remark that focusing on herself might make her more appealing to him, while obviously intended to motivate her efforts, is sure to ruin their effect.

Consider next the varieties of irrationality that arise at the level of beliefs and desires. These can be subverted and distorted by causal forces in two main ways: by drives and motivations or by inadequate cognitive processing. Since the end result can be a motivational state (a desire) or a cognitive one (a belief), we have four categories, which I now proceed to illustrate.

The motivational basis of motivations

By this phrase, I do not have in mind conscious character planning, the shaping of preferences by metapreferences. Rather it refers to nonconscious motivational mechanisms that shape our desires 'behind our back'. The best known is what Festinger called 'cognitive dissonance reduction', the natural tendency of the mind to rearrange its desires and beliefs so as to reduce the tension created by high valuations of objects believed to be unattainable or low valuations of objects believed to be inescapable.[46] Also, being faced, like Buridan's ass, with two objects that appear equally attractive creates a form of cognitive dissonance extensively discussed in chapter II.

Some applications of dissonance theory focus on the adjustments of beliefs, while others emphasize the motivated change in evaluations.

> *Example 9. The Hungarian black market.*[47] One mechanism of dissonance reduction is 'I paid a lot for it, so it must be good'. A Hungarian coffee shop begins to offer high-quality coffee to customers who are willing to pay a bit extra. Since the shop has a limited quota of coffee beans, each customer who pays the high price creates an externality for the customers who pay the official price. The official cups of coffee being increasingly diluted, more and more customers are willing to pay the premium. Yet, as more and more do so, the quality of black-market coffee approaches the initial quality of the ordinary coffee. In the end, everybody pays the higher price for coffee of ordinary quality. It would appear, therefore, that everybody has lost, in a standard n-person Prisoner's Dilemma. The twist to the story is that because of cognitive dissonance nobody experiences any subjective loss. Since everyone is paying more for the coffee, it must be better than it used to be. The Prisoner's Dilemma yields a Pareto improvement: the shop keeper gains more and the customers are happy.

It is not obvious that desires shaped by dissonance reduction are, ipso facto, irrational. They do, after all, make people happier. Desires shaped by dissonance-increasing mechanisms are more obviously irrational. Many people, for instance, have a preference for novelty that gets them into trouble:

> *Example 10. What father does is always right.* In H. C. Andersen's story of this name, a farmer goes to the market in the morning to sell or exchange his horse. First, he meets a man with a cow, which he likes so much that he exchanges it for the horse. In successive transactions, the cow is then exchanged for a sheep, the sheep for a goose,

---

[46] Festinger (1957, 1964); Wicklund and Brehm (1976). Economic applications include Akerlof and Dickens (1982) and Schlicht (1984).
[47] The example draws upon Galasi and Kertesi (1987).

the goose for a hen and, finally, the hen for a sack of rotten apples. The farmer's road to ruin is paved with stepwise improvements.[48] (Actually he is not ruined, because a pair of English tourists make and lose a bet that his wife will be angry with him when he comes back with the apples.) Although the story does not say so, it is likely that the farmer would have refused to exchange his horse for a sack full of rotten apples. Curiosity and the thirst for novelty are triggered by options which are neither too similar nor too dissimilar from the current state.[49] In Johannes V. Jensen's story of the same name – a take-off on Andersen's classic tale – the farmer goes to the market with a set of rotten apples.[50] By a series of lucky accidents, he comes back with a horse. When he tells his wife about the deals, she manages to see each of them in an unfavourable light. Although the story is not fully clear on this point, it appears that she even thought a horse for a sack of apples a bad deal. Thus her perverse attitude can probably be explained by her belief that her husband cannot do anything right, not by an inherent conservatism that would be the converse of a preference for novelty. If the latter was the case, she would probably prefer the end state over the initial state, while being opposed to each of the intermediate steps.

The motivational basis of cognitions

Dissonance reduction can also take the form of belief adjustment. Workers who take jobs in unsafe industries alter their estimated probabilities of accidents.[51] As a result, when safety equipment becomes available, they may choose not to purchase it. Here, as in other cases, misformation of private beliefs (or preferences) creates a case for government intervention.[52] In addition to direct motivational interference with the cognition, there can be indirect interference with the evidence on which cognition is based. People who dread having a dangerous disease put off seeing the doctor.

[48] von Weizäcker (1971) offers a formal model of this process.
[49] Middleton (1986).
[50] I am indebted to Hilde Sejersted for bringing this story to my attention.
[51] This example is taken from Akerlof and Dickens (1982). This otherwise excellent article is marred by the idea that people can choose their own beliefs so that, for instance, they can weigh the psychic benefits of believing that their job is safe against the cost of increased chances of accidents. Although I am sure that both the costs and the benefits of dissonance reduction influence the extent to which it occurs, I do not think they do so by virtue of conscious comparison since, as argued above, beliefs cannot be deliberately chosen.
[52] Sunstein (1986) has a general discussion of such cases.

People who fear they might be gaining weight avoid stepping on the scales.

Belief-oriented dissonance reduction is a form of wishful thinking. To the extent that it makes one feel happy, it might be thought to be a good thing. Usually, however, the pleasure of wishful thinking is of brief duration, like the warmth provided by pissing in one's pants. *Acting* on beliefs formed in this way can be disastrous and is likely to force a change in the beliefs. When action is not called for, the wishful beliefs can be more stable. The 'just-world' theory, for instance, suggests that people adjust their beliefs about guilt and responsibility so as to preserve their belief that the world is fundamentally just.[53] The best-known example is the 'blame the victim' syndrome, further discussed in II.8. While it would be perverse to say that blaming the victim is rational, it can certainly contribute to one's peace of mind. Some forms of motivated belief formation do not even have that effect. The congenital pessimist, who systematically believes that the world is as he would *not* like it to be, creates dissonance instead of reducing it. Dissonance reduction, while a threat to autonomy and rationality, is at least intelligible in terms of the 'wirings of the pleasure machine', as Amos Tversky has put it. Dissonance production indicates that the wires have been crossed and that something is radically wrong.

The cognitive basis of motivations

Under this heading fall the violations of expected utility theory that have been extensively studied over the past decade or so.[54] An important example is 'framing', that is, preference reversal induced by redescription of the choice situation.[55] People who would abstain from buying credit cards if firms impose a 3 per cent surcharge on card users may be less deterred if firms offer a 3 per cent discount on cash purchases.[56] Time preferences can be manipulated by presenting the difference between present and future consumption as a delay premium or as a speed-up cost.[57] These are

---

[53] Lerner and Miller (1978).
[54] A recent summary is Machina (1987).
[55] Tversky and Kahneman (1981).
[56] Thaler (1980).
[57] Loewenstein (1987).

examples in which the reference points or frames are imposed from the outside. A more intriguing problem arises if we ask about the principles that regulate spontaneous choice of frames.[58] It has been suggested that people choose the frame that induces the choice that makes them happy,[59] but it is far from obvious that nonconscious motivational mechanisms are capable of operating in this indirect manner.

Another set of deviations from expected utility theory arises because people do not treat known probabilities as the theory tells them to. (The problem comes on the top of their difficulties in estimating unknown probabilities.) Thus 'low probabilities are overweighted, moderate and high probabilities are underweighted, and the latter effect is more pronounced than the former'.[60] In other words, people exaggerate the difference between impossible events and low-probability events and, especially, between near-certain and certain events. Attitudes towards nuclear accidents and other great disasters may, for this reason, include elements of irrationality. The point is *not* that it is irrational to feel anxiety at the prospect of a low-probability nuclear accident. What is irrational is that this attitude, when combined with other attitudes that may also appear unobjectionable in isolation, can be made to yield inconsistent choices. 'It is not easy to determine whether people value the elimination of risk too much or the reduction of risk too little. The contrasting attitudes to the two [logically equivalent] forms of protective action, however, are difficult to justify on normative grounds'.[61]

The cognitive basis of cognitions

There is by now a massive body of evidence showing how belief formation can fail because people rely on misleading heuristic principles or, more simply, ignore basic facts about statistical inference.[62] Securities and futures markets seem excessively sensitive

---

[58] Fischhoff (1983).
[59] Machina (1987), p. 146.
[60] Tversky and Kahneman (1981), p. 454.
[61] Ibid., p. 456.
[62] Good summaries are Nisbett and Ross (1981) and Kahneman, Slovic and Tversky, eds. (1982).

to current information.[63] Baseball trainers who notice that last season's star is not living up to his past performance are rapid to conclude that he has been spoilt by success, ignoring the statistical principle that, on the average, an outstanding performance is likely to be followed by one closer to average ('regression to the mean').[64] 'Labeling' theorists of mental illness cite as evidence for their theory the fact that the longer people have been in mental hospitals, the less likely they are to get well, ignoring the alternative explanation that the probabilities of getting well may differ across people but be constant over time.[65]

Example 11. Calvinism. The previous two examples turn upon a confusion between causal and noncausal interpretation of the facts. Max Weber's interpretation of the affinity between Calvinism and economic activity invokes a similar tendency to infuse diagnostic facts with causal value. 'Thus, however useless good works might be as a means of attaining salvation, for even the elect remain beings of the flesh, and everything they do falls infinitely short of divine standards, nevertheless, they are indispensable as a sign of election. They are the technical means, not of purchasing salvation, but of getting rid of the fear of damnation'.[66] It has been argued that the mechanism invoked here is motivational, a form of dissonance reduction.[67] It could, however, be a purely cognitive tendency to confuse diagnostic and causal efficacy. When people ask themselves, 'If not now, when?' and 'If not me, who?' they commit similar fallacies, albeit very useful ones.[68] People who open only one box in Newcomb's Problem do the same.[69]

I conclude this section with a few remarks about hyperrationality. Since the concept is discussed extensively in later chapters, especially in II.3 and II.8, I content myself here with a brief

---

[63] Arrow (1982).
[64] Nisbett and Ross (1981), p. 164, referring to 'the sophomore slump'.
[65] Gullestad and Tschudi (1982).
[66] Weber (1958), p. 115.
[67] Barry (1978), p. 41.
[68] See Quattrone and Tversky (1986) for the latter fallacy and Elster (1985b) for a discussion of the former.
[69] For exposition and discussion of this problem, see the articles collected in Campbell and Sowden, eds. (1985). A perfect illustration is a circular letter issued by English Baptists around 1770: 'Every soul that comes to Christ to be saved . . . is to be encouraged. . . . The coming soul need not fear that he is not elected, for none but such would be willing to come' (Thompson 1968, p. 38).

enumeration of some main varieties. (a) Sometimes people attempt to eliminate uncertainty of beliefs or incompleteness of preferences, although the choice situation is essentially indeterminate. It is always possible to devise questions that will force a person to reveal his preferences or subjective probabilities, but often there is no reason to believe in the robustness of the results. If the outcome depends on the procedures of elicitation, there is nothing 'out there' which is captured by the questions. (b) Sometimes people look to the second decimal when they are ignorant about the first. In some contexts, this method of problem solving is as good as any other. In others, it can be very wasteful, if people differ in their assessment of the second decimal and spend resources arguing about it. (c) Sometimes people will reframe an indeterminate decision problem so as to make it appear determinate. If one option stands out along one dimension, that dimension may take on increased importance so as to make the choice an easier one. (d) Sometimes people seek out what is rational to do in any given situation instead of looking for more general rules that cover many similar cases. Focusing on rules rather than acts can economize on costs of decision (see chapter III) and also have superior incentive effects.[70] (e) Sometimes people ignore the costs of decision making. They search for the solution that would have been best if found instantaneously and costlessly, ignoring the fact that the search itself has costs that may detract from optimality.

I.5 ALTERNATIVES TO RATIONALITY

In light of earlier sections, several questions arise. How serious are these failures of rational-choice theory? Is there any reason to think that the theory has a privileged status in the study of human action? What are the alternative accounts that could supplement or replace the theory?

The failures of indeterminacy appear to me to be quite serious. One way of assessing the power of the theory is to distinguish choice situations by two criteria: the importance of the problem and the number of agents involved. 'Small' problems, that is, problems in which the options do not differ much in value from one

---

[70] In addition, focusing on rules can protect one against weakness of will.

another, do not lend themselves to the rational approach. Either the options are equally good or it is not clear that it would pay to find out which is the better, or pay to find out whether it will pay to find out. 'Large' problems,[71] in which the choice can be expected to have wide-ranging consequences, also tend to fall outside the scope of the theory. Preference rankings over big chunks of life tend to be incomplete, and subjective probabilities over events in the distant future tend to be unreliable. The theory is more powerful when applied to medium-sized problems like the purchase of a car or a house, but even here the question of optimal search is largely indeterminate.

Other things being equal, decision problems with one agent or with many agents are more likely to yield determinate solutions than problems with a small number of agents. By definition, one-agent problems have no strategic indeterminacy. With many sellers and many buyers, competition forces a unique set of equilibrium prices. With one seller and one buyer, there is often a large range of mutually acceptable outcomes and much indeterminacy concerning which outcome will be realized.[72] A rough conclusion is that rational-choice theory is applicable mainly to one-agent and many-agent problems of intermediate size. Although precise quantification is impossible, indeterminacy is not a marginal problem that can be assimilated to 'friction' or 'noise'.

The factual importance of irrationality does not lend itself to a similarly systematic analysis. The central issue is whether people deal irrationally with important problems. The issue cannot be studied experimentally, since limitations on funding rarely allow stakes to be high enough and subjects to be numerous enough to get reliable results.[73] Introspection, casual observation, historical

---

[71] See Ullmann-Margalit (1985) for an analysis of 'big decisions' which nicely complements the analysis of 'small decisions' in Ullmann-Margalit and Morgenbesser (1977).

[72] Although noncooperative bargaining theory has done much to force determinacy in such problems (Rubinstein 1982), it is mainly of use in two-person contexts. Three-person bargaining problems remain largely indeterminate even in the noncooperative approach (Sutton 1986).

[73] To get around this problem, it has been suggested that in Third World countries experiments be conducted in which five- or ten-dollar rewards represent high stakes. To get around any ethical problems, all subjects could receive the maximal reward when the experiment was completed, even though told beforehand that they would get it only if they performed well. For reasons explained in Barry (1986), severe ethical problems would still remain.

case studies and novels suggest that irrationality is quite wide-spread. Drug abuse is perhaps the most striking evidence. More generally, the widespread inability to be properly swayed by future consequences of present action points to a serious deficit in rationality.[74] Studies of 'group think'[75] suggest that political and military decisions are often made in disregard of the evidence. The motivated ignorance of the Holocaust is a massive example of irrational belief formation.[76] The vast sales of self-therapy manuals suggest that many people believe that they can talk themselves into self-confidence and self-respect. I could go on enumerating cases, but they would not add much to the general idea. Irrationality is neither marginal nor omnipresent.

Although indeterminacy and irrationality are widespread, they do not affect the normative privilege of rationality. First and foremost, rationality is privileged because we want to be rational.[77] We take little pride in our occasional or frequent irrationality, although sometimes it has to be accepted as the price we pay for other things we value. In our dealings with people, we are compelled to treat them as, by and large, rational. Communication and discussion rest on the tacit premise that each interlocutor believes in the rationality of the others, since otherwise there would be no point to the exchange.[78] To understand others, we must assume that, by and large, they have rational desires and beliefs and act rationally upon them. If a person says that he wants X and yet deliberately refrains from using the means that he knows to be the most conducive to X, we usually conclude not that he is irrational but that he does not really want X. Sometimes, of course, we may conclude that irrationality offers the best explanation of a given kind of behaviour, but even then most of the evidence about the agent that goes into that conclusion is formed on the assumption that he is, by and large, rational.[79]

---

[74] Against those who say that discounting the future only shows a 'taste for the present' and that *de gustibus non est disputandum*, I would reply, first, that much time discounting is inconsistent (Elster 1985b) and, second, that even consistent time discounting beyond what is justified by mortality tables is a failure of rationality.

[75] Janis (1972).

[76] Laqueur (1980).

[77] Føllesdal (1982).

[78] Midgaard (1980); Habermas (1982).

[79] Davidson (1980).

The explanatory privilege of rationality rests on two grounds. As just observed, rationality is presupposed by any competing theory of motivation, whereas rationality itself does not presuppose anything else. On grounds of parsimony, therefore, we should begin by assuming nothing but rationality.[80] Also, while rationality may have its problems, the opposition is in even worse shape. The dictum that you cannot beat something with nothing applies here, with some modifications. As will be clear from what I shall say about the alternatives to rational-choice theory, they are more than nothing, but they do not quite amount to something either.

Herbert Simon's theory of satisficing is intended to supplement rational-choice theory when it is indeterminate.[81] It has been applied to technical change,[82] consumer choice,[83] and numerous other problems. The strength and main weakness of the theory are its realism. On the one hand, it is true and important that many people are happy once their aspiration level has been reached. They stop searching once they have found something that is good enough. On the other hand, there is to my knowledge no robust explanation of why people have the aspiration levels they do, nor of why they use the particular search rules they do. The theory describes behaviour, but does not really explain it. Now, one might say that a similar criticism applies to rational-choice theory, which does not, after all, explain why people have the preferences they do. The hypothesis that people behave rationally is nevertheless simpler, more general and more powerful than the assumption that they are guided by their aspiration levels. In the theory of the firm, for instance, rational-choice theory needs only one assumption, namely that the firm maximizes profits. Satisficing theory needs many assumptions, stipulating one aspiration level for each

---

[80] The situation is somewhat similar to the privileged status of the assumption of selfishness. We can consistently imagine a world in which everybody behaves selfishly all the time, but not a world in which everybody behaves altruistically all the time, because altruism presupposes some nonaltruistic pleasures that the altruist can promote.

[81] I disregard the interpretation of satisficing as maximizing under constraints on information-processing capacities. Limited calculating ability is only one obstacle to first-best rationality. A more important obstacle, in my view, is our inherently limited knowledge about the value of information. Also, people with severely limited cognitive capacities may not be able to understand their limits and hence are not, subjectively, constrained by them.

[82] Nelson and Winter (1982).

[83] Hey (1981, 1982).

of the many subroutines of the firm and, when that level is not attained, one search mechanism for each routine.

Simon's theory, and other theories in the same vein,[84] are intended to *supplement* rational-choice theory, both as a guide to and as an explanation of action. They are rarely intended to *replace* the rationality assumption. Proponents of these alternatives usually grant that rational-choice theory has substantial explanatory power in the absence of uncertainty, but add that most real-life decision making is characterized by a high degree of uncertainty that is costly or impossible to resolve. This is also the point of departure of the theory offered by Isaac Levi to guide and explain decision making under value conflicts and uncertainty.[85] Under conditions of unresolved value conflict, he recommends that we use lexicographically secondary values to decide among the options that are 'admissible' according to the primary, conflicting values, an admissible option being one that is optimal according to one of these values (or to some weighted average of them). Under conditions of uncertainty, he similarly recommends the use of *security* and *deferability* to supplement the expected-value criterion. Levi also argues that many apparent violations of rationality can be understood by assuming that the agents are acting in accordance with his prescriptions. Their choices reflect reasonable ways of coping with unresolved value conflicts and uncertainty rather than cognitive illusions of the kind discussed above.[86] Levi does not try, however, to account for all the apparent violations of expected utility theory.

Other theories, offered squarely as alternatives to rational-choice theory, aim to explain what they admit to be violations of rationality. They can be classified, very roughly, into psychological, biological and sociological alternatives to the economic approach to behaviour.

Psychological theories attempt to explain the observed viola-

---

[84] Notably Heiner (1983, 1988).

[85] Levi (1974, 1986).

[86] Levi (1986), p. 33, shows that a perfectly sensible way of handling unresolved value conflicts can lead to violation of Sen's 'property alpha', which says that if a is chosen in the set (a, b), b should never be chosen in a larger set (a, b, c). Similarly he argues (Levi 1986, ch. 7) that the Ellsberg and Allais paradoxes of choice under risk can be handled without imputing irrationality to the agents who make these apparently inconsistent decisions.

tions of expected utility theory referred to earlier by providing an account that (a) is simple and intuitively plausible, (b) explains all observed deviations from expected utility theory and (c) predicts no unobserved deviations. Attempts to achieve this goal include prospect theory,[87] generalized expected utility theory[88] and regret theory.[89] This is a field where nonexperts should tread warily, and I abstain from evaluating the various proposals, beyond making the presumably uncontroversial remark that only prospect theory appears to be capable of explaining framing phenomena. I note later, however, an apparent example of irrationality through framing that is more plausibly explained by a sociological alternative to rational-choice theory.

Biological alternatives take off from findings about animal behaviour. Animals can be constrained to choose between two responses, each of which has a particular reward schedule. In variable-ratio (VR) schedules we set up a constant probability of reward for each response. The one-armed bandit of the Las Vegas variety illustrates this reward schedule. It is a mechanism with no memory: if we hit the jackpot on one occasion, we are just as likely to hit it again the next time. In variable-interval (VI) schedules we set up a mechanism with memory, so that each unrewarded response increases the probability that the next response will be rewarded. In each period the experimenter uses a chance device, with constant probabilities, to decide whether food is to be made available. Once it has been made available, it stays available. The animal does not know, however, whether it is available. To find out, and to get the food, it must make the appropriate response.

The central question is whether animals allocate their attention optimally between the two responses, that is, whether they act to maximize their rewards. Faced with the choice between two VR schedules, animals often do the rational thing and allocate all their attention to the response with the highest probability of reward. Sometimes, however, they commit 'gambler's fallacy' of distributing the stakes in proportion to the odds. With two VI schedules, the findings are also ambiguous. In a VI–VR schedule, animals usually do not optimize. Instead of equalizing the marginal return

---

[87] Kahneman and Tversky (1979); Tversky and Kahneman (1987).
[88] Machina (1983).
[89] Loomes and Sugden (1982).

of the two responses, as rationality would require them to do, they equalize the average return. They forget, as it were, that most of the VI rewards come from a few responses, and that it is not really profitable to pay attention to this schedule beyond visiting it from time to time to collect any reward that might have come due after its last visit.

Richard Herrnstein argues that the principle of equalizing average returns ('the matching law') is a more fundamental principle than utility maximization.[90] In addition to explaining allocation of behaviour across schedules, it can explain the allocation over time. Specifically, the matching law predicts that time discounting will be steeper than the exponential discount functions usually stipulated by economists. Although the empirical verdict is not yet in, there is evidence that much animal and human discounting is nonexponential.[91] On the other hand, the matching law explains only the most naïve forms of human behaviour. People can use conscious thought processes to analyse the structure of the choice situation. Unlike animals, they are not restricted to myopic learning. The matching law may describe 'prerational' behaviour, but it is powerless to explain more sophisticated choice processes.

A sociological alternative to the economic approach is the theory of social norms.[92] I define social norms mainly by their non-outcome-oriented character. Whereas rationality tells people, 'If you want *Y*, do *X*', many social norms simply say, 'Do *X*'. Some social norms are hypothetical, but they make the action contingent on past behaviour of oneself or others, not on future goals. These norms say, 'If others do *Y*, do *X*' or 'If you have done *Y*, do *X*'. The norms are *social* if they satisfy two further conditions: they are shared with other members of the community and they are in part enforced by sanctions provided by others.

Here are some examples of social norms, chosen with a view to the contrast with rational action: (a) the norm of voting is very strong in Western democracies. It accounts for most voting in

---

[90] Herrnstein and Vaughan (1980); Vaughan and Herrnstein (1987); Herrnstein (1988). A cautiously optimizing approach to animal behaviour is that of Staddon (1983, 1987).

[91] Ainslie (1975, 1982, 1984, 1986).

[92] I discuss this theory at some length in a companion volume (Elster 1989) to the present book, and the following account must be read only as a sketch of that more extended argument.

national elections.[93] Selfish voters have virtually nothing to gain from voting, while the costs are non-negligible. Altruistic voters might find voting rational, were it not for problems of strategic interaction. Altruistic voting is a game with multiple equilibria, in each of which most but not all voters go to the polls.[94] (b) The norm of vengeance practised in many traditional societies is triggered by an earlier offence, not motivated by future rewards. Indeed, from the future-oriented point of view vengeance is pointless at best, suicidal at worst. (c) In most Western societies there is a norm against walking up to someone in a cinema queue and asking to buy his place. The norm is puzzling, as nobody would lose and some could gain from the transaction. (d) Norms of dress and etiquette do not seem to serve any ulterior purpose, unlike for instance traffic rules that serve to prevent accidents.

Consider finally an example that could be explained both in terms of framing and in terms of social norms. Consider a suburban community where all houses have small lawns of the same size.[95] Suppose a houseowner is willing to pay his neighbour's son ten dollars to mow his lawn, but not more. He would rather spend half an hour mowing the lawn himself than pay eleven dollars to have someone else do it. Imagine now that the same person is offered twenty dollars to mow the lawn of another neighbour. It is easy to imagine that he would refuse, probably with some indignation. But this has an appearance of irrationality. By turning down the offer of having his neighbour's son mow his lawn for eleven dollars, he implies that half an hour of his time is worth at most eleven dollars. By turning down the offer to mow the other neighbour's lawn for twenty dollars, he implies that it is worth at least twenty dollars. But it cannot both be worth less than eleven and more than twenty dollars.

The explanation in terms of framing suggests[96] that people evaluate losses and gains forgone differently. Credit card companies exploit this difference when they insist that stores advertise cash discounts rather than credit card surcharges. The credit card

[93] Barry (1979a), pp. 17–18; Wolfinger and Rosenstone (1980), p. 8 and passim.
[94] For the reasoning behind this statement, see Oliver, Marwell and Teixeira (1985) or cases B, D and E in Schelling (1978), p. 220.
[95] I am indebted to Amos Tversky for suggesting this to me as an example of social norms.
[96] Thaler (1980), p. 43.

holder is affected less by the lost chance of getting the cash discount than by the extra cost of paying with the card. Similarly, the houseowner is affected more by the out-of-pocket expenses that he would incur by paying someone to mow his lawn than by the loss of a windfall income. But this cannot be the full story, because it does not explain why the houseowner should be indignant at the proposal. Part of the explanation must be that he does not think of himself as the kind of person who mows other people's lawns for money. It *isn't done*, to use a revealing phrase that often accompanies social norms.

Economists often argue that norms can be reduced to individual rationality. One version of the reductionist claim is that norms are 'nothing but' raw material for strategic manipulation; that people invoke norms to rationalize their self-interest while not believing in them. But this is absurd: if nobody believed in the norms, there would be nothing to manipulate.[97] A more serious reductionist argument proceeds from the fact that norms are maintained by sanctions. Suppose I face the choice between taking revenge for the murder of my cousin and not doing anything. The cost of revenge is that I might in turn be the target of countervengeance. The cost of not doing anything is that my family and friends are certain to desert me, leaving me out on my own, defencelessly exposed to predators. A cost–benefit analysis is likely to tell me that revenge is the rational choice. More generally, norm-guided behaviour is supported by the threat of sanctions that make it rational to obey the norm.

Against this argument, each of the following objections is a sufficient refutation. First, sometimes norms are followed in the absence of any observers who could sanction violations. Many people vote even when nobody would notice if they did not. Second, we have to ask why anyone would want to impose the sanctions. Perhaps they follow a metanorm to sanction people who violate first-order norms, but then we have to ask whether it is rational to follow that norm. In the regress that now arises, there must come a point at which the cost of expressing disapproval is less than the cost of receiving disapproval for not expressing it, since the former cost is approximately constant while the second

[97] Edgerton (1985), p. 3.

goes rapidly to zero. The chain of norms must have an unmoved mover, to which the rationalist reduction does not apply.

Among the alternatives to rational-choice theory, the (as yet undeveloped) theory of social norms holds out most promise. It is radically different from rational-choice theory, whereas the other alternatives are largely variations on the same consequentialist theme. They are different species of the same genus, whereas the theory of norms is of a different genus altogether. Other species of that genus might include the theory of neurotic behaviour, which is similarly rigid, mechanical and nonconsequentialist. Eventually, the goal of the social sciences must be to construct the family comprising both genera – to understand outcome-oriented motivations and nonconsequentialist ones as elements in a general theory of action. As long as this task is not accomplished, rational-choice theory will probably remain privileged, by virtue of the simplicity and power of the maximizing assumption. And in the event that it should one day be accomplished, rationality would still retain its privilege as a normative account of action.

II

TAMING CHANCE: RANDOMIZATION IN INDIVIDUAL AND SOCIAL DECISIONS

II.1 INTRODUCTION

Decision making by the flip of a coin, the toss of a die and more generally by formal or informal lotteries is perceived largely as a curiosity. Randomization is often mentioned in passing as a possible method for allocating resources, for assigning tasks and more generally for making social or individual decisions. It is occasionally discussed in more detail, with respect to specific types of decisions. Yet with the exception of Thomas Gataker's *On the Nature of Use and Lots* of 1619,[1] it has not, to my knowledge, received sustained and systematic attention.[2]

There are two main questions we can ask ourselves with respect to the use of lotteries.[3] First, under which conditions would they seem to be normatively allowed or prescribed, on grounds of individual rationality or social justice? Second, in which cases are lotteries actually used to make decisions and allocate tasks, resources and burdens? There is no reason, of course, to expect the answers to these questions to coincide. Hence we can generate two further questions. What explains the adoption of lotteries when normative arguments seem to point against them? What explains the nonadoption of lotteries in situations where they would seem to be normatively compelling? The last question is perhaps the most

---

[1] Page references are to the second edition of 1627.
[2] Mention should be made, however, of some recent work done at the Yale Law School. See notably Greely (1977) and Amar (1984).
[3] I will not discuss ordinary lotteries, i.e., betting on numbers as a source of income for the state. It seems misleading to subsume this practice under the rubric of 'referring potentially contentious decisions to lot', as does Thomas (1973), p. 140. It may be noted, however, that ordinary lotteries have their origin in the selection by lot of political representatives in Genoa. Initially people made bets on the candidates, whose names were later replaced by numbers.

intriguing and instructive one. I shall argue that we have a strong reluctance to admit uncertainty and indeterminacy in human affairs. Rather than accept the limits of reason, we prefer the rituals of reason.

The use of lotteries to make decisions itself requires the decision to use this decision mechanism rather than another. As emphasized by Gataker (pp. 55–6), lotteries reflect an intentional choice to make a decision by a nonintentional mechanism.[4] To explain and justify the decision to randomize (or not to randomize) requires a study of this higher-order decision. Who makes it? How is it made? It can be made by an individual facing a choice among several courses of action. Seeking my way out of the forest, I may decide to toss a coin when the road bifurcates.[5] It can be made by a group of individuals, who agree, by unanimity, by majority decision or some other accepted way (e.g., by lot), to allocate goods, burdens or tasks among themselves in this manner. A divorcing couple who must decide who will have custody of the children may agree to make the decision by the flip of a coin. It can be made, finally, by an administrative, legal or political agency. Hospital administrators may decide to use a lottery to allocate kidneys for transplantation.

There is a second decision to be made before the decision by lottery can take effect: one must decide how the possible actions should be matched with the outcomes that can be generated by the randomizing device. Clearly, the general solution cannot be to assign actions to outcomes by means of another lottery. At some stage, the assignment will have to be done by 'picking' rather than 'choosing'.[6] Neglect of the need for this preliminary decision led Gataker (pp. 185–6) to propose the following invalid argument against the view that lotteries show God's particular will or 'special providence'. He observed, correctly, that men often use past (unknown) events as elements in the lottery which is to guide their decisions. From this he concluded that since even God cannot alter the past, the outcome of lotteries cannot in general reflect his

---

[4] In Elster (1984), pp. 12–13, I discuss two-stage decision problems in which one intentionally decides to solve a decision problem by trial and error rather than by consciously directed search.

[5] Descartes (1897–1910), vol. 6, p. 24; Neurath (1913).

[6] On this point see Ullman-Margalit and Morgenbesser (1977).

special providence. The inference fails, since God's intervention might well come in the contemporaneous stage of matching actions with outcomes. Using his knowledge of past events, he could influence the matching so as to bring about his particular will.

The use of lotteries is associated with uncertainty, indifference, indeterminacy and incommensurability. In the absence of reasons for choosing one alternative, one candidate, one recipient or one victim rather than another, we might as well select one at random. This chapter is to a large extent an elaboration of this statement. The relation between uncertainty and lotteries is, however, more complex than one might suspect at first glance. Generally speaking, we tend to see uncertainty as an unmitigated ill. Uncertainty prevents us from planning for the future. Even more important, it prevents us from making choices that we can justify to ourselves and others as grounded in reason, whence the various tactics for uncertainty avoidance and uncertainty reduction discussed at greater length in II.3. Here I want to emphasize that the use of lotteries to resolve decision problems under uncertainty presupposes an unusual willingness to admit the insufficiency of reason. Usually, we do not want to cope with indeterminacy, but to avoid it.

Sometimes, however, we welcome an element of uncertainty, and even create it if necessary. It is true that uncertainty makes it difficult to plan for the future, but without uncertainty we might not even want to plan for the future at all. It is not easy to imagine how we would feel and behave if we knew the exact day on which we shall die, but a backwards induction argument, somewhat similar to that of the finitely iterated Prisoner's Dilemma, might apply. If life today has meaning only because there is a prospect of further meaningful days in the future, then the knowledge that on one specific day there will be no more meaning might, retroactively, remove meaning from all earlier days. This argument is, inevitably, speculative. For myself, however, I am quite sure that I would prefer a shorter life expectancy with a larger spread to a longer life with no spread at all. If I had the choice, on this issue, between an unfair lottery and a sure thing, I would take the lottery.[7]

---

[7] Formally, this is a form of preference for risk. The underlying reasons, however, are quite different. If I prefer the smaller average with the larger dispersion, it is not because I gamble on a long life but, as stated, because the certainty would be intolerable.

Our life span is substantially outside our control. Here we do not have the choice between certainty and uncertainty. In other domains, where we do have this choice, we might want to set up a lottery. By removing the knowledge about who will do what or get what at which times, one also removes incentives for opportunistic and wasteful behaviour. Since lotteries also remove the opportunity for long-term planning, their net effect may be positive or negative. I shall discuss cases of both kind. Here I want only to insist on the variety of attitudes we adopt towards uncertainty. Sometimes we face it squarely; sometimes we seek to avoid it or to reduce it. We may welcome it, and even actively promote it. Lotteries can, as we shall see, be a form of uncertainty avoidance, if they are interpreted as an expression of God's will. Today they are more frequently motivated by the acceptance of uncertainty or the active wish to promote it.

I now proceed as follows. In II.2 I discuss the nature of randomness and random choice, to bring out some conceptual and practical difficulties associated with lotteries. In II.3 I consider the use of lotteries as an aid to individual decision making. In the remaining part of the chapter I look at some varieties of social lotteries. After an overview (II.4) of actual or proposed social lotteries, I go on to consider the use of lotteries to allocate goods and burdens and to compare them with other allocation mechanisms (II.5). Next, I discuss a variety of political (II.6) and legal (II.7) lotteries. At the end (II.8) I sketch some tentative answers to the questions stated at the beginning: When are lotteries used? When ought they to be used? When and why do the answers to these two questions differ?

II.2   VARIETIES OF RANDOMNESS

In most contexts, we want lotteries to be fair. If a finite subset is selected by lot within a larger class, we want the selection to be fair in the sense of being truly random and unbiased. It is not clear, however, what it means to select randomly, nor is it always easy to do so. I first comment on three conceptual distinctions that should be made: between selections that are generated by a randomizing mechanism and selections that are inherently random; between actual randomness (in either of these two senses) and perceived randomness; and between artificial lotteries and natural lotteries. I then go on to discuss some problems that arise in the implementation and interpretation of randomness.

Randomness can be seen as a property of a process or as a property of the selections it generates. The concept of a randomizing process or mechanism might appear to be incoherent. As von Neumann once observed, 'Anyone who considers arithmetical methods of producing random digits is, of course, in a state of sin'.[8] To resolve the dilemma, we can either make use of objectively random processes at the quantum level or, more feasibly define a random mechanism in terms of the long-term patterns of outcomes. A coin is fair, roughly speaking, if and only if all independently defined subsequences of a long series of tosses converge to fifty–fifty.[9] In practice, this definition is hard to implement. Tables of random numbers have had to be modified because they turned out to have undesirable regularity properties.[10] Such revisions are difficult to justify, however, since any sufficiently long random sequence is virtually certain to have regularly looking chunks. By eliminating them, one approaches the nonrandom case of intentional mixing.[11] There is (casual) evidence that the selection of questions from different subdisciplines by university examiners in successive years is a form of intentional mixing rather than random selection. In theory, students should be able to exploit this practice to their advantage.

Could one appeal instead to the inherent randomness of the selections actually generated by the device, as distinct from the patterns in the hypothetical long-term sequence? Here again we run into problems. The notion of inherent randomness is quite deep and may ultimately defy analysis for reasons related to Gödel's incompleteness theorem.[12] Although one may sometimes be able to prove that a given sequence of numbers is random or that it is not random, no computer program can prove, for any given sequence, whether it is random or not. The notion of ran-

---

[8] Quoted after Goldstine (1972), p. 297.
[9] Feller (1968), p. 204.
[10] Lopes (1986).
[11] Feller (1968), p. 42.
[12] The following draws heavily on Chaitin (1975).

domness invoked here can be brought out by comparing the following sequences:

$$01010101010101010101$$

$$01101100110111100010$$

The first sequence can be generated by the program 'Print 01 ten times'. The simplest program that can generate the second is 'Print 01101100110111100010'. This 'incompressibility', which is used to define inherent randomness, corresponds to the intuitive idea that in a random sequence there will not be any obvious patterns. By contrast, a truly random mechanism has an equal likelihood of realizing any twenty-digit sentence of 0s and 1s. I will therefore sometimes pick a sequence which is not inherently random, although most sequences generated by a truly random device will themselves be fairly random, in a sense that can be made precise.[13]

Inherent randomness is neither necessary nor sufficient for justice by lottery.[14] Imagine that in a class of twenty pupils only ten can receive some good and that they are matched in alphabetical order with an inherently random sequence constrained to have ten 0s and ten 1s. If the choice of this particular random sequence among others equally random was not itself made randomly, the pupils might well suspect some favouritism in the choice. Conversely, if an unbiased mechanical device happened to come up with a sequence of alternating 0s and 1s, the ensuing distribution would be quite acceptable once the pupils had satisfied themselves that the mechanism was truly random.

Nevertheless, when people have no direct knowledge about the generating mechanism, they have to judge the randomness of the draw by looking at its outcome. We have seen that this assessment is problematic even if they can observe many successive draws, and it is even more tenuous when inspection of a single outcome is used to judge how likely it is to come up. There are three closely related fallacies involved here. The first is that people misperceive inherent randomness; the second that they believe a given inherently random sequence to be a more likely outcome of a random process than a given regular sequence; and the third that they

[13] Ibid.
[14] On this point see also Levi (1982).

believe that properties of a single outcome can be used to infer properties of the process.

On the first point, William Feller, referring to the pattern of German bombing over Britain in World War II, writes that 'to the untrained eye, randomness appears as a regularity or tendency to cluster'.[15] Similarly, Daniel Kahneman and Amos Tversky write that 'among the 20 possible sequences (disregarding direction and label) of six tosses of a coin, for example we venture that only HTTHTH appears really random. For four tosses, there may not be any'.[16] On the second point, Kahneman and Tversky cite an experiment concerning the distribution of twenty marbles to five children, each marble being randomly allocated to one of them. Subjects stated that the outcome 4–4–4–4–4 was less likely to be the outcome of a random process than the outcome 4–4–5–4–3, in the sense that it would occur less frequently in repeated distributions. Yet the uniform distribution is actually more likely to occur.[17] As they note elsewhere, 'a slightly uneven outcome represents both the fairness of the coin and the randomness of tossing, which is not at all represented by the exactly even result'.[18]

On the third point, the following story is illustrative:

Shortly after the reinstatement of the draft lottery in December 1969, [the renowned random-number expert Mark Kac at Rockefeller University] received a phone call from a graduate student asking him to testify in court that the sequence of birthdates chosen in the lottery was not random. The basis for the proposed court suit was given in a letter to the *New York Times* (11 December 1969) in which F. T. Haddock of the University of Michigan pointed out that there were many more birthdates from the end of the year in early positions in the draft sequence than would be expected if the sequence had been generated randomly. Kac declined the student's request in no uncertain terms, saying that he could not testify to the nonrandomness of the sequence since it is impossible to determine mathematically whether a given sequence has been generated by a random or a nonrandom process.[19]

[15] Feller (1968), p. 161.
[16] Kahneman and Tversky (1982a).
[17] Ibid., pp. 35–6. Subjects act, in other words, as if they compare classes of distributions (equal distribution vs. one child gets three marbles, one gets five and the others get four) rather than individual distributions.
[18] Kahneman and Tversky (1982b).
[19] Lopes (1986), p. 729. As Dr Kac noted in the lecture on which this account draws (and as is further discussed later), the student turned out to be right. Was Dr Kac's refusal excessively puristic? Would he have said the same about the 1940 draft lottery, also discussed below? As Aanund Hylland has explained to me, the answer depends on one's prior assumptions about the mechanism. If one has reasons to believe that the physical nature of the mechanism was such that certain patterns were ex ante somewhat possible, the likeli-

The belief that a process of selection is truly or objectively random is sufficient but not necessary for its perceived fairness. Epistemic randomness, that is, the fact that all outcomes are equally likely as far as one knows, may also be sufficient to ensure perceived fairness.[20] Consider a person who is told that a decision will be made by a die which has one side with a 50 per cent chance of coming up, four sides with 12.5 per cent chance each and one side with no chance of coming up, but who is not told which numbers correspond to which sides. For all he knows, no number is more likely than any other to come up, even though the mechanism is not an objective randomizing device. Although experiments suggest that people would rather have the decision made by a true die than by a die whose bias (if any) is unknown,[21] one might question whether they have any reason for this preference. If I assume that the number which is favourable to me has one chance in six to be matched with each side, the chance that it will come up is also one in six, as if the die were a true one.

That assumption, which is characteristic of Bayesian decision theory, should not, however, be made lightly.[22] The principle of insufficient reason, which says that in the absence of further information all possible states should be assumed to be equally probable, rests on a naïve assumption that the individuation of states is unproblematic. In the example given, it was assumed that there are six possible states, corresponding to the six sides of the die. It would be equally justified, that is, equally unjustified, however, to distinguish among three possible states: my number is on the side with a fifty per cent chance of coming up, or it is on one of the sides with a 12.5 per cent chance, or it is on the side that is certain not to come up.[23]

hood that such patterns, when observed, were generated by a biased mechanism becomes very high. It is easy to imagine, for instance, how a physical device would break down in ways that would lead to alternating 0s and 1s or all 0s, or all 1s, or long stretches with only 0s or only 1s. By contrast, it is very difficult to think of a way in which a physical device could break down so as to generate, say, the binary expansion of the square root of 2.

[20] On this point, see also Sher (1980).

[21] Ellsberg (1961).

[22] I am indebted to Isaac Levi for pressing this point on me.

[23] Some might think this an artificial construction. Although it is not, the point may be better brought out, perhaps, by the following example. Imagine that a policeman is following the trail of a criminal and arrives at a point where the road divides into three: two of them going downhill and one going uphill. In the absence of specific evidence, should he assign equal probability to the three roads or to the two states 'uphill' and 'downhill'? For historical examples, see Zabell (1987).

In that case the principle of insufficient reason tells me to prefer the loaded die, since it gives my number five chances out of twenty-four of coming up, which is better than one out of six.

It follows that a person does not act irrationally if he prefers the loaded die over the true one. Nor is the converse preference irrational. Rationality simply does not have much bite here. One is equally entitled to act as if the best that could happen is bound to happen and to act as if the worst that could happen is certain to happen (I.2). It might seem, however, as if arguments from fairness present an asymmetry. Assume that the loaded die is used and that I find out that my number was associated with the side that had no chance of coming up. I might well complain that the lottery was stacked against me, since I had no real possibility of winning.[24] *This, however, would be true of any lottery at some stage.* If I am confident that the assignment of outcomes to decisions is unbiased, the known or possible bias in the outcome-generating mechanism does not make the lottery as a whole unfair. Fairness does not require the random part in the sequence of events leading to the final decision to occur as late as possible, since one random event in the chain is enough to confer randomness on the outcome.

Epistemic randomness is the desideratum of natural lotteries, in which the decision is made contingent upon an event that is not specially arranged for the purpose. Gataker (p. 16) gives these examples: 'Suppose two by the way contending which way they shall take, put themselves upon the flight of the next fowle that crosseth them, or upon the turning of a stranger, whom they see ride before them, to the right hand or to the left'. The flight of the bird is subject to natural necessity and the turn of the stranger to intentional choice, but since these events are insulated from the information and control of the parties, they are random as far as they know. The problem is how to make sure that the events are really thus insulated. Often one party is better able to predict the natural event, or he may be in a position to influence it. When Darius and his competitors agreed to settle the empire on him whose horse should first neigh when they met in a given place on a given day, he rigged the natural lottery in his favour by arranging for his horse to be in that place with a mare so that it could be

---

[24] An analogous example from the Jerusalem Talmud is discussed in Zabell (1976).

expected to neigh.[25] The information problem can be solved by an analogy to the 'divide and choose' principle. If one person proposes to have a decision made by a certain natural event, another shall have the right of matching outcomes with decisions.[26] The manipulation problem can be solved by using a past event to make the decision. By combining these solutions, we can ensure the epistemic randomness of natural lotteries.

In decisions involving many people, the perceived fairness of natural lotteries is hard to guarantee. Instead, one would want to use a truly random device. It turns out, however, to be surprisingly difficult to implement this ideal. Thus in the 1940 draft lottery of American soldiers, 'no serial number between 300 and 600 [out of 9000] was drawn in the first 2400 draws. By pure chance, this would occur less than once in 15×10^{40} times'.[27] Although by the high standards of Dr Kac this should not in itself tell us anything about the randomness of the draw, we know from direct evidence that the mixing was in fact highly imperfect. Thirty years later history repeated itself in the 1970 draft lottery.[28] Again the physical shuffling was not sufficiently thorough, with the result that was reported in the *New York Times* and led to the telephone call to Dr Kac. The 1971 draft lottery finally got it right.[29]

One may question whether these flaws mattered at all, as long as they were unintended. The flawed draft lotteries resemble the use of a loaded die with an unknown bias, except that the fact of the bias was itself unknown to all concerned. Of the two courts that took a position on the issue, both dismissed the complaints of the unlucky draftees, but on different grounds. In *Stodolsky v. Hershey*[30] the court found that the drawing had been less than perfectly random but that there was no evidence to show that it was so far removed from randomness as to violate the presidential proclamation requiring 'random selection'. Hence the record was 'too slight' to justify the 'profound consequences' of setting up a new lottery. In *U.S. v.*

[25] Herodotus, *The History*, bk. 3, 84–7.
[26] For a related proposal, see Sher (1980), p. 207.
[27] Fienberg (1971).
[28] Ibid.
[29] Rosenblatt and Filliben (1971).
[30] 2 S.S.L.R. 3527 (W.D. Wisc. 1969).

Kotrlik & Gaevert[31] the court insisted that the selection was random
'as the term is usually understood and used in ordinary English'
since 'there was no plan, purpose or pattern in the drawing of the
numbers'. The court, in other words, defined randomness epistemically. The earlier decision, by contrast, had defined randomness as
'that quality which makes the selection of any one sequence of the
366 numbers as likely as the selection of any other sequence of the
366 numbers'. From the context it is clear that this refers to objective equiprobability. In my view, the latter decision got it right, not
because of the irrelevant argument from usage but because the
epistemic notion is the appropriate one in this context. In II.6 I
consider cases in which objective randomness may be required.

The process of selecting jurors at random can be even more
difficult to carry out. I am not here referring to gross and intentional bias, like that described by Hans Zeisel in 'Dr. Spock and the
case of the vanishing women jurors'.[32] Rather I have in mind the
problems that can arise in the best-intentioned efforts to draw a
truly random sample, as in *State v. Long*.[33] Here the defence successfully claimed that the process of jury selection in Atlantic City
did not give each person the same chance to be selected for jury
service. For instance, the source list used for the random draw
contained about 180 000 names, whereas there were only 130 000
people in the relevant age group. Hence almost 40 per cent of the
people had double opportunity to be selected for jury duty. Also,
the use of fifth-letter alphabetization as a criterion of selection
'meant that many people in the same panel would have the same
fifth letter in their last name. This explained how some panels had
large numbers of Jewish names (e.g., Wise*m*an, Feld*m*an) or Italian names (e.g., Fera*r*ro, Dina*r*do)'.[34] These practices were held to

[31] 5 S.S.L.R. 3693 (9th Cir. 1972). General discussions of the legal attitude towards randomization are Winick (1981), pp. 412–20, and Capron (1975), pp. 155–63.

[32] Zeisel (1969). In Dr Spock's trial the venire of 100 jurors contained only nine women, as
a result of two successive and grossly biased selections.

[33] 499 A.2d 264 (N.J. Super L. 1985).

[34] Hans and Vidmar (1986), p. 57. First names are no more reliable. 'In the town of
Mannheim, for example, statistics were compiled regarding the number of children in
each family. The sample comprised the families whose names had the initial letters A, B
and M. It turned out, however, that names with these initials were especially numerous
among Jewish families, and as the children of Jewish families were particularly numerous, the enquiry gave a misleading result' (Jensen 1926, pp. 429–30). Assignment of
cases to judges by the first letter of the defendant's last name can also create bias, as
reported by Coons (1987), p. 112, n. 137.

violate the defendant's constitutional right to a jury drawn from a representative cross-section of the community. The value of this right is further discussed in II.6.

I have been assuming, as do most writers on this topic, that the random process is an equiprobabilistic one. Each member of the relevant group has the same chance of being selected. Or, more weakly, as far as anyone knows no member has a larger chance than any other of being selected. Could one have allocation with weighted probabilities, so as to give different individuals different chances of being chosen for the burden, benefit or task in question? The suggestion might appear absurd. The point of lotteries, presumably, is to facilitate choice when the options cannot be ranked in strict preference order. The use of weighted probabilities would, however, seem to presuppose that the options can be ranked in an order of priority, the candidates more likely to be chosen being the more worthy ones to be chosen.

It is true that equiprobability is the rule,[35] but there are exceptions. In Georgia's land lottery of 1832 'each citizen was entitled to one chance, unless he belonged to a favoured group – orphans, Revolutionary War Veterans, head of a family and the like – in which case he was given two chances'.[36] If we ask why these were favoured, the answer is obvious: because of their special need or contributions. If we ask why the lottery was not held exclusively among people in the favoured categories, the answer is also clear: the authorities did not want a settlement whose population was composed exclusively of orphans, veterans and heads of families.

A contemporary example of weighted lotteries is provided by the Dutch procedure of admission to the 'closed studies' of medicine, chemistry and veterinary science.[37] Figure II.1 illustrates how the system works in medicine. At the individual level the weighted lottery strikes a compromise between rewarding achievement and providing equal opportunity. At the social level, it embodies a compromise between efficiency and equity. The compromise is widely regarded as acceptable, as shown by Fig. II.2, which links scholastic standing and preference for admission procedures.

It comes as no surprise that preference for the straight lottery is

[35] Fishburn (1972), p. 19.
[36] Wilms (1974), p. 54.
[37] Hofstee (1983).

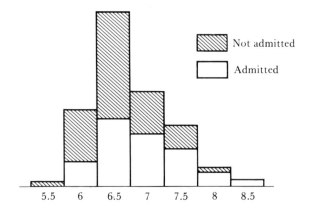

Fig. II.1. Effects of weighted lottery with overall selection rate of .45. (After Hofstee 1983.)

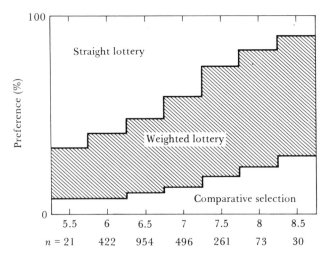

Fig. II.2. The relation between scholastic standing and preference for admissions procedures. (After Hofstee 1983.)

most frequent among weak students and preference for selection on merit most frequent among strong students, just as the preference for equal pay tends to be most frequent among unskilled workers and the preference for pay according to skill most frequent among skilled workers.[38] It is more surprising that the corre-

---

[38] See Messick and Sentis (1983) for a general argument for the view that perceptions of fairness are dictated by self-interest.

lation is so imperfect and that, in fact, the percentage of students who prefer the weighted lottery increases almost monotonically with their scholastic grades. Many of the best students, that is, prefer a system in which they stand a chance of being turned down over one in which they are certain to be accepted. What matters to these students is that the system be sensitive to achievement, not that it be sensitive only to achievement.

Selective law enforcement could similarly be organized as a weighted lottery, with the more serious crimes having the greater likelihood of being pursued, without smaller offenders knowing that they can go about their business with no risk of punishment. Perhaps this is how police attention actually *is* allocated. Spot checks by the Internal Revenue Service and similar institutions probably use weighted lotteries, with larger incomes being more likely to be singled out for inspection than smaller ones, although information about their practices is hard to come by.

Two distinctions may be mentioned at this point. Assume that we have to assign m goods, burdens or tasks randomly to n persons, with $m < n$. We can do so either by picking m persons at random or by having a separate lottery for each person giving him a chance of m/n of being selected. (The distinction can also be applied to nonequiprobabilistic choice.) The procedures are equivalent at the individual level and, if m and n are large, approximately equivalent at the aggregate level. The separate lotteries would be more time-consuming, since they require n separate acts while the direct selection requires only m acts. The two systems could also differ with respect to perceived fairness. Some people might feel that separate lotteries, being more individualized, are also more fair. Moreover, individual lotteries could be decentralized, by each person setting up his own lottery. In some contexts this could be an important advantage.[39]

---

[39] The distinction between one collective lottery and many individual lotteries throws light on the distinction between utilitarianism and theories of justice which, like that of Rawls (1971) or Dworkin (1981), insist on the 'separateness of persons'. Suppose that behind the veil of ignorance we are asked to make a choice among three social arrangements. In A, everybody is moderately well off. In B, everybody is well off, with the exception of one innocent person who is chosen at random to be executed as a scapegoat, as in Shirley Jackson's story discussed in II.4. Arrangement C is like B, except that now a separate lottery is conducted for each person, giving him a $1/n$ chance of being executed. From the utilitarian point of view, B and C are indistinguishable. If either is preferred to A, both are. From a Rawlsian perspective, C could be preferred to A and A would be preferred to

The other distinction is between truly random selection, by either of these two procedures, and the selection of every nth individual in some independently given ordering. The latter can differ from the former in two respects. First, the selectors might be able to influence the outcome, by selecting the ordering (alphabetical versus reverse alphabetical) or the starting point. When testifying before a U.S. Senate committee on jury selection, Hans Zeisel was asked, 'You mean if you just took every third name on the voters list, you wouldn't be getting a random sample?' His answer was, 'No. You would have to be very careful to start the names so that one's friend does not come on the jury list because he is ninth or 12th'.[40] Second, the individuals to be selected might be able to detect the periodicity and to manipulate their own place in the order. A proposal to carry out spot checks on every tenth car on the road, for example, might suffer from this defect.[41]

We should consider, finally, a very different interpretation of selection by lot, as the revelation of God's will. Proverbs 16:33 has it that 'the lot is cast into the lap; but the whole disposing thereof is of the Lord'. From the Old Testament until the early modern age, divinatory, divisory and consultory lotteries were often used for the purpose of discovering God's will.[42] A late example is from

B. In C, each person takes his chance. In B, one person is sacrificed for the sake of society. I believe it follows from the Rawlsian approach to justice that such sacrifices are objectionable, whereas risky choices made by individuals on their own behalf are not. This argument applies independently of the distinction between maximizing average welfare and maximizing the welfare (or amount of primary goods) of the worst off.

[40] Federal jury selection (1967), p. 136.

[41] An interesting case of this kind, treated by the U.S. Supreme Court [*Delaware v. Prouse*, 440 U.S. 648 (1978)], concerned the constitutionality of spot checks of cars for the purpose of examining the driver's licence and the car's registration. The majority held that such checks were unconstitutional, whereas roadblock stops in which all cars were checked were allowed. The argument was not that 'random', 'discretionary' and 'capricious' stops were to be disallowed because of the risk that police officers might abuse their power by seeking to obtain revenge or profit from selecting one car rather than another. Rather the Court's argument was that spot checks involved 'a possibly unsettling show of authority' and thus might 'create substantial anxiety', unlike roadblocks and traffic checkpoints where 'the motorist can see that other vehicles are being stopped'. In a concurring opinion Justice Blackmun assumed that the Court's 'reservations [about less intrusive checks] also includes other not purely random stops (such as every 10th car to pass a given point)'. It is not clear whether he was relying on the need to restrict potentially abusive discretion or on the need to minimize anxiety. To achieve the latter objective, the policy of stopping every tenth car would have to be made publicly known, for example, by roadsigns. The objective of detecting defective cars might suffer from the publicity, however, because owners of defective cars could change their place in the queue.

[42] For an extremely full survey see Gataker (1627); also Lindblom (1964).

1653, when 'a London congregation proposed that a new Parliament should be selected from nominees chosen by each religious congregation "by lot after solemn prayer (a way much used and owned by God in the scriptures)" '.[43] In this function, lotteries, whether formal or informal,[44] are but one of many equivalent devices used to force God's hand, the best-known alternatives being the ordeal and the duel.[45] On this interpretation, there is no need to make lotteries fair, since God's hand could always steer the die or the coin so as to make the right side come up, just as he could ensure the victory of the weaker party in a duel. Similarly, there would be no reason to have a preference between trial by fire, in which God had to intervene miraculously to save the innocent, and trial by cold water, in which intervention was required only to prove guilt.[46] Nor would there be any need to take great care in selecting the pool of eligibles for a lottery. 'If a lot were God's sentence, what need men be so curious in examining and trying the fitness and unfitness of those that they admit to a lot?'[47] That people did in fact care about these procedural matters testifies to their ambiguous attitude towards the methods.

According to Aquinas, 'No miraculous effect is expected [in duels], unless the combatants be very unequal in strength and skill'.[48] The equally matched duel, in his opinion, was a chance device that served as a means of decision, not as a means of proof,[49] and hence did not constitute an unlawful tempting of God. A puzzling case is a thirteenth-century duel in Bologna between two champions fight-

---

[43] Thomas (1973), p. 141.
[44] An instance of an informal lottery is opening the Bible at random in the hope that the selected verse might offer guidance to action. See Thomas (1973), p. 139, and Donagan (1983), who refers to an instance in which 'by a Catch-22 argument, a randomly opened Bible on one occasion forbade the practice itself' (p. 317). (Gataker 1627, p. 346, refers to a similarly self-undermining consultation by Saint Francis.) The practice goes back to the *sortes Virgilianae* of the classical world, amusingly described in Rabelais, *Gargantua and Pantagruel*, 3:11–12. Rabelais brings out the large scope for discretionary interpretation of the randomly selected texts.
[45] This distinction is slightly misleading, as witnessed by the existence of 'ordeal by lot'. For surveys of these techniques for revealing God's will, see Nottarp (1956); Lea (1973, 1974), p. 195; Bartlett (1986).
[46] Thomas (1973), p. 260, suggests that 'the choice of method was . . . determined according to whether or not the accused was already believed to be guilty'. If so, the motive would have been to minimize God's need to intervene miraculously.
[47] Gataker (1627), p. 200.
[48] Thomas Aquinas, *Summa Theologica*, II.II.95.8.
[49] For this distinction see Nottarp (1956), pp. 269–70.

ing on behalf of their principals. 'When the champions were in the lists a child placed inside the garments of each a card bearing the name of his principal, and until the combat was ended no one knew which of them represented the plaintiff and which the defendant'.[50] Was God supposed to guide the hand of the child? Or was he supposed to guide the thrusts of the champions? Or was the whole practice nothing but an elaborate lottery with no religious meaning?

Gataker's view was that the use of lotteries to reveal God's will was lawful only when expressly commanded by God.[51] Instances were the command to use lotteries to divide the land of Israel (e.g., Num. 26:52–6) or to detect the guilty (Josh. 7). Otherwise the use of lotteries to reveal God's will was a blasphemous and superstitious tempting of God. Aquinas, while holding broadly the same position, had a slightly more lenient view: 'If, however, there be urgent necessity it is lawful to seek the divine judgment by casting lots, provided due reverence is observed'.[52] To support his view he cites Augustine (*Ep. Ad Honor* 180): 'If, at a time of persecution, the ministers of God do not agree as to which of them is to remain at his post lest all should flee, and which of them is to flee, lest all die and the Church be forsaken, should there be no other means of coming to an agreement, so far as I can see, they must be chosen by lot'. Gataker's interpretation of this passage from Augustine seems more plausible. One should decide by lot who should 'retire and reserve themselves for better times; that so neither those that stayed might be taxed of presumption, nor those that retired themselves be condemned for cowardice' (p. 66). There is no reason to see Augustine's lottery as a way to 'seek the divine judgment' when it can be explained by these more simple and mundane considerations.[53]

---

[50] Lea (1974), p. 195.
[51] Gataker (1627), pp. 14–25.
[52] Aquinas, *Summa Theologica*.
[53] The same argument applies to the other text from Augustine cited by Aquinas in support of his view: 'If thou aboundest in that which it behooves thee to give to him who hath not, and which cannot be given to two; should two come to you, neither of whom surpasses the other either in need or in some claim on thee, thou couldst not act more justly than in choosing by lot to whom thou shalt give that which thou canst not give to both'. Again nothing supports the view that Augustine was recommending the lottery as a means to find the divine judgement. Indeed, the phrase 'thou couldst not act more justly' directly suggests the other interpretation.

II.3   RANDOMIZATION IN INDIVIDUAL DECISIONS

In discussing the use of lotteries in individual decision making,[54] I shall distinguish between parametric and strategic decision making. The latter is characterized by a strong form of interdependence of decisions: to make up my mind I must anticipate what others will do, knowing that they are similarly deciding on the basis of anticipation of my decision. In the former, the environment, including the behaviour of other people, can be taken for given or at least as dependent only on my actual behaviour, not on anticipations about my behaviour. Both types of decision have scope for randomization. Parametric decisions call for a lottery when the agent is indifferent or his preferences are indeterminate. Strategic decisions call for a lottery when there is no equilibrium point in pure strategies. In a parametric decision, decision by lot is never rationally prescribed, although sometimes rationally allowed. (The habit of always using lotteries to resolve parametric decisions when they are rationally allowed may, however, be rationally prescribed as a means of economizing on costs of decision.) In a strategic decision randomization is sometimes rationally prescribed.

In parametric decisions, or 'games against nature', decision by lot would seem useful when we are unable to make up our mind about what to do, or when the effort required to make up our mind does not seem worth while, or when the lottery has good incentive effects. The last reason, while very important in social lotteries, has only a minor role in the making of individual decisions. The most important example is probably randomization in designing experiments. 'The medical experimenter who selects which patients are to receive a new treatment for a disease and which are to receive the standard treatment or none at all, can unconsciously select for the new treatment patients that are health-

---

[54] The distinction between individual and social lotteries is somewhat inadequate, in that it does not capture cases in which two or more individuals freely agree to have some allocative decision made by randomizing, without there being any institution that can force them to stick to their decision. In particular, randomizing is often the theoretical solution to bargaining problems. In III.5 I discuss private custody bargaining in this perspective and conclude that randomizing devices are not likely to be much used. I believe this conclusion carries over to other real-life cases of bargaining.

ier and have therefore a better chance of recovery. Randomization prevents the exercise of such bias'.[55] This is almost a two-person problem, in which the conscious self (which seeks truth) uses a lottery to prevent the unconscious self (which seeks success) from succumbing to the pleasure principle. Since I do not believe such cases to be frequent outside experimental contexts, I shall focus on lotteries related to uncertainty and indeterminacy.

First, we could use lotteries when there are several options that are equally and maximally good. These options may be indistinguishable, as in the choice between identical cans of Campbell's tomato soup, or they may differ in ways that exactly offset each other so as to leave us indifferent among them. Next, we could use lotteries when the top-ranked options are incommensurable, for either of the two reasons discussed in I.3. In some contexts we may be unable to rank or compare the outcomes of the various actions we can take, namely if the outcomes differ along several dimensions so that we are unable to make the necessary trade-offs. In other contexts we may be able to attach values but not numerical probabilities to the outcomes. Finally, the top-ranked options may be equally good as far as we know, and it is not worth the trouble to find out more. Although we are confident that one option would prove superior if we took the time and effort to find out more about them, it may not be rational to do so because the difference is expected to be small compared with the cost of acquiring the additional information.[56] Driving through a foreign city without a map is a case in point.

Some of these choices are trivial, in the sense that it does not matter much which option we choose. It may be important to make a choice, but unimportant which choice we make. Buridan's ass illustrates this predicament. Lotteries can also be appropriate for highly consequential choices, however. The choice of a career (I.3) or the choice between two women to whom I might propose marriage may not lend itself to rational decision grounded in properties of the options. Instead, I might decide to toss a coin or use some equivalent procedure. The choice of procedure may be

---

[55] Suppes (1984), p. 211.
[56] Strictly speaking, the first category, of choice under indifference, should be subsumed under this heading, since one can (almost) always break a tie by finding out more about the options.

governed by quasi-superstitious considerations, as exemplified by the following thought experiment.

Suppose Jack is unable to make up his mind whether to propose marriage to Jill or to Mary. He cannot make himself toss a coin between them, since this, he feels, would be an excessively impersonal and frivolous way to make such an important decision. He decides instead to have the decision made by a natural lottery or by fate, by proposing to whomever of the two he first meets in the street. As far as he knows both outcomes are equally likely, yet he prefers this epistemically random procedure to the flip of a coin. Assume, however, that he later learns that Jill was out of town so that there was no real chance that he would have run into her. Then he might well reconsider or regret his decision. He might feel that Jill 'hadn't had a chance'. By this he might mean that he deprived 'fate' of the opportunity of steering the outcome, assuming that fate never operates such 'uphill' moves as recalling Jill to town by her father's illness.[57]

By this story I want to suggest that visibly arbitrary chance is often repulsive. Even when we have no reason to decide one way or another, we would like the outcome to be determined by reasons. To have it both ways, we can tie our decision to natural causality in the hope that it will reflect some underlying purpose or pattern in the universe, such as fate, God's will or the natural interconnections among all things. There is a large overlap between lotteries and the various forms of divination, from prayer through astrology to witchcraft, memorably described by Keith Thomas in *Religion and the Decline of Magic*. Theologians made clear distinctions among these practices. Some of them were held to be legitimate, but most of them were condemned as blasphemous and superstitious. In the popular mind they all came together in an undifferentiated belief that the universe was not random and that it was possible to unlock its secrets. The permutations were endless. Sometimes people used a lottery to choose a propitious time to consult the astrologer.[58] Sometimes it was held that 'no prayer could be effective unless offered at an astrologically propitious moment',[59] whereas one fa-

---

[57] For the distinction between uphill and downhill moves in thought experiments and scenarios, see Kahneman and Tversky (1982c).
[58] Thomas (1973), p. 402, n.86.
[59] Ibid., p. 432.

mous astrologer 'said prayers before setting a figure'.[60] According to Sir Thomas Browne, ' 'Tis not a ridiculous devotion to say a prayer before a game at tables'.[61] Several 'went so far as to declare that astrological diagnosis was the only sure way in which witchcraft could be discovered'.[62]

The purpose of these techniques was partly cognitive, partly practical. In a world of uncertainty and misery – Thomas refers to 'the hazards of an intensely insecure environment'[63] – people want to know the causes of their misfortunes as well as what to do about them. The idea that suffering can strike blindly and randomly is hard to tolerate. While the most satisfactory belief is perhaps that someone else is to blame for one's misfortunes, it may be better to think oneself blamable than to believe that no one is to blame.[64] If people, for instance, believe that the world is basically just, we would expect the unfortunate victims also to blame themselves. There is some evidence for this view in the 'just world' studies initiated by Melvin Lerner.[65] The explanation, even if unfavourable to oneself, at least provides a *meaning* for the events in question. Since human beings are meaning-seeking animals, they are uncomfortable with the idea that events are merely sound and fury, signifying nothing.[66]

Human beings are also reason-seeking animals. They want to have reasons for what they do, and they create reasons when none exist. Moreover, they want the reasons to be clear and decisive, so as to make the decision easy rather than close. Several findings support this view. We do not like to make close decisions, perhaps because of the potential regret associated with them. There is a tendency for the arguments that go into a close decision to be

---

[60] Ibid., p. 450.
[61] Quoted in ibid., p. 135.
[62] Ibid., p. 757.
[63] Ibid., p. 5.
[64] Thomas argues (ibid., p. 763) that the tendency of many of these practices, including witchcraft, to make the sufferer believe in his own guilt was also socially valuable. Although he does not explicitly say that the social benefits enter into the *explanation* of this tendency, this conclusion is almost irresistibly suggested by the highly functionalist bias of his book taken as a whole.
[65] See notably Lerner and Miller (1978) and Rubin and Pepau (1973). The strongest result in the latter article is not the reaction *to* the losers in the draft lottery, but the reaction *of* the losers, who tended to lose self-esteem. Other findings point in different directions. Hoffman and Spitzer (1985) did not find that lotteries generate moral entitlements that can serve as the disagreement point for bargaining games.
[66] See also Elster (1983a), sec. II.10.

rearranged in retrospect, so that the chosen option emerges as clearly superior to the others.[67] Sometimes this process of adjustment takes place before the choice, to permit avoidance of the unpleasant state of mind associated with a close race among the options. It has been suggested that in such cases one unconsciously looks for a framework within which one option, no matter which, has a clear advantage over the others, and that, having found such a framework, one adopts it for the time being and chooses the option which it favours.[68]

Similar findings about the tension created by predecision ambiguity are reported in unpublished work by Amos Tversky.[69] In his experiment, subjects were given a description of two apartments that differed in price and in distance from campus, and told that they could either choose one of them now or go on looking at some other apartments that might or might not be available. If they took the latter option, they ran the risk of the two apartments becoming unavailable. Before making a decision, subjects reviewed the entire set of options. Some subjects were placed in a high-conflict condition, in which one apartment scored high on the first dimension and low on the second, and vice versa for the other. Both apartments, however, were quite good on both dimensions. Other subjects were placed in a low-conflict condition, in which one apartment scored higher than the other on both dimensions. Here, however, both apartments were relatively poor in both respects. In the first condition, more subjects decided to search further than in the second. The desire to resolve ambiguity and to make a clear-cut decision apparently mattered more than the desire for a good apartment.[70]

Keith Thomas argues that one cause of the decline of magic in the late seventeenth century was the increased 'ability to tolerate ignorance which has been defined as an essential characteristic of the scientific attitude'.[71] It follows that explicit lotteries should be more frequently used, with no attempt to dress them up as an

---

[67] See, e.g., Brehm (1956); Festinger (1957); Veyne (1976), p. 708 and passim.

[68] Shepard (1964).

[69] Tversky (1987).

[70] In a variant of this experiment, the second condition is replaced by one in which a third option is added that is dominated by one of the others on both dimensions. More people then choose the dominating option, thus violating the principle that choice be independent of irrelevant alternatives. (Having heard about this finding at second or third hand, I cannot give a precise attribution.)

[71] Thomas (1973), p. 790.

expression of fate or God's will. But he also suggests that people in contemporary societies are just as averse to the recognition of uncertainty, ignorance and indeterminacy. 'The investment programmes of modern industrial firms, for example, often require decisions to be taken about future policies at times when it is often impossible to form a rational view of their outcome. It is not surprising that industrialists sometimes use barely relevant statistical projects to justify what is essentially a leap in the dark'.[72] Speculating along similar lines, I would suggest that Bayesian decision theory itself is an expression of the desire to have reasons for everything. The idea, for instance, that in the absence of specific information all outcomes should be deemed equally probable cannot be justified in logic, because of the problem of individuating states of the world. It does, however, have firm psychological foundations, in the desire to force a determinate solution to all decision problems. The toleration of ignorance, like the toleration of ambiguity more generally, does not come easily.[73]

In an early and penetrating analysis of this problem Otto Neurath wrote:

One can think of all kinds of men in situations in which no further deliberation can help. There is not the slightest reason to doubt that a great military leader like Napoleon is frequently incapable of deciding by means of reflection exactly what he should do. Nevertheless the method of more or less admitted button counting is an object of abhorrence and ridicule to most contemporaries. However, since these contemporaries are not in possession of complete insight either, the question is which substitute for button-counting do they apply.[74]

Among the substitutes enumerated are the following. First, there is 'instinct', or (as I would call it) judgement. Neurath observes that the proper place of instinct is not as a substitute for reflection: 'This view misuses instinct by consciously introducing it as a mere stop-gap, whereas its significance is evident wherever it rules from the start'. He adds, however, that 'part of the significance of instinct is that it did not allow vacillation to occur in periods when cool calculation played a minor role, and in this

[72] Ibid., p. 791.
[73] Loevinger (1976).
[74] Neurath (1913). I am grateful to A. Soulez for drawing my attention to this brilliant article, in which I found Neurath to anticipate a number of conclusions at which I had arrived independently.

respect it avoided waste of energy'. Second, he considers the belief in oracles, omens, prophecies and the like. On the one hand, he observes, 'great military leaders, politicians and other men of action . . . often show a pronounced tendency toward superstition'. On the other hand, 'individuals whose weak character does not allow them to influence events energetically [tend] towards the more complicated forms of prophecy and often [create] a highly randomized structure of omens'. Third, Neurath mentions the use of authorities, including majority voting: 'Somebody may indeed approve the majority principle only because it enhances the ability to act; it is a beloved substitute for the unloved drawing of lots'. In II.6 I argue that it is rather the other way around: because of the indeterminacies in majority voting, we might sometimes as well use a lottery.

Consider next lotteries in strategic decision making. Here, the purpose of randomization is not to resolve indeterminacy, but to keep other people uncertain about what one is doing. A simple example is randomized bluffing in poker.[75] A more complex example is taken from the hunting practices of the Naskapi, an Indian tribe in the Labradorian peninsula.[76] To determine the direction in which to hunt, they burn the shoulder blade of a caribou over a fire so as to produce cracks and spots in it. The blade is then held in a predetermined position with reference to the local topography, and the cracks and spots used to indicate the direction. It has been conjectured that a useful effect of this randomized procedure is to prevent regularities in the hunting patterns which might be detected by the hunted.[77] Although the randomizing device is probably biased, in that cracks and spots are more likely to form in certain ways than others, the 'regularity stemming from this source may to some extent be lessened because the Naskapi change campsites'.[78] This effect, if indeed it exists, might or might not explain the practice itself, depending on the presence of either intentionality or feedback in the process.

The Naskapi play a game against nature, but against a part of

[75] As Alvin Roth has pointed out to me, one can also use pure strategies to decide when to bluff, e.g., by bluffing if and only if one is dealt the two of diamonds. Here one random event, namely the dealing of the cards, is used for two different purposes.
[76] The following draws upon Moore (1957).
[77] Ibid., p. 71.
[78] Ibid., p. 72.

nature that is capable of rudimentary learning. Fully strategic action, however, takes place in the presence of fully strategic others, who are capable not only of learning from the past but also of anticipating the future or, for that matter, the present. For simplicity we may consider strategic games in which the players have to make simultaneous decisions such that the outcome for each depends on the decisions of all. In these games, it is also in general true that the decision of each depends on the expected decisions of all. For a long while it was thought that this interdependence leads to an infinite regress.[79] The modern notion of an equilibrium point has clarified the problem. It is defined as a set of choices such that no player can improve his outcome by unilaterally deviating from it. The fundamental theorem of game theory, proved by John Nash around 1950, is that all noncooperative games, that is, games in which players decide independently of one another, have an equilibrium point.[80] An equilibrium point may consist of pure strategies, so that to each player there is associated one physical action he should take. It may also, however, consist of mixed strategies, that is, a weighted lottery over the pure strategies. For instance, it may tell one player to use a 60–40 lottery going north and going south, and the other to use a 70–30 lottery between the same options.

Explicit, conscious randomizing in strategic interaction is rare, with one exception. To see why, two observations are sufficient. First, mixed strategies are never dominant. It is never the case, that is, that a random choice of strategy is prescribed regardless of what the other players do. Hence mixed strategies will at most be chosen under conditions of perfect information that are rarely fulfilled in practice. Second, mixed strategies are never uniquely optimal. If a player expects all the other players to stick to their equilibrium strategies, it follows by definition that he cannot do better by deviating from his equilibrium strategy. It can also be proved, however, that he can do no worse for himself if he devi-

---

[79] Rémond de Montmort (1713) wrote that 'Les questions sont très simples, mais je les crois insolubles. Si cela est, c'est un grand dommage car cette difficulté se recontre en plusieurs choses de la vie civile. Quand deux personnes, par example, ayant affaire ensemble, chacun veut se régler sur la conduite de l'autre'.

[80] The truth of this statement depends on certain assumptions about the strategies open to the players and about their preference orderings.

ates from it, choosing instead any probabilistic combination of the pure strategies that enter into the equilibrium strategy with a nonzero probability. He might then well reason as follows. 'Suppose one of the other players makes a mistake, or is less than perfectly rational or less than perfectly well-informed. To protect myself against this eventuality, I should really choose my maximin strategy,[81] that is, the strategy that makes the worst that could happen to me as good as possible. If the other players stick to their equilibrium strategies, I have nothing to lose, and if they don't I have something to gain. On further reflection, moreover, I must conclude that they are probably thinking along similar lines, being as rational and as cautious as myself. To preempt their preemptive deviation from equilibrium, I must deviate myself.' The smallest chink in the assumption that all players are rational and well informed, and that all know this, and so on, would make the whole equilibrium unravel.

The exception to this statement arises in two-person zero-sum games, in which one person's gain is always another person's loss. Here the equilibrium strategies are also the maximin strategies of the players, so that the cautious fall-back option is also the strategically rational one. Since military conflicts often approximate the zero-sum condition, it is not surprising that we find mixed strategies being used in the deployment of troops. However, nobody cares much about ex ante rationality. Ex post success is what counts. 'Imagine a congressional investigation of a military commander, or an agency chief, who has adopted a specific pure strategy which has been ruinous. What would be the reaction if his defense hinged on the fact that he adopted this pure strategy by the throw of dice?'[82] If the commander or agency chief acts out of self-interest, he would be best advised to use the maximin pure strategy, even knowing that this may not be optimal against what the opponent will do.

There is a possible behavioural defence of mixed strategies that extends also to non-zero-sum games, stated as follows by Leif Johansen:

---

[81] Within the set of probabilistic combinations of the pure strategies that enter into the equilibrium strategy with a nonzero probability.

[82] Luce and Raiffa (1957), p. 76.

When the decision-makers ponder the situation, they will go through various stages of reasoning, thinking of what the other players will do as well as of what would be the best decision on one's own part. When no equilibrium exists in pure strategies, this reasoning will not lead to a unique conclusion about what the decision-maker should do. Each time a player, tentatively, comes to a conclusion about what he should do, he will get second thoughts about what the others will do, and then again abandon the tentative conclusion about [his] own decision. For instance, when all players are similar, an individual decision-maker who tentatively arrives at a non-random decision, will immediately think of what happens if the other actors are thinking along the same lines, and he will realize that his tentative decision does not look like a good decision. Without having studied the theory of non-cooperative equilibria, including solutions in terms of mixed strategies, a decision-maker would sooner or later have to take a more arbitrary decision, which could perhaps be described as a random decision.[83]

The problem is that there is no reason for the randomly chosen strategies to be chosen with the precise numerical probabilities assigned to them by the theory.[84] Perhaps we could expect this to happen if the optimal mixed strategies are equiprobabilistic ones (cf. Harsanyi's argument cited in I.3), but not otherwise.

II.4   SOCIAL LOTTERIES: AN OVERVIEW

I begin with a list of cases in which lotteries are currently used to allocate tasks, scarce goods or necessary burdens to individuals, or in which they have been used in the past for these purposes, or in which their use has been seriously proposed or at least envisaged. In II.5 through II.7 I consider some of the cases in greater detail.

There are not many instances of social decision making by lot in contemporary Western societies. The two major examples are the draft[85] and the selection of jurors.[86] Lotteries have been used occasionally to allocate scarce medical resources such as kidney machines[87] and they play a role in regulating inheritance in some countries.[88] Lotteries play a mostly trivial role as tiebreakers in

---

[83] Johansen (1987).
[84] Johansen is aware of this problem and attempts to deal with it in terms of the theory of fictitious play (see Luce and Raiffa 1957, pp. 442–6). He is also aware of the shortcomings of this procedure.
[85] For a survey, see Fienberg (1971). An eloquent argument for lotteries in the draft is found in Harvard Study Group (1967).
[86] For a full discussion of American jury selection, see Hans and Vidmar (1986).
[87] 'Scarce medical resources' (1969), p. 660.
[88] Herzfeld (1980).

various political contexts.[89] A dramatic example occurred in Sweden after the election in 1973 resulted in an exact tie between the socialist and the nonsocialist blocs in Parliament, and decisions had to be made by the toss of a coin since the constitution did not provide another way of resolving impasses. In the United States, oil-drilling leases are partly allocated by lotteries.[90] In several countries, admission to high schools, universities and professional schools sometimes is determined by random drawing, either within a pool formed by substantive criteria or, as in Holland, using weights determined by these criteria. Lotteries are frequently used in sports and games, to decide who plays first or to match teams with each other or teams with players.[91] Lotteries and similar procedures are sometimes used to select questions in school and university examinations. Spot checks by the Internal Revenue Service and similar institutions are sometimes done on a quasi-randomized basis.[92] Public housing is allocated by lotteries in several countries. In Israel, for example, applicants for housing are ranked on a point system that takes account of dependents, present housing and other variables. Those with many points participate in lotteries for the best housing, those with fewer points in lotteries for the less attractive.

In the past lotteries have been used more widely. The best-known cases are probably the choice of political representatives by

---

[89] South Dakota uses lotteries to break ties in congressional elections. In Tennessee the choice between two candidates with the same number of votes is left to the governor. In Massachusetts equality of votes means that no candidate is elected, and the situation is treated as if the incumbent had died in office. If the election is very close, courts will sometimes order a new election.

[90] Haspel (1985).

[91] In the United States, more complex sport lotteries include the following. In the National Basketball Association, it was formerly the case that the team that finished last in a given season had the first choice of players for the next season, the next to last had the second choice and so on. Because of the incentive to lose created by this practice, the order is now determined by a lottery among the bottom eight teams. In the supplementary draft for the National Football League, the rights to choose players are allocated by an inverse weighted lottery. The World Champions get their name placed in a hat once. The last, the twenty-eighth-place team, gets its name placed in the hat twenty-eight times. (I am indebted to Mark Kishlansky for supplying information about these practices.)

[92] Institutions of this kind face two optimization problems. First, what pattern of randomization should it announce to the public to achieve maximal deterrence? Second, what pattern of randomization should it actually use to maximize revenue from fines and payment of unpaid taxes? Because these institutions are allowed to proceed secretly, and because the public does not have the information to infer the true pattern from observed behaviour, the two patterns are not constrained to coincide.

lot in the Greek and Italian city-states.[93] Lotteries also played a role in Roman elections. The selection of jurors by lot was introduced in Athens in the fifth century B.C., and the random assignment of judges to cases a century later.[94] The selection of religious officials and the assignment of sacred offices have been carried out by lot in many societies, the best known being the selection by lot of the apostle to succeed Judas (Acts 1:26). The allocation of land to settlers by means of a lottery was a regular practice in the United States in the nineteenth century[95] and is reported at several places in the Old Testament (e.g., Num. 26:52–6 and 33:54). Various kinds of draft lotteries were common in France from the late seventeenth to the late nineteenth centuries.[96] The practice of decimation, that is, killing one hostage or one treacherous soldier out of ten, has been common. Often, the choice has been left to the victims themselves, as illustrated in Graham Greene's *The Tenth Man*. It was one of the customs of the sea to choose the victim of cannibalism by lottery when the situation was desperate enough to justify this step.[97]

Gataker reports the following examples, among many others. According to Origen, angels' places in heaven are assigned to them by lot (p. 61). In Geneva, priests are selected by lot 'to visit the infected at the pesthouse in times of general infection by epidemic disease' (p. 66). 'In desperate cases, [the Jews] decided sometimes by lot who should slay each other' (p. 89), an obvious reference to Massada. 'In Egypt it is reported that they were wont yearly by lot to assign each man or each kindred what land they should till' (p. 104). Cambises's army 'for want of victuals by lot sequestred a tenth part of themselves to make meat of' (p. 110). A Nestorian abbot cast lots to decide 'between his heretical monks and the orthodox bishops, to be therefore informed whether of them held the truth: which being cast, says the story, it went with the bishops, whereupon he and his monks, the most of them, came home unto them' (p. 330).

There have been many proposals to use lotteries to regulate

---

[93] Headlam (1933); Staveley (1972).
[94] MacDowell (1978).
[95] For a description of one case, see Dale (1983). The procedure used was a combination of lottery, choice and queuing.
[96] Sturgill (1975); Badeau (1882), pp. 289–96; Choisel (1981).
[97] Simpson (1984), p. 140.

choices that are now made on other grounds. It has been seriously argued that political representatives should be chosen by random drawings among the votes, to facilitate the representation of minorities.[98] Similarly, it has been proposed that when there are cyclical majorities, one alternative should be selected at random.[99] Also, by allowing the alternatives themselves to take the form of lotteries certain perverse decisions can be avoided, although the procedure also creates further difficulties.[100] Another proposal is to reshape the political system so that power devolves from parliament to decentralized committees, whose members are chosen by lot.[101] It has been suggested that randomly switching babies among families at birth, although undesirable because of the implied violation of family autonomy, would have the good effect of ensuring equality of opportunity.[102] It has been proposed, furthermore, that broadcasting licenses and procreation rights be allocated in this way.[103] Various writers have argued that employers should use lotteries to choose among minimally qualified applicants for jobs,[104] that layoffs should be decided by lottery,[105] that elections should be randomly timed,[106] that members of congress should be randomly assigned to committees,[107] that custody of children in disputed cases should be decided randomly (see chapter III), and that allocation of medical resources should rely on lotteries as a main mechanism.[108] In *U.S. v. Holmes* the issue was who, if anyone, would have been thrown overboard from a leaky and overcrowded lifeboat. The crew had thrown fourteen male passengers overboard, but the judge said that the victims ought to have been chosen by lot among all concerned, crew as well as passengers. Lot, he said, is 'the fairest mode, and, in some sort, an appeal to God, for selection of the victim. . . . In no other than this

---

[98] Ackerman (1980), pp. 286–9; Amar (1984).
[99] Ackerman (1980), pp. 291–3.
[100] Zeckhauser (1969).
[101] Burnheim (1985).
[102] Fishkin (1983), p. 57.
[103] Greely (1977).
[104] Hapgood (1975); Divine (1976).
[105] Greely (1977), p. 125; Ireland and Law (1982), pp. 19–21.
[106] Lindbeck (1976).
[107] Thaler (1983).
[108] Kilner (1981). For a very specific proposal of this kind, involving alternate stages of lotteries and selection on medical criteria, see Katz (1973).

or some like way are those having equal rights put upon an equal footing, and in no other way is it possible to guard against partiality and oppression'.[109]

I conclude this overview with two uses of the lottery concept in fiction. Shirley Jackson's short story 'The Lottery' describes, in chillingly trivial detail, a small New England village in which the inhabitants each June choose, by a multistage lottery, one among themselves to be stoned to death. The impact of the story comes from the utter lack of any perceived *point* to the sacrificial lottery, except for the mumblings of an old man that the harvest would be bad were they to give up the lottery, as other villages are said to be doing. The biblical ancestors of this story would seem to be the choice by lot of a scapegoat in Lev. 16:7–10 and the lot by which Jonah was selected to be thrown overboard as responsible for the tempest threatening the ship (Jon. 1:7). The analogies are imperfect, however. The goat to be sacrificed was not the scapegoat, but the other goat upon which the Lord's lot fell. Rather the scapegoat was driven into the wilderness, as were most human scapegoats in classical Greece.[110] When human scapegoats were actually sacrificed, there is no evidence that they were chosen by lot among the population at large.[111] Rather the victims tended to be criminals, poor or otherwise repulsive persons. Being like dirt, they symbolized the dirt to be wiped out. The story of Jonah, by contrast, refers to a specific crisis, not to a periodically recurring sacrifice as in Shirley Jackson's story. Moreover, Jonah was not a scapegoat in the sense of a symbolic victim: he was actually believed to be guilty of something. Hence Shirley Jackson's story unites elements which as far as I know have never been found together in actual societies: the periodic character of the sacrifice, the selection of the victim from an unrestricted pool, the use of a lottery to select the victim, the subsequent killing of the victim and the purely symbolic (nonretributive) significance of the rite. Could it have happened? I doubt it.

---

[109] *U.S. v. William Holmes*, 1 Wallace Junior 1, 26 Fed. Cas. 30. For discussion of a similar (fictitious) case, see Fuller (1949).

[110] Burkert (1985), pp. 82–3.

[111] A possible exception is provided by Frazer (1963), p. 660, who cites a text to the effect that 'the human victim chosen for sacrifice . . . may be either a freeborn or a slave, a person of noble or wealthy parentage, or one of humble birth'. The actual choice mechanism is not explained, however.

Jorge Luis Borges's short story 'The Lottery in Babylon' describes a society in which virtually all matters are left to chance,
including the use of the chance mechanism itself.[112] The very
operation of lotteries is tainted by randomness, uncertainty, se-
crecy and fraud, until all members of society become their covic-
tims and coperpetrators. The story is probably inspired by the
story of Heliogabalus, described as follows by Gataker. 'That mon-
ster of men, Heliogabalus, a second Nero, used to propound to
whom he pleased, both in public and private, certain mixed lots,
some matter of gift, some matter of charge, of such extreme ineq-
uity, that some were neither mended nor impaired at all, but
mocked only, some were made, as we say, and others utterly un-
done' (p. 157). A modern Heliogabalus is described in Graham
Greene's *Doctor Fischer of Geneva or the Bomb Party*. The rich Dr
Fischer likes to humiliate his guests by offering them Christmas
crackers which have either a large cheque or a small bomb in
them. In these stories, lotteries are synonymous with capricious
and arbitrary behaviour, in contrast to Shirley Jackson's story, in
which they are part and parcel of the social order. These are
indeed the two faces of social lotteries, which combine the regularity of an institution with unpredictability of outcome. The great
advantage, and sometimes the great disadvantage, of lotteries is
that one can count on not being able to count on the outcome.

II.5 SCARCE GOODS AND NECESSARY BURDENS

To discuss arguments for and against the use of lotteries to assign
goods and bads, scarce goods and necessary burdens, I shall compare them with a number of other allocative mechanisms which
can rival as well as be complementary to chance mechanisms.
There are two ways in which substantive criteria such as need,
productivity and merit can be used in combination with lotteries.
First, they can be used to define the pool from which the random
selection is made or, less frequently, to eliminate some of the
randomly chosen candidates. I know of no instance of social lotteries without some preselection or postselection scrutiny on the basis

[112] For an attempt to draw some lessons for political theory from this story, see Goodwin
(1984).

of need, merit and the like. We must then ask why the criteria used in the scrutiny could not also be used to select the candidates. Answers will be suggested at various places in this chapter.

Second, substantive criteria can be used to define the probabilities in weighted lotteries. In addition to the actual examples cited in II.3 concerning land lotteries and admission to medical school, the following proposal, further discussed in II.8, is worth citing:

> When a resource is scarce, always to prefer the parent or the younger patient will have the effect of excluding people without children and people not necessarily very advanced in years. Because it is harsh to deprive treatable patients of any hope of cure, and because no principle of preference is clearly right, it may be desirable to devise a compromise system. This might be done, for example, by establishing separate waiting lists for patients in different age groups and for those with or without families. Patients could be selected from one waiting list with greater frequency than from another.[113]

In assessing and comparing these allocative mechanisms, three criteria should be kept in mind. First, there is the inherent fairness or goodness of the decision that results, disregarding incentive effects and strategic adaptations. Next, there is the impact of these 'second-order' allocations on the 'first-order' allocations of a certain part of society's resources to the domain in question.[114] It has been argued, for instance, that 'if random selection or the market were the main basis of scarce resources allocation, there is all the more likelihood that scarcity would be significantly alleviated as holders of political and economic power attempted to reduce the chance that they themselves would be excluded'.[115] Similarly, the introduction of the draft lottery and the end of deferment for (most) students may have contributed to political pressure to end the Vietnam War, as influential parents faced the prospects of seeing their children sent to die. Other things being equal, we would want second-order mechanisms that did not shape or preempt the political first-order choices.[116] Finally, we

---

[113] 'Scarce medical resources' (1969), p. 665. In Poland there are usually two queues for consumer goods, the normal one and the one that consists of those who have the right to buy without queuing up, such as pregnant women, the handicapped and very old people. To regulate the queues there is 'an unwritten rule that buying is realized in turns: one "privileged" person, one "normal", etc.' (Czwartosz 1988, p. 6).

[114] For this distinction, see Calabresi and Bobbit (1978), pp. 19–22 and passim.

[115] Kilner (1981), p. 266.

[116] Assuming that 'we' here refers to politicians, this amounts to saying that they ought to discourage second-order mechanisms that would give them an incentive to make bad first-order decisions, given their known tendency towards opportunistic behaviour.

would need to consider the 'third-order' decisions made by the individuals who apply for the scarce goods (including exemptions from burdens) or by other means make themselves eligible for them. The incentive effects may be socially valuable, as when people work hard to get into school, or undesirable, as when people mutilate themselves to avoid military service. Indeed, there are interaction effects among all three levels. A given second-order principle may generate decisions at the third level which in the aggregate influence social wealth and thus the first-order decisions about how to allocate it.

Absolute equality

When a good can be infinitely divided without loss of value, it is often divided equally among all applicants or potential beneficiaries. When it cannot be thus divided, the principle of absolute equality dictates that it should not be given to anyone. A striking example is the following: 'According to the Jerusalem Talmud . . . if a group of men is surrounded by pagans who demand that one of the men be handed over to be killed or else all the men will be killed, the men must allow themselves to be killed rather than hand over a single Jew'.[117] Similarly, Solomon's first decision, to cut the child in half, followed the principle of absolute equality at the expense of efficiency. Usually, however, the principle of absolute equality is not applied when the good cannot be divided without loss of value. Instead, lotteries offer themselves as a natural alternative, substituting equality of chance for equality of outcomes. A clear example is in St. John, 19:23–4: 'Then the soldiers, when they had crucified Jesus, took his garments and made four parts, to every soldier a part, and also his coat: now the coat was without seam, woven from the top throughout. They said there-

---

[117] Leiman (1983). Rosner (1986), pp. 347–8, interprets the principle as expressing the idea that one may not destroy human life to save another human life. In light of the following, the interpretation is not compelling: 'If, however, the pagans designate the victim by name, Rabbi Johanan . . . rules that the victim may be handed over even if not guilty of a capital offence' (Leiman 1983). Hence the idea seems rather to be that of avoiding moral responsibility for selecting the sacrificial victim. (For another example of this reluctance to assume responsibility, see Glover 1977, p. 102). A more clear-cut Talmudic example is that of the two people in the desert and one pitcher of water, sufficient to save one but insufficient to save both (Rosner 1986, p. 348). Here several commentaries say that both should drink and both should die.

fore among themselves, Let us not rend it, but cast lots for it, whose it shall be'.

Lotteries are preferred to physical division when division reduces the value of that which is to be divided. Cutting a child in two would reduce its value to nothing. Cutting a seamless coat in four parts would reduce its value substantially. In these cases, the criterion for value reduction is that each applicant would rather have the undivided object than the parts into which it is divided, even were he to get them all. In other cases, the criterion must be stated in terms of increasing marginal utility or productivity. Thus if time spent with a child has increasing marginal utility, both parents would prefer coin tossing to decide custody over time sharing or joint custody. (That statement, however, presupposes risk neutrality. Sufficient parental risk aversion would offset increasing marginal utility and make the parents opt for time sharing.)[118] Because of learning effects it is often more efficient to have half the age group perform two years of military service than to have the whole group do service for one year. In some cases, division reduces not only the value but the amount of that which is to be divided. It might seem obvious that work sharing is a better solution to the unemployment problem than random layoffs, yet under quite reasonable conditions a shorter working day could lead to increased unemployment.[119]

Queuing

There are two ways of seeing the relation between lotteries and queuing. First, they can be conceived as alternative and rival mechanisms for allocating scarce goods. Thus the first-come first-served approach to the allocation of kidney machines has been contrasted with allocation by lottery. Many hospitals use the former, but at least one has used the latter.[120] In an empirical study of perceived justice, subjects were asked what was the fairest procedure for allocating tickets to a concert: by queuing, by lottery or by an auction.

---

[118] This distinction is meaningless in standard (von Neumann–Morgenstern) utility theory, in which the attitude towards risk is already incorporated into the utility function. I believe, however, that the problem of child custody brings out very well the reality of the distinction, and hence the limited validity of the theory.

[119] Hoel (1986).

[120] Katz (1973), p. 402; 'Scarce medical resources' (1969), pp. 659–60.

Somewhat surprisingly, perhaps, the procedures were ranked in the order just mentioned.[121] The reason may have been that using the queue could be seen as allocation by effort, albeit a totally unproductive one. In that case queuing that requires only the mailing or deposit of a claim would be less highly valued. Second, however, queues can be seen as a kind of 'natural lottery',[122] related to but distinct from artificially generated random selection. The allocation of intensive care units in a hospital can hardly be made other than on a first-come first-served basis, derived from the random order in which accidents occur. Hobbes argued that primogeniture was a form of natural lottery, on a par with the principle of first seizure.[123] The argument is somewhat specious. Primogeniture, while impartial (nobody intended the first born to be the firstborn), can hardly be said to be fair (each child did not have an equal chance of being the firstborn).

I distinguished between queues which involve a strenuous if wasteful standing in line and those which simply require the mailing or depositing of a claim. Examples of the former are queues for consumer goods in Eastern Europe[124] or for university admission in France, where would-be students and their relatives stand or lie in queue for days. Examples of the latter are the recent (January 1987) queuing by mail for U.S. nonrestrictive immigrant visas or for nursery school places in Italy, where parents deposit a claim when their children are born. In the former case, resources wasted by waiting in the queue can easily absorb much or all of the surplus to be allocated.[125] Furthermore, we must distinguish between queues which are formed by voluntary decisions (e.g., queues for immigrant visa or for consumer goods) and those formed by natural processes (e.g., queues for intensive care units or for kidneys).[126] The former, unlike the latter, depend on individual skills and lend themselves to strategic calculation. For a queue to be assimilable to a natural lottery, it must be organized in a way that does not waste resources, and the order in which people enter the queue should reflect a truly random process. Even

---

[121] Kahneman, Knetsch and Thaler (1986).
[122] Kilner (1981).
[123] *Leviathan*, I.15.
[124] Czwartoz (1988).
[125] Barzel (1974); Johansen (1987).
[126] Löwy (1986).

when queues are used under these conditions, their explanation may, however, be a different one. Order in the queue can serve as proxy for need: if a patient becomes steadily more ill as time goes on, his need for medication or treatment may also increase.

Rotation

When the allocative situation recurs regularly, rotation is an obvious alternative to lotteries. It is used mainly, perhaps only, in the matching of individuals with political, legal and administrative offices. One might think that rotation is just a temporal division of the good or burden, especially similar to equal physical division of, say, a cake. Yet because it often matters when a task is to be performed, whereas it does not matter who gets which of several identical pieces of cake, the two mechanisms are quite different. Rotation can be combined with lotteries in two ways. First, the order of rotation may be chosen randomly in advance from the set of all possible sequences. This practice was often observed in Republican Rome, to fix the order in which rotating offices were to be allocated.[127] It has the advantage of giving individuals time to prepare themselves for the task, but also the drawback of inviting corruption and bribery.

Another system, with the converse vices and virtues, is that of lotteries without replacement. Concerning the allocation of temple duties in Jerusalem it has been noted that 'with respect to the burning of the Incense, a highly valued duty, sampling without replacement was used in preference to the usual sampling with replacement, so as to ensure that all new priests take a turn before a new round started'.[128] It has also been argued that 'it is a mistake . . . to suppose that it was basically sortition which kept the [Athenian] democracy in being and ensured that power remained at least nominally with the popular Assembly. More fundamental by far was the principle of rotation – the rule, applied in all but a few cases, that no citizen should hold any one office for more than once in his lifetime'.[129] Given the small number of citizens and the

---

[127] Pauly-Wissowa, *Realencyoplädie des klassischen Altertum*, art. 'Lösung', p. 1498.
[128] Hasofer (1967).
[129] Staveley (1972), p. 55.

large number of offices to be filled by lot, every Athenian could in fact expect to hold office about once in his lifetime.[130]

Need

In many cases, it might seem obvious that scarce resources should be allocated by need rather than by lottery. Medical resources, unlike grace, should not fall impartially on barren and on fertile ground, but be directed to the persons whom they can most benefit. To use chance instead of reason is 'an abdication of moral responsibility'.[131] A general answer to this argument (II.8) is that the abdication of reason can be a most rational procedure. It remains to be shown, of course, that the answer applies to the present kind of case. To show that it might apply, consider first decision costs. Fine-tuned considerations of differential needs for medical resources might, even when feasible, be very expensive for the community.[132] The temptation to reject such reasoning as inhumane should be resisted. The selection of patients to treat is a costly element of the medical process which has to be assessed in terms of its benefits no less than any other element in the process, such as expensive diagnostic procedures that are used to decide whether to treat a given patient.[133]

Another, less controversial kind of decision cost is incurred by the patients rather than by the community. If the selection process is long and time-consuming, there is a risk that patients might die who otherwise would have survived or, at the very least, that they will suffer considerably and needlessly while waiting. As explained in chapter III, a similar argument applies to child custody decisions. In such cases more coarse-grained methods of selection, such as random choice, might be preferable. Even then, of course, one would usually have to take some account of need in forming the pool of eligibles among whom to draw lots for the scarce good.[134]

---

[130] Headlam (1933), pp. 49, 188. As he points out, 'it made all the difference whether any citizen might be elected, or whether nearly every citizen must be elected' (p. 50).
[131] Belliotti (1980), p. 255. Belliotti does not suggest that the patient's need be the sole criterion. Instead, he advocates the use of a point system.
[132] This is one of the arguments for random selection in Katz (1973), p. 401.
[133] See, e.g., Menzel (1983).
[134] An elaborate four-stage procedure of this kind is proposed by Katz (1973). A three-stage procedure is proposed by Rescher (1976).

A more fundamental problem arises from the indeterminacy of the very notion of need. First, there is a conceptual indeterminacy. Does allocation according to need mean that one should give the good to the persons who would benefit most from it?[135] Or that it should be given to those at the lowest welfare levels? The two criteria, the first in terms of marginal needs satisfaction and the second in terms of levels of need satisfaction, coincide under some circumstances,[136] but not always. Some people who are at a very low welfare level because of a handicap that reduces their productive efficiency may also, because of the same handicap, be inefficient converters of goods to welfare. (What is more far-fetched, people who are already at high levels of welfare may, because of their culture and refinement, be more able to derive additional welfare from the scarce good.)[137] Second, difficult problems arise concerning interpersonal comparisons of welfare.[138] In addition to the usual sort of obstacles to such comparisons, a special difficulty arises in the case of life-saving medical resources. Assuming, for the sake of argument, that a newborn infant may benefit more from life-saving medication than a twenty-year-old person, many would feel that the latter should nevertheless have priority because he has more to lose.[139] Finally, the preference revelation problems associated with the measurement of welfare suggest that we would often find it impossible in practice to carry out finely grained comparisons of needs. These ambiguities suggest random choice as a good procedure in some cases. In many cases, of course, the differences in need are uncontroversial. A person who will die of cancer within a week is a less worthy candidate for a kidney transplant than a young and otherwise healthy person.

---

[135] Elster (forthcoming) discusses this distinction in more detail.

[136] They coincide if all individuals derive the same amount of welfare from a given material situation and if their marginal welfare is always decreasing with increasing amounts of goods.

[137] Leibniz, for instance, held this view, at least with respect to certain goods (Elster 1975, pp. 151–3).

[138] These problems arise both in comparing welfare levels and in comparing welfare increments. Those who believe that levels are more easily compared than increments might prefer something like the maximin criterion. Those who believe that increments lend themselves more easily to comparison might prefer utilitarianism. See, e.g., Sen (1982), ch. 12.

[139] Many arguments for abortion seem to assume a similar asymmetry.

Productivity

One can allocate scarce resources where they do the greatest good for society, as distinct from allocating them to the person who has the greatest need for them. It might be the case that X has a greater need than Y for higher education, in either of the senses distinguished above, but that Y, because of his superior resources, would be able to use the education more productively. One person might have a greater need for military exemption, and yet be chosen for service because of his fighting skills. A worker might have a greater need for his job, and still be laid off if he is less efficient than another. From the social point of view, the use of chance rather than productivity might also seem to be an abdication of moral responsibility.[140] Yet, assuming that we do take that point of view, several difficulties remain. Costs of decision might make it pointless to use very fine tuned methods of screening for productivity, even assuming their reliability. Moreover, the reliability of screening is quite dubious. Tests for school admission are often bad predictors of school performance and of later job performance.[141] The selection of research proposals according to their scientific merit does somewhat better than random selection, but it is very far from perfect.[142] Hence there is something to be said for first forming a pool of those who possess minimal levels of qualification and then selecting randomly within it. Not much is lost by way of efficiency, and much is gained by way of fairness. If necessary, the lottery could use weighted probabilities.

In addition, one may argue that productivity is not the proper criterion. The 'Captain's Dilemma' discussed by Lawrence Kohlberg is intended to bring out this point.[143] In his story, one of three persons must be thrown overboard lest the boat capsize and all die. Of the three, one is the captain, who is indispensable for navigating the boat. One is an old man with a broken shoulder. If he goes overboard, there is an 80 percent chance that the other two would survive. The third is a young and strong man in whose absence the others would merely stand a fifty-fifty chance. Kohl-

---

[140] This position is strongly argued by Basson (1979).
[141] Hapgood (1975).
[142] Cole, Cole and Simon (1981).
[143] Kohlberg (1981), pp. 205–11.

berg argues that the captain should draw straws between the old man and the young man. The lottery, while suboptimal from the efficiency perspective, is preferable on the Rawlsian grounds of enhancing the life prospect, as seen from behind the veil of ignorance, of the worst-off member of the group.

Although Kohlberg's reasoning is multiply confused,[144] something like his conclusion does follow from the premise that one should maximize the survival chances of the persons with the lowest chances.[145] It is questionable, however, whether that premise can be justified in Rawlsian terms. To protect the worst off makes sense if we are maximizing their actual welfare. It is more dubious whether it also makes sense to maximize their expected welfare when the potentially worst outcome is equally disastrous for all concerned. Expected welfare is not a primary good: in fact, it is not any kind of good at all.[146]

Contribution and desert

Sometimes goods are allocated according to earlier contributions. They serve, then, as a reward for good behaviour (or as a punishment for bad behaviour). When the link between contribution and reward is established ahead of time so that the individuals concerned can count on it and plan accordingly, I shall refer to it as desert. Contribution and desert are backward-looking principles, unlike need and productivity, which are forward-looking. Reward according to desert may nevertheless have good effects on productivity, by creating an incentive to good behaviour. The allocation of grades to students and of bonuses to workers are examples.

[144] First, Kohlberg misstates Rawls's original position as one in which the parties know that they have 'an equal probability of being the weak man or the strong man'. On that interpretation of the veil of ignorance, the utilitarian conclusion, which he wants to avoid, follows unavoidably. Second, he gets his numbers wrong when he says that 'if a lottery is used, the old man's probability of living is 50%'. The correct number is 25%. Third, he inconsistently reintroduces utilitarian considerations when he says that the lottery is justified because 'the strong man's chances of life decrease only 30 percent by the use of a lottery, compared to the 50 percent decrease in life chances of the weak man if he is ordered to go'. Moreover, these numbers are also wrong: the strong man's chances decline from 80 to 40%, whereas the weak man's increase from 0 to 25%.

[145] What follows is not that the parties would choose an even-chance lottery behind the veil of ignorance, but that they would choose a lottery giving the weak man eight chances out of thirteen to remain in the boat and the strong man five.

[146] Broome (1984a).

Also, a seniority system of layoffs creates an incentive for workers to stay in their firm, thus reducing turn-over rates and increasing productivity.[147] These effects are not forthcoming when, as in the demobilization of American soldiers at the end of World War II, the system is not known in advance.[148] Here the order in which the soldiers were allowed to leave the army depended on how many points they scored on a composite scale on which contributions to the war effort, that is, length and danger of service, were a major component, together with number of family dependents. In another well-known example from the same war, productivity took precedence over contribution, when scarce penicillin was given to soldiers with venereal disease to get them combat-ready rather than to soldiers who had been hurt while fighting.[149]

Lotteries may be used to supplement the principle of desert, in the allocation of punishment for criminal behaviour. When it is impossible or undesirable to prosecute all known or easily detected offenders, the police should not be allowed discretionary power to select whom to prosecute, because they might use it to get back at personal enemies or to obtain favours.[150] Instead, they should use a nondiscriminatory procedure, such as selecting randomly whom to prosecute or proceeding on a first-come first-served basis when that is more feasible. The age-old practice of decimation is an example. The chosen individuals get (we assume) what they deserve, and hence the allocation follows the principle of desert; yet the choice of whom to select for this treatment is random. Similarly, we have the authority of Augustine and Aquinas for the legitimacy of selecting recipients of charity by lot.

Auctioning

Most of the goods discussed above, including exemption from burdens, can be allocated by auctioning, that is, by creating a market system. This can be combined with a lottery in two ways. First, one can let people pay for a chance of being selected. This is

---

[147] Freeman and Medoff (1984), p. 107 (positive relation between seniority and turn-over rates) and p. 174 (positive relation between turn-over rates and productivity).
[148] Stouffer et al. (1949), vol. 2, ch. 11.
[149] Beecher (1969), pp. 279–81.
[150] Davis (1971), ch. 6. See also Aubert (1980), p. 91, and Feinberg (1980), p. 282.

the practice followed in the U.S. oil-lease lottery program. At present, each person can buy only one lottery ticket for a given parcel of land, but it has been argued that the system could be improved by allowing any number of tickets to be bought, thus more closely approximating a market system.[151] Second, the people selected by lot may be able to sell their right to the good, or buy exemption from an undesirable duty. Most examples known to me fall in the second category, that is, paying someone to take one's place to perform a task for which one has been chosen by lot.[152] Where draft lotteries have been used, the practice of buying substitutes has sometimes been allowed,[153] although often expressly forbidden.[154] Alternatively, citizens have been allowed to buy their way out by paying a tax the proceeds from which were used to induce volunteers.[155] A striking example of combined market and lottery is Greene's *The Tenth Man,* in which one of three selected by lot to be shot by the Germans offers his entire fortune to anyone who is willing to take his place and finds a volunteer who accepts the offer.

II.6 POLITICAL LOTTERIES

The political and the legal systems may be represented by the flow chart shown in Fig. II.3.

In this process, each stage except the second has occasionally been organized as a lottery. The proposal, if not the practice, of organizing the second stage as a lottery can also be documented. In this section I consider lotteries in the first and the second stages, as well as some other applications of lotteries to politics. I have already had the occasion to say something about the use of

[151] Haspel (1985).
[152] An example from the first category: students who are admitted to medical school at the University of Bergen are reported to pay about £2000 to exchange their place for a similar place in Oslo.
[153] Choisel (1981), p. 46. In Norway between the two world wars military service was regulated by a two-stage lottery. In the first stage, about one-third of the age group was exempted by lot from the regular three-month service. In the second, some of the conscripts were chosen by lot for an additional three-week service, for which it was possible to buy a substitute. (I owe this information to Magne Skodvin.)
[154] Sturgill (1975).
[155] In France this system was introduced by Napoleon in 1855. The system of substitutes was reintroduced in 1868 (Choisel 1981). De Bohigas (1968) has a good account of the contemporary debates.

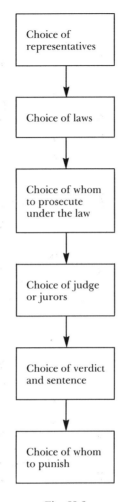

Fig. II.3

lotteries (including weighted lotteries) in the third stage. The last three stages are discussed in the next section.

Today, lotteries have virtually no role in the political process beyond that of occasionally being used as tiebreakers.[156] In the

---

[156] Also, in the British House of Commons private member bills are often dependent on the outcome of a lottery before they can be brought forward, since time in Parliament is a scarce resource.

past, however, they were widely used to select members of legislative or executive assemblies. Even today the proposal of random selection of candidates is often discussed and sometimes advocated. Traditionally the unit of equiprobabilistic political lotteries was the candidate: each member of a given group should have the same chance of being selected. In addition, lotteries were often used in elections to ensure a fair voting procedure. In modern discussions, by contrast, the unit is the voter: each person should have the same chance of having his preferred candidate selected.

Selections of representatives and officials by lot occurred primarily in the Greek and Italian city-states. In Athens all officials (ca. 600) and council members (500) were chosen by lot, with the exception of generals and a small number of magistrates for whom special qualifications were needed (100 altogether).[157] The latter were chosen by direct election. With the exception of these technical tasks, virtually everyone was supposed to possess the competence required for governing the city. Nevertheless, the random selection was sometimes preceded by a nomination process and always followed by scrutiny of those who had been selected. 'Some protection must have been seen to be needed against the appointment by lot of the truly incompetent'.[158] For some tasks it was important to choose the best, whereas for others it was sufficient to ensure a minimal level of competence. Yet the important fact to note is that even the latter had this protection clause. Similarly, the Athenians had various devices to protect themselves against the potential excesses of simple majority voting on all issues.[159] The combination of random choice of officials and simple majority voting in the assembly was potentially so unstable that no society adopting it could survive without some quasi-constitutional restrictions.

---

[157] These numbers are taken from Hansen (1979). The best discussion of Athenian lotteries remains Headlam (1933); see also Mulgan (1984).

[158] Staveley (1972), p. 60. Headlam (1933), p. 96, has a different view of the *dokimasia*, as the scrutiny was called. In his opinion it served only to exclude candidates who were formally disqualified from holding office and not to evaluate the competence or capacity to do well in office.

[159] Among these were the *graphe paranomon,* whereby a citizen could be indicted by the courts for having made an illegal proposal in the assembly, even when it had been approved by the latter. See Hansen (1974). New legislation was subject to control by the *nomothetai,* a group of individuals chosen by the assembly with the authority to approve or reject laws passed by the assembly. See MacDowell (1978), pp. 48–9. (For a different interpretation, see Hansen 1986, ch. 4.)

The Athenian system was quite complex, often requiring two-stage lotteries. It was transparency itself, however, compared with the practices of the Italian city-states. Venice, for instance, had an extremely elaborate procedure for selecting the doge:

The ducal election lasted five days, with two stages of the process allotted to each day. Thirty members of the Great Council, exclusive of patricians under thirty years of age, were selected by lot. Retiring to a separate chamber, this group of thirty reduced themselves by lot to nine, who then elected forty men by a majority of at least seven votes each. After electing the forty, the nine returned to the hall of the Great Council with their list of nominees, 'without looking at, speaking or making a sign to anyone'. These nominees were announced to the chamber and checked to insure that no clan had more than one representative, a precaution followed at every stage of the election. The group of forty assembled in a separate room and reduced their number by sortition to the twelve men who were to elect the next group of twenty-five by at least seven votes apiece; although forbidden to nominate themselves, the twelve could elect a member of the previous group of forty. The twenty-five were reduced by lot to nine, who elected forty-five patricians by the usual majority of seven votes. The forty-five drew lots to select eleven of their number, and the Eleven (the Undici) elected the Forty-One (the Quarantouno) that then elected the doge by at least twenty-five votes.[160]

The crucial step apparently was that whereby the nine, selected by two successive lotteries from the Great Council, elected the forty. 'Although it could hardly be legislated, it was presumed that the nine . . . would then elect forty important politicians'.[161] From then on the process was one of bargaining and jockeying for position within a narrowly circumscribed elite. Since no one was assured of victory, no group could 'impose its will without an overwhelming majority or substantial good luck'.[162] This 'ingenious attempt to find a middle ground between an election by the Great Council and one by a simple conclave of the governing circle'[163] was fairly successful in preventing factional strife among the patricians. It did not open politics to the popular orders, unlike the Florentine system, to which I now turn.

We may consider fourteenth-century Florence to be an example of a society in search of, or at least in need of, constitutional

---

[160] Finlay (1980), pp. 141–2. A similar, although simpler, system was used in fifteenth-century Barcelona (Carrère 1967, p. 39).
[161] Finlay (1980), p. 143.
[162] Ibid., p. 144.
[163] Ibid., p. 143.

constraints.[164] The development of the Florentine electoral system in this period could be summarized, perhaps, as the transformation of 'instant politics', in which no institutions could ever be taken for granted, into (or at least towards) a regime capable of commanding durable assent. To understand the tensions which the political process was supposed to resolve, we can first note that Florentine society in this period was divided both vertically and horizontally. The vertical divisions were, first, between the aristocratic oligarchy and the guildsmen and, second, among various groups of guildsmen. The horizontal divisions were factions within the oligarchy, similar to, if less violent than, those between the Guelfs and the Ghibellines in the preceding century. Many of the electoral struggles in the period concerned the modalities of guild representation in city politics. Although corporatism, a political system based directly on the guilds, was regularly proposed and occasionally realized, the general tendency was towards a regime based on loyalty to the city and its political regime rather than to one's profession.

The object of electoral politics was the election of members to the city government (the Signoria) and to various committees. Every two months these bodies were appointed anew, by a process which in general included four stages. First, candidates had to be nominated; then, the nominated candidates had to be scrutinized for approval; then, among the approved candidates a certain number had to be selected by lot; and finally, among the selected candidates those were rejected who did not satisfy various conditions of eligibility, the main ones being that neither the candidates themselves nor their close relatives should recently have held office. Each of these stages was, naturally, a focus of controversy, since the formal rules for nomination, scrutiny, selection and rejection shape and biase substantive outcomes.[165] Before we consider the process more closely, we should observe the very short time of office, constant throughout the period. The Florentines, apparently, did not trust anyone to hold power for long. In this they may well have acted wisely, but it is clear that the high turn-over rate invited problems of stability, continuity and legitimacy. The

---

[164] The following draws extensively on Najemy (1982).
[165] Przeworski (1988).

ingenious if incomplete solution to these problems will occupy us in a moment.

Before we consider the solutions to the two specific problems of guild representation and high turn-over rates, the ground rules for proposing solutions and getting them accepted must be explained. The legislative assembly chose the mode of election of the government. In part of the period the assembly deliberated anew for each election, thus creating an extremely unstable system in which not only the set of officeholders but also the methods of electing them could change every two months. This extreme of untrammeled democracy was, however, the exception rather than the rule, since the assembly, or those to whom it delegated its authority, could in principle choose many successive governments with one fell stroke. I return to this important, indeed unique, feature of the Florentine system.

To create a system which transcended guild interests, numerous solutions were proposed and some of them put to the test. Although there was general agreement that guild representation on the Signoria must be ensured, there was controversy over how it should be realized. The guilds, naturally, wanted to be able to nominate their representatives. The oligarchy wanted the representatives of the guild to be nominated from the outside – for example, by the existing Signoria. An intermediate proposal was to have representatives from any given guild nominated by members of the other guilds or to have guild nominators convened by district rather than by guild. These conflicts can be viewed cynically, as an attempt by the oligarchy to break the power of the guilds or by the major guilds to break the power of the minor ones (or vice versa), but they can also be viewed as an effort to overcome guild particularism in favour of loyalty to the city as a whole. From the last point of view, one should note the 'constitutional' element of checks and balances in the intermediate proposals.

The more important task was to overcome the destabilizing forces resulting from the short period of office. The solution that came to be worked out was to have the officials for many successive governments nominated, approved and selected simultaneously, with a selection process based on lottery. Disregarding numerous variations and qualifications, the system in force in the third quarter of the century worked roughly as follows. Every three years various bodies, the most important of them the advisory colleges from the sixteen administrative districts, nominated candidates for office. The nomination process resulted in a large number of candidates, usually several thousand. These were presented to a scrutiny committee of 144 members, most of whom were appointed directly by the existing government. The committee voted in secret on each candidate, a two-thirds majority being required for approval. The names of the approved candidates were then placed in bags, from which were drawn at random, every two months, the names of those who would serve on the Signoria for the next period. Since the bags were not exhausted during the three-year period nor discarded after the end of the period, there were always several overlapping bags in existence. The rule was to start with the oldest bags and to proceed to the more recent as the oldest became exhausted or the names drawn from them were ineligible for some reason. As a consequence there was a many–many correlation between governments and scrutinies, as distinct from the one–one correlation of modern elections.

The consequences of this complex arrangement were manifold. The fact that a large number of citizens were nominated for office contributed to the legitimacy of the system, especially since it was never made public who survived the scrutiny. The knowledge that 'my turn may come' on some future extraction of names from the bags probably prevented many citizens from rocking the boat. In addition, since the random element in the system prevented anyone from knowing who would hold office when, no faction could influence or bribe future officeholders. This was an important guarantee for the guilds against the powerful oligarchy, as were the restrictions on eligibility which prevented individuals of the same family from holding office frequently. Moreover, the lack of clear correlation between scrutinies and governments ensured that electoral discontent lacked any obvious target of attack. Randomness in itself ensures that a corrupt government cannot be directly traced to a corrupt electoral mechanism, and the system of overlapping bags must have made it even more difficult to perceive any malevolent hand at work behind a bad outcome.

Against this, of course, both the temporal lag between nomination and officeholding and the element of randomness had some undesirable consequences, as was well summarized by Leonardo Bruni in the early fifteenth century:

Experience has shown that this practice was useful in eliminating the struggles that so frequently erupted among the citizens competing for elections [under the previous system]. But as much as extraction by lot is beneficial to the republic in this respect, just as much and even more is it harmful in another, namely, that because of the chance of the draw many unworthy persons are placed in the magistracy of the priorate. For the same care is not taken in staffing offices to be drawn in the future as in electing present ones, and we certainly give more attentive consideration to present matters and tend to be more negligent in judging those things ordained for an uncertain future. This practice of extraction by lot also extinguishes any motivation for prudent conduct, since, if men were forced to compete in direct elections and openly put their reputations on the line, they would be much more circumspect [in their life and behavior].[166]

In other words, the system reduced the prescrutiny incentive of the nominated candidates to behave well, since the motive of the scrutinizers to pay attention to behaviour was reduced by time and uncertainty. It also reduced their postscrutiny incentive, since in a random draw nothing they did could affect their probability of being chosen. For these reasons, perhaps, the system was later modified into a two-track system, in which nearly half of the government was drawn from another set of bags filled with names carefully selected by and from the oligarchy. With this final modification, the system survived for another century. The de facto elite dominance ensured stability and continuity, as well as legitimacy among the oligarchy, while the broad popular participation made for legitimacy among the citizens at large.

Before discussing proposals of random voting in modern democracies, I shall add a few words about the use of lotteries in antiquity to ensure fair voting. Sparta elected its elders by the method of the 'shout', an early form of the applaudometer contemptuously dismissed as 'childish' by Aristotle.[167] 'The candidates proceeded one by one before the assembled citizens in an order which was determined by lot, and as they did so, the people expressed the extent of their approval by shouting. Meanwhile, a small group of men were confined in a nearby building from which they could see nothing of the proceedings, and there they noted on tablets their impression of the relative loudness of the

---

[166] Cited after Najemy (1982), p. 313.
[167] *Politics*, 1271a.

cheers raised for each of the candidates as they passed by'.[168] The one who was judged by the panel to have received the loudest acclaim was then elected. Presumably the reason the candidates had to enter in random order was to ensure the spontaneity of the proceedings.

Roman elections also made subsidiary use of lotteries in two contexts, both of which were related to the fact that the Romans voted in tribes rather than individually.[169] They used lots to select the tribe in which should vote those Latins who happened to be present in Rome at the time of the vote. More important, they used lots to overcome flaws in the voting system. In some elections, the tribes voted successively and the returns from certain tribes were announced before others were called to vote. Clearly, the former could easily exercise an influence on the latter. To prevent some tribes from having a systematic advantage over others, the order in which the tribes were called to vote was determined by lot.[170] In other elections, the tribes voted simultaneously, but the returns were declared successively until as many candidates as there were places to be filled had received a vote from the absolute majority of the tribes. At that point, the counting stopped and the returns from the remaining tribes were discarded. To prevent inequality of influence, the order in which the tribes had their returns read was determined by lot. Clearly, the problems could have been solved by more direct methods. When tribes voted successively, one could have waited until all had voted before reading out the results. When they voted simultaneously, one might have chosen the candidates with the greatest number of votes from all tribes. The Romans' patchwork solution may have served the goal of equalizing the influence of all tribes over time, but hardly that of fairness towards the candidates, which may tell us something about the relative importance attached to these goals.

Modern discussions of random elections emphasize, as I said, the voter rather than the candidate as the unit of selection. An election should be decided by choosing a 'random dictator' from

---

[168] Staveley (1972), p. 74. For discussions of the use of 'the shout' in seventeenth-century England, see Kishlansky (1986), pp. 61–2, 181. He argues, however, that here it should not be seen as a primitive form of majority voting, as it clearly was in Sparta.

[169] The following draws upon Staveley (1972), pp. 152–6.

[170] This is a simplification, but not, I think, a misleading one for the present purposes.

the electorate. This proposal would appear strange, to say the least, yet surprisingly there are a large number of arguments to be made for it. Not surprisingly, however, the counterarguments are even stronger.

Perhaps the main argument for lottery voting[171] is that it reconciles honesty with self-interest. It has been known for a long time that many methods of aggregating individual votes into social decisions are plagued by the problem that it sometimes pays to be dishonest. By misreporting his preferences, an individual may be able to ensure a social decision which is better – according to his true preferences – than the decision which would be made if he reported them correctly. The Comte de Borda, having proposed a procedure which was vulnerable to this kind of strategic behaviour, insisted that 'my scheme is intended only for honest men'. If people follow their self-interest, however, they often have an incentive to deviate from honesty. If they do, the social decision may be disastrously bad, with no claim to being the 'popular will'.

Even those who deny (as I do) the omnipresence of opportunistic self-interest would agree that it would be desirable to have a political system which did not rely heavily on people being honest when it is in their interest to be dishonest. Could one not design a system in which it is never in people's interest to misrepresent their preferences? It turns out that lottery voting is the only system which achieves this. Somewhat more precisely, the only voting procedure which is Pareto-optimal, nondictatorial and strategy-proof is 'random voting', the simplest case of which exists when the probability of an option being chosen is equal to the proportion of individuals who rank it as their first choice.[172]

A second advantage of lottery voting is that of reducing the problem of the 'wasted vote'. Under a deterministic voting system there is little point in voting for a candidate if his victory is confidently expected in any case, whence the notoriously low participation rates in the American South. Similarly, there is no point in voting for a candidate who has virtually no chance of being elected, whence the difficulties of new parties in attracting votes. Sometimes, of course, one may want to increase the majority with

---

[171] I adapt this terminology from Amar (1984).
[172] Gibbard (1973, 1977).

which one's candidate is elected, so as to give him the moral authority or mandate needed to carry out major reforms. Similarly, a vote for a doomed candidate can give a show of respectability to his cause. These, however, are secondary considerations. The problem of the wasted vote is real enough. It would be solved by lottery voting, which ensures that each vote counts equally, that is, increases by the same amount the likelihood of the candidate's being elected.

This may be discussed somewhat more precisely. Under a deterministic voting system, a voter will be decisive if and only if his vote is pivotal, that is, if the other votes are exactly evenly divided among the candidates. (I assume for simplicity that the number of other voters is even.) Under lottery voting he will be decisive if and only if his vote is drawn at random to dictate the choice. The probability of the latter event is $1/n$, where n is the number of voters. The probability of being pivotal depends on the assumptions we make about the distribution of votes.[173] The simplest assumption is that each voter is equally likely to vote for either party. In that very special case, the probability of being pivotal is larger than the probability of being a random dictator. For instance, with an electorate of 1 million the chance of being pivotal is approximately 8/10 000. If, however, we assume that each of the other voters is somewhat more likely to vote for party A than for party B, the chance of being pivotal soon becomes very small. In an electorate of 1 million, the chance of being pivotal is smaller than the chance of being a random dictator if the probability that others will vote for A exceeds 0.50018.

Another advantage of lottery voting is that it ensures that there will be no permanently unrepresented minorities. In many societies there exist minorities whose members differ from the majority along many critical political dimensions, such as race, religion, language and wealth. If the creation of a separate polity is impossible because the number of minority members is too small or because the members are dispersed over the whole national territory, lottery voting can ensure that their voice is nevertheless heard. It is not, however, the only way of achieving this goal. One might guarantee the representation of parties that reach a certain

---

[173] The following draws upon Owen and Grofman (1984).

percentage of the national vote, even if they do not make it past the post in any single district. This is, for instance, the practice in Sweden and in West Germany. In Israel, where there is only one electoral district, it is achieved automatically.

Finally, lottery voting has the populist value of blocking the emergence of professional politicians. The system 'would create a legislature of rotating citizen-legislators instead of a group of lifetime lawmakers'.[174] The pressure from special-interest groups on legislators would be less effective, because their ability to influence reelection chances would be reduced. Hence legislators would be freer to enact the public interest. Moreover, a steady stream of new representatives would improve the assembly's ability to perceive what that interest consisted of, since it would be made up largely of people who had recently been active in community life.

Against all these advantages, lottery voting has several disadvantages which explain why it has never been adopted and suggest that it never will be. Most obviously, the lack of continuity among the representatives counts against the proposal. Lottery voting would make it more difficult for representatives to learn from experience. What Tocqueville identified as a major problem of democracies, that 'each generation is a new people'[175] and that 'after one brief moment of power, officials are lost again amid the everchanging crowd',[176] would be vastly exacerbated under a system of lottery voting. Disproportionate power would accrue to the bureaucracy, which would, even more than today, be an element of stability in the ceaseless flux of politicians coming and going. On balance, therefore, populist goals would be badly served by the system.

Moreover, having to think about reelection is not simply a source of vulnerability to special-interest groups. It is also a form of accountability to the electorate without which the temptation to plunder the spoils of incumbency might be overwhelming. Furthermore, the predictable rise of numerous small parties would make the Fourth French Republic a paradigm of stability by comparison. With a combination of lottery voting and a large number

---

[174] Amar (1984), p. 1298.
[175] Tocqueville (1969), p. 473.
[176] Ibid., p. 207.

of small parties, the laws of probability would ensure that even a large majority on a specific issue would often be reversed after the next election. The system might soon take on the surrealistic air of Borges's 'The Lottery in Babylon'. Finally, the risk of some lunatic fringe coming into power would not be acceptable, even if the chance were very small. If we are concerned about the risk of nuclear accidents with a probability of happening of about 10^{-7}, we might well have reason to be afraid of less likely political accidents which could have disastrous effects on a much larger scale.

The second stage of the political and legal processes could also be organized on a random basis. I do not know of any regime which has actually adopted this practice, but it is not inconceivable that the proposal might be implemented as a practical solution to the problem of cyclical majorities. If an individual prefers a to b, b to c and c to a, we would probably say that he has not thought carefully about the problem and that he would get his preferences straight by reconsidering. Ideally, one might want to say the same about an assembly of cyclical majorities. If the assembly gave itself more time for deliberation and rational discussion, it would achieve or at least approach unanimity.[177] In practice, for reasons that need not be spelled out in detail, this will not happen. There will often be a need to aggregate preferences which are sufficiently different from each other for cycles to arise. In such cases one might say that, for all practical purposes, the assembly has no preference and that one might as well choose one motion at random. This proposal would be certain to meet strong opposition. We have, I believe, a deep-rooted desire that the proximate causes of our decisions be reasons. A similar and probably more acceptable device, one step removed, would be to have the order in which the alternatives are held up against each other set at random, to remove the possibility of agenda manipulation. Since the motion finally adopted depends crucially on the order of voting,[178] random agenda setting effectively approximates random legislation.

Consider two general arguments for democracy. On one conception, democracy is good because and to the extent that it allows

[177] This view is notably associated with Jürgen Habermas. For a discussion, see Elster (1983a), ch. 1, sec. 5.
[178] For a summary of recent findings see Riker (1982), ch. 7, and Ordeshook (1986), ch. 6.

expression of the popular will, or at least does so better than any other system. In light of the Arrow–McKelvey–Schofield impossibility theorems,[179] this view cannot be defended, since the notion of the popular will is incoherent. On another conception, democracy is to be recommended on procedural grounds, 'as a way of picking out, without reference to inherently arguable claims to superior competence, a unique' decision.[180] Neither agenda manipulation nor random choice satisfies the first conception, since nothing does. Random choice, unlike agenda manipulation, satisfies the second conception of democracy.

I shall conclude by considering, in increasing order of plausibility, three other proposals to randomize aspects of the political process. First, Assar Lindbeck has suggested that elections could be randomly timed.[181] He does not specify what he has in mind, but one rule might be that at the beginning of each quarter one decides with a given probability whether an election should be held at the end of that period, the whole process beginning two years after the preceding election. If the probability is 15 per cent, there is a 73 per cent chance that an election will be held within four years of the preceding one and a 93 per cent chance that it will be held within six years. One might also consider nonconstant probabilities. The rationale for this policy would be to prevent or dampen the 'political business cycle' created by the tendency for each government to begin with austerity and end with potlatch. Against this advantage one would have to consider the negative effects of lack of predictability. The government would be unable to plan effectively, and others would be unable to count on the (temporary) stability of governmental action and policies. Also, governments might end up giving more rather than less thought to reelection, effectively acting as if each quarter were the last.

Second, Richard Thaler has proposed that the assignment of members of Congress to congressional committees be done ran-

[179] Arrow showed, loosely speaking, that no system of aggregating preferences can eliminate the possibility of cyclical social preferences. McKelvey and Schofield showed that this possibility is the rule rather than the exception and that, moreover, the cycles cover the whole policy space rather than being restricted to a small subset of it. See Riker (1982), pp. 181–8.
[180] Barry (1979b), p. 195.
[181] Lindbeck (1976), p. 18n.

domly.[182] Once again, the advantages and disadvantages are fairly obvious. On the one hand, random assignment would break the system of entrenched power by seniority, which has been a major obstacle to rational policy making in the United States. On the other hand, there would be a loss of continuity and no possibility of matching committee membership with experience or inclination. On balance, the proposal might be a good idea, at least compared with current U.S. practice. It might be a good thing for congress members to acquire a varied experience. They ought, after all, to be generalists rather than specialists. Being professional politicians with a trained staff, they would suffer smaller transition problems than most other people.

Third, one might consider random redesigning of electoral districts.[183] Ideally, reapportionment following population changes should be guided only by the principle of ensuring equal influence of all voters.[184] In practice, the parties in power can and do use reapportionment to increase their electoral chances. To avoid this, one could institute random designing of the districts whenever the inequality exceeded a certain level, constrained by the principle of equal influence and by topological considerations such as convexity. One might also try to ensure some temporal continuity – for example, by having an upper limit on the number of voters who would not have in their new district a majority from their old district. Against this, one could argue, however, that a good side effect of the random reapportionment might be the reshuffling of the political cards, so as to break the power of old alliances and create, on a small scale, the possibility for the periodic renewal of politics called for by Thomas Jefferson and others. Random reapportionment would, in my opinion, be clearly superior to the current American system. It might be thought to be inferior to other methods, such as periodic (nondiscretionary) adjustment of the number of representatives to keep pace with demographic changes. If the idea of renewal through reshuffling is taken seriously, it might even be superior to those other methods.

[182] Thaler (1983). Kishlansky (1986), p. 36, has a brief reference to a similar proposal in the seventeenth-century House of Commons.

[183] As observed by Amar (1984), pp. 1294–6, lottery voting would also eliminate incentives to gerrymander. The present proposal achieves the same aim without incurring the prohibitive costs of lottery voting.

[184] Behind this simple phrase lies a very complex reality. See Still (1981) and Rogowski (1981).

II.7 LEGAL LOTTERIES

The final three stages of the flow chart set out in II.6 are the selection of judiciary decision makers and their decision making. The practice of choosing judges and jurors by a random device is frequently observed and easy to justify. The use of lotteries to choose a verdict or sentence has also been observed, although more infrequently. It might be thought, however, to be inherently repulsive and irrational. I shall argue that there are cases in which the best way for courts to decide is by the flip of a coin or some similar device. Finally, and more briefly, I shall discuss the use of lotteries to decide which condemned criminals shall actually have to serve their sentence.

Compared with the choice of jurors, the assignment of judges and magistrates to cases is a little-discussed issue. Magistrates in Athens and judges in Rome were sometimes allocated by lot.[185] In one Norwegian local court, each of three judges is assigned three to four of the numbers between 0 and 9. Cases are numbered in order of arrival and matched with judges by their last digit. For all practical purposes, this is a lottery system.[186] In Germany, as noted earlier, judges are assigned to cases by the first letter in the defendant's last name. An individual judge will, for example, get all defendants whose last names begin with *H*. Because large companies therefore tend to meet the same judge, the system has been criticized for systematic bias.[187] The assignment of judges to cases has been especially controversial in the American context. Benjamin Cameron, a judge on the Fifth Circuit of Appeals that dealt with a number of civil rights cases arising in the wake of *Brown v. Board of Education,* claimed that judges were systematically assigned to these cases in order to favour liberal and progressive views. Although the claim had little substance, it led to the development of a ' "fail-safe" system that separated the assignment of judges to panels from the scheduling of cases'.[188] Assuming no communication between the judge that assigned panels to sit on designated dates in specific cities and the clerk who would calen-

---

[185] In Athens this practice was introduced a century after the establishment of randomly selected jurors (MacDowell 1978, p. 40). For the Roman lotteries 'inter collegas', see Pauly-Wissowa, art. 'Lösung'.

[186] I am indebted to Kirsten Sandberg for information about this practice.

[187] Coons (1987), p. 112, n.137.

[188] Bass (1981), p. 241.

dar the cases, this is equivalent to random assignment, unless they are both influenced by some common factor.

The random selection of jurors is widely practised. It was invented, together with the democratic jury itself, in Athens some time before the middle of the fifth century B.C.[189] From those who volunteered, six thousand were chosen by lot to be jurors for the year. Juries for the various courts were made up out of this list of six thousand. In the beginning each juror was allocated to one court for the year. Later, probably because of trouble with corrupt juries, a different system was introduced. At the beginning of the year the six thousand were divided into panels (probably ten), and each morning panels were randomly assigned to the various courts. Later still, the units of random assignment became the individual jurors, possibly because of the need to have an odd number of jurors so as to avoid ties. The juries were large, with several hundred members. They decided both the question of guilt and the penalty (if any) by majority vote and secret ballot. In the case of a tie the defendant was acquitted, although the use of odd-numbered juries and fines imposed on abstaining jurors made this event unlikely. The choice of penalty was made by a procedure reminiscent of modern final-offer arbitration.[190] 'In any trial in which assessment . . . of a penalty or compensation was required, . . . the successful prosecutor proposed a penalty, the unsuccessful defendant proposed another (naturally a lighter) penalty, and the jurors voted for one or the other; no compromise between the proposals was possible'.[191]

Juries are widely used in modern Western societies. Their strongholds are in the Anglo-Saxon and the Scandinavian countries. In the United States, on which the following discussion will be concentrated, the process has at least two stages: selection of a panel of jurors and selection of the jury from the panel. Sometimes the panel itself is chosen from a larger subset of adult citizens. In Norway, that larger subset is appointed nonrandomly by the municipal board. To settle the defendant's guilt or innocence,

---

[189] The following draws upon MacDowell (1978), pp. 33–5, 252–4.
[190] On this practice see H. Farber (1980).
[191] MacDowell (1978), p. 253. The use of this principle with Athenian juries seems to be due to two factors. First, the jurors were too numerous to reach a compromise by deliberation. Second, the multidimensionality of the possible penalties made compromise by voting impracticable (cycles might easily have arisen).

fourteen people, seven men and seven women, are drawn at random from the subset. Of these, both the defence and the prosecution reject two, leaving a total of ten. The gender constraint does not operate in these challenges, so that in theory the final jury might have as much as a 7–3 bias. The four jurors selected to fix the sentence are, however, constrained by law to be two men and two women.

There are a number of arguments for choosing jurors at random. First, all citizens ought to have an equal chance to assume the privilege (or the burden) of jury service. Call this the *equal-chance argument*. If jury service is seen as a privilege, as it usually is, the equal-chance argument can be justified by the educative effects of jury service. As Tocqueville makes clear, it cannot be taken for given that what is good for the citizens is also good for the parties in the case. 'I do not know whether a jury is useful to the litigants, but I am sure it is very good for those who have to decide the case. I regard it as one of the most effective means of popular education at society's disposal'.[192]

Second, random selection of jurors has good incentive effects, by making it more difficult to bribe or threaten those who have to decide the case. Call this the *incentive effect argument*. This consideration has always been an important argument in jury selection, at least in societies with a generally high level of violence and corruption. Unlike the first argument, it is clearly grounded in concern for the goodness of the decision.

Third, random selection of jurors is often defended on the grounds that the defendant or litigant has a right to be judged by an impartial and representative group of his peers. Call this the *fairness argument*. It will be further discussed below. I shall make the assumption, to be questioned later, that fairness requires the actual jury to be a representative cross-section of the community, and not simply drawn from a larger panel with this property.

To these three goals correspond three different concepts of randomness. The equal-chance argument requires an objectively random process in which each person has the same chance as any other of being selected. For the incentive effect argument, epistemic randomness is sufficient. If the point of random selection

[192] Tocqueville (1969), p. 275.

of jurors is to eliminate the risk of bribery, the epistemic impossibility of knowing who will be selected is more important than objective equiprobability of being selected.[193] The fairness argument, as I have specified it, requires stratified randomization. In Norway this takes the form of selecting equal numbers of men and women, but on other dimensions of stratification the groups will not have equal representation. If the jury is stratified by race, for instance, the races will be represented in the jury according to their representation in the population. There is a clear hierarchy among these methods. Stratified randomization will achieve all three goals. Unstratified randomization will achieve the first and the second goals, but not the third. An epistemically random process that is in fact biased will achieve only the second.

I shall consider the fairness argument in more detail.[194] American legal doctrine is that no defendant has a right to a representative jury, only the right to have a jury drawn from a representative cross-section.[195] The process shall not be biased, although the end state may well be. Yet often end states are what we care about. To bring the question into focus, I shall quote from the dissenting opinion of Justice Marshall in the recent case of *Lockhart v. McCree:*[196]

There is no basis in either precedent or logic for the suggestion that a State law authorizing the prosecution before trial to exclude from jury service all, or even a substantial portion of a 'distinctive group' would not constitute a clear infringement of the defendant's Sixth Amendment right. 'The desired interaction of a cross section of the community does not take place within the venire; it is only effectuated by the jury that is selected and sworn to try the issues'. . . . The right to have a particular group represented in the venire is of absolutely no value if every member of that group will automatically be excluded from service as soon as he is found to be a member of that group. Whether a violation of the fair cross

---

[193] See testimony by H. Zeisel, 'Federal jury selection', p. 131.
[194] I am indebted to Akhil Amar for clarifying these issues (or at least making me less confused).
[195] See, e.g., Ely (1980), p. 139. See also *Taylor v. Louisiana* (419 U.S. 522, 1974), p. 538: 'It should also be emphasized that in holding that petit juries must be drawn from a source fairly representative of the community we impose no requirement that petit juries actually chosen must mirror the community and reflect the various distinctive groups of the population. Defendants are not entitled to a jury of any particular composition . . . ; but the jury wheels, pools of names, panels, or venires from which juries are drawn must not systematically exclude distinctive groups in the community and thereby fail to be reasonably representative thereof' (majority opinion, Justice Marshall joining, Justices Rehnquist and Burger dissenting).
[196] 106 S. Ct. 1758 (1986).

section requirement has occurred can hardly turn on *when* the wholesale exclusion of a group has taken place.

It is clear, from the sentence quoted by Justice Marshall from a dissenting opinion he gave in an earlier case,[197] that he wants to justify the right to a jury drawn from a fair cross-section by end-state considerations. The decision reached by the jury will be substantively better, and not simply procedurally more just, if the jury contains a variety of viewpoints. The effect of excluding 'any large and identifiable segment of the community . . . is to remove from the jury room qualities of human nature and varieties of human experience'.[198] A related, but slightly different argument is the importance for the defendant of having someone on the jury capable of understanding his situation, behaviour, culture and language. 'What may appear to white jurors as a black defendant's implausible story may ring true to black jurors with a greater knowledge of the context and norms'.[199]

From this it seems to follow that the jury should be a stratified random sample, ensuring that there will be some men and some women, or some whites and some blacks, proportionate to their presence in the community. To ensure the desired variety and communication, their presence on the jury itself, not simply on the earlier panels, should be guaranteed. This is especially true when juries are small. Although the Supreme Court found that the goal of providing a fair possibility of obtaining a representative cross-section of the community was not 'in any meaningful sense less likely to be achieved when the jury numbers six, than when it numbers twelve',[200] this statement is demonstrably false.[201] Equal or proportional representation on the panels would satisfy the equal-chance argument or the incentive argument. The fairness argument requires more.

The objection will be raised that a small jury can be stratified only along a small number of dimensions, whereas a potentially unlimited number of dimensions could be relevant. No jury of ten

[197] *McCray v. New York,* 461 U.S. 961.
[198] *Taylor v. Louisiana,* p. 532. The cited sentence is actually a quote from the opinion of Justice Marshall in an earlier case.
[199] Hans and Vidmar (1986), p. 50.
[200] *Williams v. Florida* 399 U.S. 78 (1970), p. 100.
[201] Zeisel (1971).

or twelve can be a microcosm of a large community. To this I have three answers. First, the number of dimensions of stratification can exceed the number of people on the jury, if each person represents several dimensions. Instead of having, say, a young person, a black and a woman on the jury, one might have a young black woman. Second, one might limit oneself to a small set of dimensions which historically have given rise to massive and systematic bias, race and gender being the most important. For civil-liberty reasons the set would probably have to be severely restricted in any case. One could hardly, for instance, ask people selected for the panel about their sexual orientation, even when this would be relevant to the case. Third, and this is my main reply, one might give the defendant the right to choose the dimension(s) of stratification.[202]

The conclusion that I draw from Justice Marshall's opinion is not the one he wanted to draw himself. He was concerned exclusively with the *systematic* exclusion of certain groups, not with the exclusion that might happen through accidents of random selection. Yet if both kinds of exclusion can lead to the same end result, and if end results are what matters, how can the distinction be justified?[203] The answer must be that end results will be biased less frequently if the process is truly random. The reply might not satisfy the black defendant facing an all-white jury drawn in an impeccably random manner, but, or so the argument would go, in the long run the goals of the legal system are best served in this way. Against this I submit that a stratified random selection would have the same long-term benefits as unstratified selection, as well as being more fair in individual cases.

I turn now to the final stage of the legal system, that of legal

[202] Would the same right have to be granted to the prosecution? I do not think so. The equal right of defence and prosecution to eliminate jurors does not imply an equal right to ensure the presence of jurors of a certain kind. The rationale for the defendant's right would be his need to have someone on the jury capable of understanding his language, culture and norms. There is no corresponding rationale for the prosecution.

[203] This also seems to be the argument of Justice (now Chief Justice) Rehnquist, dissenting in *Duren v. Missouri* 439 U.S. 357, pp. 372–3, and writing the majority opinion in *Lockhart v. McCree*, p. 1767. Once one recognizes the illogic of the standard doctrine, which accepts bias in jury composition but not in jury selection, there are two ways to go. Either one requires balance in jury composition as well as in jury selection (this is the argument presented above) or one accepts bias in selection as well as in composition (this is the view to which Chief Justice Rehnquist seems to be committed).

decision making. By and large, of course, random selection is not allowed at this stage. When it occurs, it is punished. One example comes from England, where a 'decision of 1665 allowed . . . juries to cast lots to resolve their differences as an alternative to a retrial when agreement could not be reached. (This decision was set aside eleven years later, however, and by the eighteenth century it had become a serious misdemeanour for juries to reach their decision in this way).'[204] More recently, the Louisiana Judiciary Commission recommended disciplinary action against a Baton Rouge city judge who gave the appearance of deciding cases by tossing coins,[205] on the model of the judge in Rabelais who after laborious and time-consuming presentation of evidence invariably decided his cases by the fall of the dice.[206] There are, nevertheless, civil-law cases in which the practice would seem to be justified. And there are several older cases in criminal law which show that random judgements have not always been perceived to be abhorrent even if they would not be accepted today.

In a classic article John Coons discussed the curious lack of any place for compromise in the law, arguing that it is related to the 'winner take all' attitude that underlies Western law, as distinct from the law of many other societies.[207] In the light of the possibility of random decisions, this cannot be quite right. A lottery is a form of compromise in which the winner does get all. Rather resistance to compromise must be due to the resistance to acknowledging the indeterminacy of fact or law. The elaborate system of the law presupposes that judges must and therefore can reach a clear-cut decision. The decision may be close, but it is not allowed to be indeterminate. As arguments for this principle, Coons mentions incentive effects on litigants, juries and judges. More cases might be brought, and each case might be less carefully considered, if compromises were allowed. 'Resolving factual issues against good men is often a distasteful duty. Remove that duty, and it is likely that more and more cases will begin to seem close'.[208]

Nevertheless, there are cases in which compromises seem to be

[204] Thomas (1973), p. 141.
[205] Fishburn (1978), p. 137.
[206] *Gargantua and Pantagruel*, 3:39–40.
[207] Coons (1964).
[208] Ibid., p. 762. The same point is made in Neurath (1913), p. 9.

inevitable or desirable. In chapter III child custody litigation is offered as one example. Paternity suits may also require compromises. Coons discusses the case of two men who are equally likely to be the father of a given child and says that under American law 'precedents suggest' that one of them will be held solely and fully responsible.[209] The selection of one rather than the other might be made by a lottery, but other considerations, such as income, could also be relevant.[210] In Sweden, however, the possible fathers share[211] equally in the financial responsibility, thus substituting 'an unvarying error of fifty per cent in all such judgments for an error of one hundred per cent in half of these same judgments'.[212] The Swedish practice seems to recommend itself on utilitarian grounds, assuming decreasing marginal utility of money and roughly similar utility functions.

If 50–50 chances of paternity call for a lottery or for equal division, what should we do in 51–49 cases? (I assume these to be reliable, objective possibilities.) Coons would apparently follow the mainstream and make the man with the slightly greater chance of paternity fully responsible. This, however, seems absurd. Rather, a 51–49 compromise should be imposed, whether a physical or a probabilistic one. A compromise would also be called for in 80–20 cases, since a 20 per cent chance of innocence would certainly constitute 'reasonable doubt' according to the usual criteria. In that case, however, a lottery might not be acceptable. If full responsibility were given to the man with only a 20 per cent chance of being the father, he would probably think the decision monstrously unjust, whereas he might well accept to pay 20 per cent of the child support.

Let us assume, however, that the latter option is not available, that is, that we are dealing with a case in which (a) we can assign unequal objective probabilities concerning the relevant facts and (b) no physical compromise is possible. In such cases, if there are

[209] Ibid., p. 758.

[210] Financial considerations are doubly relevant. Giving financial responsibility to the more affluent man is in the interest of the child (and of the mother). Also, under standard circumstances the more affluent man will be hurt to a lesser extent by the financial sacrifice.

[211] Or rather shared. With modern techniques for blood testing on a number of inheritable factors, 50–50 chances are the exception. Courts then routinely award full responsibility to the man with the highest probability of being the father.

[212] Ibid., p. 757, n.4.

any, a lottery using weighted probabilities might seem to recommend itself. As to the perceived injustice of the less probable candidate being chosen, we may appeal to an insightful observation by Francis Allen.[213] We should not ask, 'Who is the father?' but 'Who engaged in illegitimate or illicit activity which was within the scope of risk, of which this little bundle now is the concrete manifestation?'[214]

I conclude with some examples of the way that lotteries have been used to decide criminal cases. I do not think there are any arguments for incorporating lotteries in present-day criminal law. Here the defendant should have the benefit of doubt, a principle that has no application in civil cases. In old legal codes lotteries were nevertheless used to decide the most serious cases, such as murder. The most frequently cited instance comes from the old Frisian law.[215] When a man was killed by an unknown hand, a two-stage lottery was held among seven suspects selected by the accusers. In the first stage, an even-chance lottery was held to decide whether one of them was guilty or whether all were innocent. If the lot showed one of them to be guilty, a second lottery was held to decide who was guilty. In all likelihood, the Frisians believed that the lottery was a divinely inspired method of proof, not just a man-made method of decision. As noted above, however, trial by battle could be seen as a form of decision-making lottery and was explicitly viewed as such by Aquinas and, in a somewhat inconsistent manner, by Frederic II.[216] A further, intriguing case comes from 'several Swedish and Finnish law cases from the 17th and 18th centuries in which by drawing lots it was decided who of several accused should be sentenced to death for murder. In those cases all those accused had attacked the victim but it was impossible to ascertain which of them had dealt the mortal blow'.[217] The underlying idea probably was that of *lex talionis*: a life should be given for a life, but not more than one for one.

Another question concerns whether sentencing should be allowed to be unpredictable and arbitrary, that is, epistemically ran-

---

[213] Allen (1964), p. 798.
[214] On the issue of 'moral luck' which arises here, see Williams (1981), ch. 2, and Nagel (1979), ch. 3.
[215] Lea (1973), pp. 107–8.
[216] Bartlett (1986), pp. 123–4.
[217] Eckhoff (1974), p. 216.

dom.[218] A much-quoted opinion of Justice Stewart in *Furman v. Georgia* argues strongly against this practice:

These death sentences are cruel and unusual in the same way that being struck by lightning is cruel and unusual. For, of all the people convicted of rapes and murders in 1967 and 1968, many just as reprehensible as these, the petitioners are among a capriciously selected random handful upon whom the sentence of death has in fact been imposed. My concurring Brothers have demonstrated that, if any basis can be discerned for the selection of these few to be sentenced to die, it is the constitutionally impermissible basis of race. . . . But racial discrimination has not been proved, and I put it to one side. I simply conclude that the Eight and Fourteenth Amendments cannot tolerate the infliction of a sentence of death under legal systems that permit this unique penalty to be so wantonly and so freakishly imposed.[219]

In legal contexts like this one, 'random' is often synonymous with 'whimsical', 'capricious' and 'arbitrary'. The concept differs, therefore, from the objective or mathematical notion of randomness.[220] It refers to the fact that different judges or juries may decide similar cases differently or that even the same judge may reach different decisions on similar cases. Although the latter meaning is closer to the ordinary sense of the term, the former is more central to the legal doctrine.[221] Much of the debate around *Furman* turns, for instance, on the idea of 'comparative proportionality'.[222] In a recent article John Coons argues that such inconsistency across judges is an inevitable feature of legal decisions, considered to be 'systems of bounded randomness'. He does not believe, however, in replacing randomly deciding judges by a mechanical chance device. 'People resist having their noses rubbed in the randomness of the system. . . . Randomness may be inevitable, but it must express itself indirectly or even covertly at that point in the process where the human decider is selected'.[223] Judges, unlike coins or dice, can be moved by argument, even if the argu-

---

[218] See Davis (1971), pp. 133–41, for a general discussion of arbitrariness and discretion in sentencing. He notes (p. 140, n. 69) that the problem is especially serious in those American states where sentencing cannot be appealed.

[219] *Furman v. Georgia* 408 U.S. 238, p. 309 (1972).

[220] It also differs from the notion of discrimination, which contains a systematic component not present in the idea of arbitrariness. In legal practice, however, the concepts are hard to disentangle from each other (Nakell and Hardy 1987).

[221] Coons (1987) discusses both varieties.

[222] Nakell and Hardy (1987), pp. 47, 252–3.

[223] Coons (1987), p. 110.

ments affect only the second decimal of a number whose first decimal is chosen at random.

Finally, even after the verdict has been pronounced and the sentence chosen, the court might use a random device to decide whether it should actually be carried out.[224] For instance, one out of ten or one out of two on death row might be randomly chosen for execution and the others have their sentence commuted into prison for life. The practice of decimation as punishment for mutiny or treason shows that the idea is not wholly removed from reality. If minimizing loss of death is the main objective of capital punishment, random execution of death sentences might well be the optimal solution, if the increased number of killings caused by the reduction of deterrence is offset by the smaller number of executions. Similarly, random serving of prison sentences would save the taxpayers some money, since fewer people would go to prison.

Against the gains from carrying out sentences in a random fashion one must count, first, the reduced deterrence effect and, more important, the moral uproar the practice would not fail to provoke. It would be widely perceived as a mockery of justice if one convicted embezzler or burglar out of three was allowed to leave the court a free man. Equal risk of punishment ex ante would not matter compared with the unequal punishment ex post. An expected punishment is no more a form of punishment than the expectation of a good is in itself a good.[225] There is, I believe, an irreducible retributive element in the system of justice. Many people would accept the use of deterrence arguments in the determination of the proper sentence for various types of crimes, *on the condition that the sentences would actually have to be served.*

II.8 WHY LOTTERIES?

I now turn to the questions raised at the beginning of this discussion. The focus is on social lotteries, with occasional comments on individual decision making.

---

[224] This notion has been entertained by Aanund Hylland (personal communication) and David Lewis (1989).
[225] Broome (1984a).

The first question concerned a factual problem: when have lotteries, in one form or another, actually been used to make individual or social decisions? I have tried to provide a reasonably exhaustive answer to this question. I am sure there are many cases that have escaped me, but I would be surprised if I have missed any major examples. The question is: what pattern, if any, emerges from the survey? Here are some generalizations.

First, as observed by Gataker (p. 68), 'lotteries are most frequent in democracies or popular estates'. The Italian city-states, though not democracies in our sense, provide an example. Here political lotteries were used to prevent or dampen the murderous conflicts among factions of the oligarchy that would have arisen if instead the officials had been elected. Athenian democracy was different. Election by lot was a natural compromise between the principle that the people should rule directly and the practical impossibility of having everybody involved in the day-to-day matters of government. To Gataker's claim we have to add, however, that modern democracies invariably favour elections over lot. One might deny, however, that elections *are* democratic.[226] From the point of view of the Athenians, 'election could be seen as an aristocratic, we might say 'meritocratic', rather than a democratic device, because it was aimed at finding the best candidates. Election might imply that all citizens are equally good judges of merit, but not that they are equally meritorious'.[227]

Second, lotteries are more frequently used when they can be interpreted as the expression of God's will. In Athens itself the selection of officials by lot may have had a religious origin, although later it became a wholly secular institution.[228] Although official Christian doctrine after the twelfth century did not favour this interpretation of lotteries, it lived on for a long time. Thus understood, the outcome of a lottery is not a random event, but the result of an intentional act.

Third, the most pervasive use of lotteries throughout history appears to have been in assigning people to administrating legal and political tasks and in allocating burdens to people. The selec-

---

[226] Pope (forthcoming) offers a sustained argument along these lines.
[227] Mulgan (1984), p. 546.
[228] Staveley (1972), pp. 56, 251, n.90. Mulgan (1984), p. 544, asserts, however, that 'a completely rational and secular interpretation of the lot is probably mistaken'.

tion of jurors and that of soldiers are recurring examples. The use of lotteries to allocate scarce goods, by contrast, has been common. I offer this generalization with some hesitation, but it seems to be supported by the facts I have surveyed. Although any allocation of a burden can also be represented as the allocation of a good – namely, exemption from the burden – there is a clear difference in practice between selecting one soldier from a village for military service and selecting one person from a large pool for a kidney transplant. There seems to be less willingness to use lotteries for allocating gains than for allocating losses.

The second question I raised concerned the normative justification of lotteries, in terms of individual rationality, economic efficiency or social justice. Let me begin by discussing one frequently cited and in my view invalid reason for adopting lotteries: they prevent those who are not chosen for the scarce good from losing self-esteem. It has often been noted that a perfect system of reward according to contribution, desert or productivity can have bad effects on the self-perception of the losers.[229] It is easier to retain one's self-respect after receiving a bad grade or failing to be promoted if one can blame it on some nonrational element in the screening process, such as the selecting agent's bias, corruption or incompetence. The denial of custody may not be felt to be stigmatizing if the judge is obviously biased and irrational. Psychological studies suggest that procedural fairness together with an unfavourable outcome generates dissatisfaction,[230] contrary to the frequently held view that people prefer losing fairly to losing unfairly.[231]

Examples like these might seem to provide an argument for introducing a known element of randomness into the system, but a moment's reflection shows that this would hardly work. If an inexpensive and reliable system of screening according to the relevant criterion was available, the deliberate choice of an imperfect system for the purpose of enhancing the self-respect of the losers would not be acceptable. Imagine, for instance, that in a class of fifty students it was known that one out of ten A papers had been randomly selected to receive the grade of B, in addition to the

---

[229] Hapgood (1975), p. 38; Greely (1977), p. 120; 'Scarce medical resources' (1969), p. 663.
[230] Musante (1985).
[231] Mashaw (1985), pp. 162–3.

papers correctly graded B. Surely the knowledge that a prior, correct ranking had been made would make some of the B-graded students insist on getting the correct grades. By contrast, a naturally imperfect system, as distinct from one deliberately designed to be imperfect, might well have preservation of self-respect as a desirable side effect. Applicants for a job might thus welcome the employer's using a lottery because of the decision costs associated with fine-tuned screening, although they would hardly ask him to use a lottery were there no such costs. Here, as elsewhere, self-respect is essentially a by-product that cannot be achieved by actions designed for the sole purpose of enchancing it.[232]

An apparent counterexample to this argument is found in the use of lotteries to avoid loss of esteem and self-esteem in seventeenth-century parliamentary elections in England. Mark Kishlansky argues that before the civil war, a predominant concern of the electorate was to achieve consensus and avoid contests:

> The principle of parliamentary selection – and, judging from the available evidence, the reality as well – was unified choice. 'By and with the whole advice, assent and consent', was how the town of Northampton put it when enrolling the selection of Christopher Sherland and Richard Spencer in 1626. Communities avoided division over parliamentary selections for all the obvious reasons – cost, trouble, fear of riot, challenge to magisterial authority – and for one other: The refusal to assent to the choice of an M.P. was an explicit statement of dishonor. Freely given by the will of the shire or the borough, a place in Parliament was a worthy distinction. Wrested away from competitors in a divisive contest, it diminished the worth of both victor and vanquished.[233]

Sometimes, nevertheless, consensus was not reached and election day approached with more candidates than seats to be filled. The local gentry would then, often successfully, try to persuade the candidates to avoid the impasse 'by lot or hazard . . . or any other equal way'.[234] When the number of candidates matched that of seats, disagreement might still arise over who was to have the first place. On one such occasion,

the justices explained to the two candidates, 'we have bethought ourselves of some mediation therein and such as can be no blemish to either of your reputa-

---

[232] For other arguments to this effect see Elster (1983a, ch. 2, sec. 8); also Elster (1988a).
[233] Kishlansky (1986), pp. 16–17.
[234] Ibid., p. 78. The phrase is from a contemporary report on an election in 1614. On that occasion the offer to use a lottery was rejected by one of the candidates. For cases in which lotteries were successfully employed, see ibid., pp. 71, 141.

tions to consent unto'. They proposed that on the evening before the county day [the candidates] meet with the sheriff at Chelmsford and draw lots for the first place. 'And by that means fortune to be the director without touch to either of your credit'.[235]

To be rejected by fortune was less dishonourable than to be rejected by the community. It could be inferior, nonetheless, to being selected by the community. One candidate, explaining why he refused the casting of lots proposed by the magistrates, said that he would not have it appear 'that the freeholders of the said country had forborne to make election of him in regard of these rumors and reports'.[236] Ideally, one would present oneself for office only if one was certain to be selected. When misunderstandings or lack of coordination led to a surfeit of candidates, a lottery might save the honour of all concerned, unless too many insults had been exchanged, in which case nothing short of victory would do. The process was essentially noncompetitive, and lotteries were used only to resolve unwanted contests in a peaceful way. Hence they do not really constitute a counterexample to the claim that one cannot deliberately introduce a random element to console the losers in competitive processes.

Indeterminacy is a fundamental reason for using lotteries. The simplest form of indifference is equioptimality. When there are several candidates who are equally and maximally good, one might as well toss a coin among them. In social decisions, this presupposes that 'goodness' is measured in an objective, rigorous way. Counting votes to choose among political candidates is an example. Other examples are the point systems used for admission to medical school in Norway, for promotion in the U.S. Civil Service or for demobilization in the U.S. Army in 1945. With equality of votes or points, lotteries can be used as tiebreakers. In individual choices indifference can also be a purely subjective matter.

A more complex form of indeterminacy is equioptimality within the limit of what it pays to find out. The costs of fine-tuned screening of candidates who pass a threshold of minimal qualification may be prohibitively high, compared with the social gains from choosing the best. If several candidates are equally good as far as

[235] Ibid., p. 68.
[236] Cited in ibid., p. 81.

one knows or would want to know, one might as well choose randomly. This argument works best when the selection criterion is productivity. Hiring workers, selecting soldiers or admitting students to law school are choices properly guided by social gains rather than by the deserts of the applicants.[237] In the choice of a custodial parent one should weigh the costs and benefits to the child of fine-tuning, as further argued in chapter III. If both parents are fit to have custody, random selection of the custodial parent might be in the best interests of the child. Applicants who are rejected by the lottery may well think that their right to a fair evaluation has been violated, but I do not believe they have any such right. They have a right to equal concern and respect, and that right is not violated by the lottery.

A third variety of indeterminacy is sometimes referred to as incommensurability. Here comparisons of the claims or the options is inherently impossible or unreliable, not just costly or difficult. In individual choice this situation can arise when preference orderings are incomplete or when it is impossible to assign numerical probabilities to the outcomes of action (I.3). In social allocation it can arise in several ways. First, within a given dimension of choice, interpersonal comparisons may be inherently controversial. Consider the allocation of medical resources according to such criteria as social utility, need and past contributions to society. How do we compare the social utility of a tax lawyer and a public defender?[238] How do we compare a teenager and a middle-aged man with respect to levels or increments in needs satisfaction? How do we compare the past contributions to society of a general and a factory worker? I am not implying that such comparisons are always impossible, only that they often are. Second, there is in general no reliable, intersubjectively valid trade-off across these dimensions. The point system used for demobilization in the U.S. Army may seem to be an exception. The assignment of weights to the several dimensions, as well as the choice of the dimensions themselves, were made after a careful opinion survey among the civilian and noncivilian population.

It is unlikely, however, that the scheme could be duplicated in

---

[237] This is denied by Sher (1987), pp. 122–3, but perhaps only because he does not consider the costs of fine-tuned decision.
[238] 'Scarce medical resources' (1969), p. 662.

more complex settings, such as the selection of transplants or the drafts of soldiers for an ongoing war. The choice of observable proxies for contribution, productivity and need would be highly controversial, as would the assignment of weights to these variables. In any case, Arrow's impossibility theorem tells us that we cannot in general expect to construct a social ranking on the basis of individual rankings.[239] Somewhat more precisely, we cannot hope to piece together the interpersonal comparisons made by different persons into one consistent ranking with a claim to be *the* social comparison.[240] The demobilization scheme succeeded because the main variable, contribution to the war effort, could be easily quantified and because there was general agreement that this *was* the main variable. When consensus fails, we might as well use a lottery.

To say that we might as well use a lottery is not to say, however, that a lottery is rationally or morally required. If there is no detectable, relevant difference among the candidates, all are equally worthy and hence it might appear that no wrong is done by using other methods of allocation. Thus it has been argued that one might as well select the most beautiful, the ugliest, the tallest (and presumably the shortest) people in the pool.[241] One reason for preferring lotteries is their salience. Among the innumerable criteria that could be used in situations of indeterminacy, they stand out as being simple, mechanical and universally applicable. Another reason is that criteria related to manipulable properties of people create incentives for wasteful behaviour (as discussed later). More generally, any given property may turn out to be highly correlated with other criteria that one would *not* want to use for allocating the scarce goods. Tall and beautiful people, for in-

---

[239] As a matter of fact, the opinion survey that was used as a basis for the scheme contained inconsistencies. Thus 55% thought that a single man with two campaigns of combat should be released before a married man with two children who had not been in combat; 52% rated eighteen months overseas as more important than two children; and 60% rated two campaigns as worth more than eighteen months overseas. A propos this finding, Stouffer et al. (1949) write that 'a high degree of internal consistency on such intricate hypothetical choices was hardly to be expected' (p. 528), thus suggesting that the problem was one of individual inconsistency. Had they written after the publication of Arrow's impossibility theorem a few years later, they might have preferred the interpretation in terms of collective inconsistency.

[240] This statement refers to the work of Hylland (forthcoming), extending (and slightly weakening) Arrow's theorem to the problem of aggregating interpersonal comparisons.

[241] Mavrodes (1984).

stance, tend to earn more. The general presumption against need-less departures from equality counts against giving them preferential access. To prefer short and ugly people would reinforce the irrational social attitudes that define these traits as handicaps which justify compensation.

Another fundamental reason for using lotteries derives from incentive effects. The uncertainty surrounding the impact of lotteries on individuals cuts both ways. Ignorance of the future can remove the incentive for wasteful behaviour – but also for socially useful behaviour. Which effect dominates depends on the general level of honesty and of the complexity of social organization. For the Florentines it probably made sense for political officials to be chosen randomly and to serve for a very short period, lest they use the office to enrich themselves or to consolidate their faction. The lottery may have prevented their society from degenerating into anarchy, given the general level of dishonesty and distrust.

Incentive effects can justify lotteries even when rational criteria are available and fully determinate. We may be confident that citizen X is more qualified than citizen Y to hold office and yet fear, assuming equal degrees of dishonesty, that a forewarned X could be more dangerous than an unforewarned Y and *a fortiori* more dangerous than an equal chance of an unforewarned X and an unforewarned Y. We might think that physical ability, which is an easily measured factor, is the only relevant criterion in the selection for military service and yet use a lottery to reduce the incentive for self-mutilation. We might believe that people with professional experience ought to have some priority in admission to medical school and yet use a lottery to prevent people from wasting years of their life accumulating points.

Two sorts of undesirable incentive effects are removed by lotteries. Consider the argument for choosing jurors and political officials by lot or the argument for random timing of elections. If the alternative to randomization is to have the decisions made by those who stand to profit from them, one would expect the prosecution to choose the jurors most likely to be favourable to them or the government to choose the date of election that would maximize its chances of winning. If, however, the alternative to randomization is to have the decisions made by an impartial mechanism that allows them to be anticipated, one would expect friends of the defendant to bribe the jurors or the government to let the timing of economic policies be governed by the date of election. By creating maximal uncertainty about the outcome, on-the-spot randomization can be superior both to discretionary decision and to predetermined selection.

Incentive effects arise at several levels. Random selection prevents officials from using their discretionary power to play favourites, punish enemies, enrich themselves or simply bask in the arbitrary exercise of power. In addition to this top-down effect there is a bottom-up effect that prevents potential appointees or recipients from bribing and threatening officials. More generally, randomizing prevents recipients of scarce resources from trying to make themselves more eligible, at cost to themselves or to society. Self-mutilation to avoid military service has been a sufficiently serious problem for many societies to have made it a criminal offence. Self-mutilation to increase the chance of medical treatment is at least conceivable. Finally, to the extent that the chosen individuals have themselves favours to dispense, randomization can deter third parties from extending bribes or threats. Often, the presence of third parties is the reason that officials and appointees would conspire in the first place, since they provide the kickback funds out of which both are paid.

Yet uncertainty about who will do what and what will happen later can often be inefficient. No one has an incentive to invest time and effort to qualify himself for a position which is assigned randomly. One might think that allocating research grants by random choice would not make much difference, since peer review is both costly and unreliable. That argument, however, assumes that the pool of applicants would remain the same in the random system, which it would obviously not if grants were known to be allocated in this manner.[242] I have quoted Leonardi Bruni's comments on the Florentine electoral system, and notably his observation that the 'practice of extraction . . . by lot extinguished any motivation for prudent conduct'. Since the anticorruption and antifactionalism arguments for random assignment to office also presuppose that the term of office must be short, the system also removed the incen-

---

242 Cole (forthcoming).

tive for long-term planning in office.[243] It is similar in that respect to the systematic rotation of officials practised in Imperial China to prevent them from forming alliances with the local gentry[244] or to the Soviet practice of rotating managers.

Lotteries and rotation have better worst-consequences and worse best-consequences than a system that allows officials to hold office for some time or to form bonds with the local population. They would therefore be chosen by a constituent assembly acting on Hume's 'maxim, that in contriving any system of government, and fixing the several checks and controls of the constitution, every man ought to be supposed to be a knave, and to have no other end, in all his actions, than private interest'.[245] Yet in mature political systems, in which some measure of public-spiritedness in public officials can be counted on, the uncertainty has more bad effects than good ones.

Incentive effect arguments also apply against John Harris's proposal to have a 'survival lottery' that would allocate scarce resources for transplantation by choosing donors randomly in the population.[246] Each donor would give several organs, thus allowing many lives to be saved at the expense of one.[247] The proposal has met with numerous objections. On utilitarian grounds, which were also the basis for the proposal itself, it has been argued that the scheme would remove 'the natural disincentives to imprudent action', since people would know, for instance, that they could eat what they liked without worrying about heart problems.[248]

As noted earlier, lotteries are sometimes used to regulate inheritance, but never to my knowledge to allocate the whole of an estate randomly to one heir.[249] One might ask why the latter practice has never been observed. Equal division of a property

---

[243] This point is related to, but distinct from Tocqueville's argument, cited earlier, that high turn-over rates prevent officials from learning.

[244] Skinner (1977), p. 341.

[245] Hume (1963), p. 40.

[246] Harris (1975).

[247] A state of technology is assumed that allows all organs to be transplanted with certainty of success.

[248] Singer (1977).

[249] A partial exception is found in Danish law. When several heirs want the same object in the estate, it is allocated by a lottery. In the final accounting, the object thus allocated is evaluated below market value, so that the surplus is effectively allocated randomly (Krabbe 1944). The earlier law said that the whole estate should be divided into an equal number of equally valuable parts, to be allocated randomly.

may be fair, while efficiency often requires a single heir, usually chosen by primogeniture. Would not random choice of the sole heir be a superior system, combining fairness and efficiency? The answer (or part of it) is that random choice would lack one of the two efficiency features of primogeniture. It would, like primogeniture, allow for economies of scale. It would not, however, give the heir time to prepare himself for the job of running the family farm. In fact, equal division might also be more efficient than random assignment of the whole estate to one person, if the inefficiency generated by uncertainty exceeded that generated by diseconomies of scale. The negative incentive effect that would be created by lotteries might explain why they are never observed in these cases. They could also explain the relative rareness of ultimogeniture.

A final and frequently cited value of lotteries is that of promoting fairness.[250] It is difficult to assess this claim, because of the vagueness of the notion of fairness.[251] In most cases it probably reduces to the view that when there are no relevant differences among the candidates or applicants, one should use a lottery since the alternative (i.e., using irrelevant differences) would be unfair. Fairness, on this conception, means simply that relevantly like cases should be treated alike. But there could be a stronger version of the claim. It would argue that even when there are relevant differences, people should be treated alike. In a fundamental sense, which dominates the relevant differences, all persons are equally worthy. Any human life, for instance, is as valuable as any other, irrespective of quantity (i.e., expected life span) and quality (i.e., ability to enjoy life). Hence any person should have equal access to or, in cases of indivisibility, equal chance of access to scarce resources.[252]

Thus starkly stated, the argument is unacceptable. At the very least it would have to be extended in a maximin direction: unequal access or unequal chances are acceptable if they increase the

---

[250] We must distinguish between two issues. The first, discussed in II.2, is: when is a lottery fair? The second, discussed later, is: when is it fair to use a lottery?

[251] For a useful discussion, see Broome (1984b).

[252] Jewish ethic, for instance, endorses the premise of this claim (Rosner 1986, p. 346). The conclusion drawn is not, however, that one ought to use a lottery. Rather the principle advocated is that of equal physical division or, when the good is indivisible, of not giving it to anyone. For an explicit version of the strong fairness claim, see Kilner (1981).

access or chances of those who are worse-situated. 'In a lifeboat, we may want especially to treat those without whom the boat will probably not reach shore. Similarly, in a disaster, the best course may be to treat first any one who can help treat others'.[253] Using a weighted lottery (or multiple queues) could increase everybody's chance of getting the scarce good, if the inequality created opportunities or incentives that in the end would make the good less scarce. The regulation of access to medical or technical education by a weighted lottery could be justified by this argument.

Even thus improved, the argument is unacceptable. Productivity is not the only reason to deviate from equality. We also make distinctions on grounds of need. A person who is sure to die in a few weeks should not be a candidate for a kidney transplant. We make distinctions on grounds of contribution and desert. In many contexts, fairness as equity – to each according to contribution – is more plausible than fairness as equality.[254] There was nothing unfair about the demobilization scheme used by the U.S. Army.

In these cases, we might still ask whether fairness requires the relation between need or contribution and allocation to be deterministic or probabilistic. John Broome has argued[255] that when people have unequal claims to a scarce, divisible good, fairness requires that their chance of receiving it be proportional to the strength of their claim. The claim of old people to a kidney transplant being weaker than that of young persons, they should have a smaller, but nonzero chance of receiving it. Lottery voting may also be interpreted in this way, as a way of matching strength of claims with probability of being chosen. Under Broome's proposal, all claims would be respected, not in the sense of being satisfied, but in the sense of having a chance of being satisfied proportional to their strength.

One objection to the proposal is that in small groups there is a non-negligible chance that all or most winners would be people with weak claims. Fairness ex post would be violated in favour of fairness ex ante. This difficulty could be removed by stratified randomizing, analogous to the multiple queues mentioned earlier. Imagine that ten kidneys are to be allocated among twenty

---

[253] Kilner (1981), p. 265.
[254] For this distinction, see, e.g., Deutsch (1975).
[255] Broome (1987).

recipients, ten old people who would live another five years with the kidney and ten young people who would go on to live for twenty more years. If expected life extension is used to weigh the probabilities,[256] each old person would have one chance in five of receiving a transplant and each young person four chances in five. Under an unstratified weighted lottery, all or most recipients might turn out to be old. Stratified randomization would ensure that two old people and eight young people would be selected.[257]

Even thus modified, the fairness of the proposal is not obvious. Is it fair to select two old people at the expense of two young people who (by assumption) are more needy? Tentatively, I would argue against Broome's proposal. Once we have decided to use, say, need as the criterion for allocating the scarce resource, it seems perverse to adopt a procedure that is sure to withhold the good from some very needy persons while giving it instead to some who need it much less. The proposal lacks psychological stability, because it would appear monstrously unjust to high-need persons who were denied the good. But the question requires clarification. As argued later, the appearance of justice should not be the main determinant of institutional practice.

The third question – what explains the use of lotteries in situations where normative reasoning counts against using them – will be treated briefly, since I do not believe there are many such cases. When lotteries were interpreted as God's will, there must have been occasions on which one consulted the die without the justification of indeterminacy. Although the church insisted that one could not ask God to spare one the trouble of acting prudently, the warning was far from always heeded.[258]

Gataker argues (p. 68) that in democracies lotteries tend to be used even 'though such indifferency indeed be not always allowable, nor such equality stand ever with equity'. The democratic passion for equality can easily be carried to extremes and force the

---

[256] I assume that the life extension could be a measure of need. Similar arguments could be carried through using number of family dependents as a measure of need. One might also use a different criterion altogether, such as length of combat service if the potential recipients are soldiers. Or one could have a point system incorporating several criteria. The argument presupposes only that one has somehow reached agreement on some way of measuring strengths of claims.

[257] This proposal is discussed in 'Scarce medical resources' (1969), p. 665.

[258] Thomas (1973), pp. 99–103.

use of (even-chance) lotteries even when need, contribution, productivity or entitlement would point unambiguously to a different
allocation. More generally, democracy creates a preference for
nondiscriminating allocation procedures – equality, even-chance
lotteries, queuing, rotation – that minimize the need for discretionary and potentially controversial comparisons among people.
The basic axiom of political democracy that people have to be
treated as equal in wisdom even when in fact they are not (IV.5)
tends to carry over to other arenas and force institutions to treat
people as equal in need or merit when in fact they are not.

Third, and more conjecturally, there may be instances of misplaced uses of lotteries that derive from overemphasizing the positive incentive effects created by uncertainty and neglecting the
negative effects. I alluded to this problem before, in the discussion
of Florentine politics. I can well imagine that firms that make
random spot checks of their employees could neglect the negative
'atmosphere effects'[259] created by such practices.

The final question is why lotteries are so rarely used when there
are so many good arguments for using them. I shall discuss several, closely related explanations. They are all connected to the
argument from indeterminacy.

People want to have reasons for what they do.[260] More spe-
cificially, they want reasons to be the proximate determinant of
their choice. In the argument for using a lottery, reason also inter-
venes, but at an earlier stage in the decision process. The decision
not to use reason to make the final choice may be the most rational
one, as recognized in Pascal's 'Il n'y a rien de si conforme à la
raison que ce désaveu de la raison'[261] or Descartes's 'La principale
finesse est de ne vouloir point du tout user de finesse'.[262] In an
earlier work I discussed other examples of this rational abdication
of reason, using Ulysses's binding himself to the mast and addic-

---

[259] For a discussion of such effects, see O. Williamson (1975), pp. 37–103.

[260] 'Humans generally prefer to order their affairs through reason rather than through
random or arbitrary action' (Summers 1974, p. 26). In Summers's view, procedural
rationality is to be valued independently of the outcome to which it leads: 'Of two legal
processes yielding more or less the same results, only one of which is rational process,
we should generally prefer the rational one' (ibid.). I discuss process values below.

[261] *Pensée*, 272.

[262] Descartes (1897–1910), vol. 4, p. 357.

tion control as paradigm examples.[263] In that case, the argument for abdication was that one could not trust oneself to make the right decision when the time came to make it. Here the argument is that there is no right decision.

The two arguments are, however, somewhat related. Sometimes we know that we could find the decision that would have been optimal if found costlessly and instantaneously. By investing more time, effort and money we may be able to rank the options on the relevant dimension of choice. We may also know, or be in a position to know, that the benefits from finding out are small compared with these costs. Yet because of what one might call *an addiction to reason* we do not use a lottery, but go on looking for reasons, until triumphantly, we find one. I believe the child custody case further discussed in chapter III brings this out with special poignancy. To promote the best interests of the child, the compulsive rationalist searches for evidence of fitness and unfitness of the parents while, in the meantime, the damage done to the child by the process of searching exceeds the benefits to be expected from the search. It is more rational, then, to resist the sirens of reason.

People also dislike making close decisions, as shown by the evidence for prechoice and postchoice tension when the decision seems likely to be a close one (II.3). To reduce the tension, they adjust the weights of the various criteria so as to make one option appear clearly superior to the others. Fear and anticipation of regret may be the driving force in this mechanism.[264] The explicit and conscious use of a lottery implies that the decision is extremely close, and hence that there is a large likelihood for later regret if more becomes known about the situation. Again, this may lead to overinvestment in the search for more information.

A further, related reason is the inability to keep the ex ante perspective firmly in mind. A decision that turns out to be wrong

---

[263] Elster (1983a), ch. 2.

[264] This language should not be taken to be as intentional as it may appear to be. I do not suggest that people consciously adjust the weights because they consciously anticipate regret. If they tried, they would not succeed, because they would still remember the unadjusted weights (Elster 1983a, ch. 2). Rather the experience of regret following close decisions sets up a reinforcement process which, unknown to the persons themselves, shapes the attitude in later decisions of this kind.

in an ex post sense may nevertheless be the best that could have been made at the time of choice. A military commander who chooses his plan of attack by the flip of a coin, to confound the enemy, may be harshly criticized if it goes wrong. To reduce anticipated blame, he may choose the pure strategy with the highest security level attached to it. Equality ex ante can also be a fragile motivation. It may seem acceptable as long as the coin is hovering in the air, but when it comes down the losing party may protest that he was never given a fair hearing.

This leads to the final source of resistance to lotteries: the attachment to process values. The following argument is probably representative of much legal thinking on the subject:

> Random selection . . . denies the citizen's demand for participation in and accountability for the method of allocation. In merit or need determinations, the potential recipients can argue with the allocating official about his satisfaction of the relevant criteria, and if the good is denied the citizen can blame the official. The lottery eliminates both options. It may thus have the cost of political withdrawal if citizens begin to feel they cannot affect the decision-making process. More damaging is the thought that random systems of allocation cut down on social interaction, producing the psychological alienation of being treated as an object. The frustrations engendered by the unaccountable allocation of the lottery may be the greatest cost of random selection.[265]

Against this I prefer the view argued in the following passage:

> While I recognize that there is something unseemly about granting a television license by drawing lots among generally qualified applicants, and that a flip of the coin is out of the question as a method of deciding whether or not a particular offender should receive the death penalty, it does not follow that a process which gives the appearance of rationality should always be chosen over one which concedes that rational choice among competing demands is not possible at a given level of information. It is undoubtedly true . . . that law often has symbolic offices to fill; but it is also true that law must *be* fair as well as *seem* rational.[266]

There are several arguments for attaching importance to procedural or process values. First, one may argue that in the long run respecting procedural values leads to better substantive outcomes, even if in a given case they may appear burdensome and pointless. Process values, far from being opposed to utilitarianism, may be defended on rule-utilitarian grounds. If judges are allowed to decide indeterminate cases by the toss of a coin, they may come to

[265] Greely (1977), pp. 122–3.
[266] Katz (1973), p. 391.

find indeterminacy in more cases, thereby endangering the cause of outcome-oriented justice.

Second, one may argue that even when the outcome is substantially the same whether or not these values are respected, they have an independent importance. Defendants or claimants should, for instance, be allowed to challenge experts even if no difference in the final decision is to be expected. Even if the current practice of assigning child custody by assessment of parental fitness is epistemically random, it is superior to explicit randomizing in that it allows the parents to present their case.[267] The costs to the legal system created by the more time-consuming method of decision are overridden by the principle that justice must not only be done but ought also to be seen to be done. I find this argument hard to evaluate. On the one hand, the actual demand for participation cannot be a sufficient justification. As noted by Robert Summers in his discussion (and defence) of process values, 'participatory governance . . . is commonly overvalued'.[268] It may well be true of many contemporary societies that everybody would be better off if everybody insisted less on insight, participation and appeal. On the other hand, a legal and administrative system that appears opaque and unintelligible to the citizens will easily fall into disrepute. A legal system which is responsive to the need for understanding is a public good which must be upheld against short-term cost–benefit considerations. This, however, is also an outcome-oriented argument.

Third, one may argue that some process values are so important that they should be respected even when the final decision is thereby made substantively less good. Someone who accepts my argument that fine-tuned assessment of parental fitness in custody cases undermines the goal of substantive justice, which is to protect the interests of the child, might still believe that the gain in process value more than offsets the loss in outcome value. Summers cites two cases of this kind.[269] First, prohibition of involuntary stomach pumping of persons suspected of drug offences may have 'bad result efficacy' and yet be required to protect individual dignity. As Summers recognizes,[270] an act-utilitarian argument

---

[267] Here I neglect the cost to the child. This is considered in the next paragraph.
[268] Summers (1974), p. 43.
[269] Ibid., pp. 17–18.
[270] Ibid., pp. 34–6.

against such practices is also available: their possibly useful results might be offset by the certain discomfort and humiliation of the individual subject to them.[271] Another explanation of this value would be squarely rule-utilitarian: privacy and dignity need protection against the constant temptation of government to focus on the short-term benefits of violating them and to neglect their long-term value.[272] And even if the argument for privacy is not based on outcome-oriented considerations, it could be overridden by them. Invasions of privacy that would be unacceptable if the purpose were to detect drug offences might be fully justified if the purpose were to stop people from transmitting AIDS to their partners.

Summers's other example poses a greater challenge:

> Many law creating bodies are popularly elected and operate by majority rule. But it is arguable that these features have almost as much bad efficacy results as they have good. It is at least true that democratic legislatures create their share of bad laws. Yet the participatory features of democratic legislatures are nevertheless good for what they are, apart from results. They comprise a form of participatory governance which is good for its own sake and therefore qualifies as a process value.

Again, the argument could be met with utilitarian considerations. Tocqueville, for instance, praised democracy 'much more on account of what it causes to be done than for what it does. It is incontestible that people often manage public affairs very badly, but their concern therewith is bound to extend their mental horizon and shake them out of the rot of ordinary routine'.[273] Here, however, utilitarianism is not sufficient. Tocqueville's argument, like many utilitarian considerations, cannot stand the light of day. For democracy to have these desirable side effects outside the political realm, the participants must also believe in the political value of the system.[274] The value is not that of producing decisions which express the popular will, since there is no such thing. Rather the value derives from indeterminacy. Since all claims to

---

[271] This was the Supreme Court's argument against discretionary spot checks of automobiles (see note 41).

[272] 'The good things that freedom brings are seen only as time passes' (Tocqueville 1969, p. 505). 'We will rarely know what we lose by a particular restriction of freedom' (Hayek 1982, vol. 1, p. 57).

[273] Tocqueville (1969), pp. 243–4.

[274] Elster (1983a), ch. 2, sec. 9.

natural superiority are inherently arguable, people must be assigned equal political rights or equal political chances.

I believe, therefore, that in most cases the alleged independence of process values from outcomes evaporates on closer inspection. The cart of procedural justice ought not to be put before the horse of substantive justice. If current beliefs about procedural values go against substantive justice, they may have to be respected for the time being, but on purely pragmatic grounds: no system of justice can work if people do not believe in it. The perceptions of procedural justice are local, context-specific[275] and bound up with accidents of history and politics. Legal and political theory ought to be concerned with aligning process values with substantive values, not with finding an optimal compromise between them.

The basic reason for using lotteries to make decisions is honesty. Honesty requires us to recognize the pervasiveness of uncertainty and incommensurability, rather than deny or avoid it. Some decisions are going to be arbitrary and epistemically random no matter what we do, no matter how hard we try to base them on reasons. Chance will regulate a large part of our lives, no matter how hard we try to avoid it. By *taming chance* we can bring the randomness of the universe under our control as far as possible and keep free of self-deception as well. The requirements of personal causation[276] and autonomy[277] are reconciled by the conscious use of chance to make decisions when rational argument fails. Although the bleakness of this vision may disturb us, it is preferable to a life built on the comforting falsehood that we can always know what to do.

Otto Neurath characterizes the belief that we can always have good reasons for our decisions as *pseudorationalism*. Whereas Cartesian 'rationalism sees its chief triumph in the clear recognition of the limits of actual insight', pseudorationalism 'leads partly to self-deception, partly to hypocrisy'. To conclude the present chapter I can do no better than to quote his further comments on this distinction:

[275] For documentation, see Kahneman, Knetsch and Thaler (1986).
[276] De Charms (1968).
[277] Elster (1983a), ch. 3.

The attitude of Thomas Hobbes in the matter of religion . . . rarely finds approval. His idea that some order is better than none enrages every pseudorationalist who hopes to reach a decision by an adequate measure of thinking. Hobbes' intolerance is purely external, a means to an admitted political end. He simply feels unable to decide which of the positive religions is preferable. It appears to me that this behaviour of Hobbes is the only one possible for an honest rationalist in many affairs of life; however, whether rationalism is at all suited to regulate public life is another question. But once tradition and community feeling are weakened, there is no choice but that between rationalism, which undoubtedly leads to drawing lots, and pseudorationalism which falsifies thinking and feeling. . . .

Let us go back to the parable of Descartes. For the wanderers lost in the forest, who have no indication at all as to which direction to follow, it is most important to march on energetically. One of them is driven in some direction by instinct, another by an omen: a third will carefully consider all eventualities, weigh all arguments and counter-arguments and, on the basis of inadequate premises of whose deficiencies he is unaware, take one definite direction which he considers the correct one. The fourth, finally, will think as well as he can, but not refrain from admitting that his insight is too weak, and quietly allow himself to decide by lot. Let us assume that the chances of getting out of the forest are the same for the four wanderers; nevertheless there will be people whose judgment of the behaviour of the four is very different. To the seeker after truth whose esteem of insight is highest, the behaviour of the last wanderer will be congenial, and that of the pseudorationalist third wanderer most repellent. In these four kinds of behaviour we can perhaps see four stages of development of mankind without exactly claiming that each of them has come into full existence.[278]

---

[278] Neurath (1913), pp. 9–11.

III

SOLOMONIC JUDGEMENTS: AGAINST
THE BEST INTERESTS OF THE CHILD

La principale finesse est de ne vouloir point du tout user de finesse.

Descartes, Letter to Princess Elisabeth

Simplicity is the ultimate sophistication in deciding a child's placement.

Goldstein, Freud and Solnit, *Before the Best Interests
of the Child*

III.1 INTRODUCTION

Few situations are as agonizing as child custody disputes in divorce cases.[1] It is agonizing above all for the parties directly involved: the parents and the children. For some parents, the child is such an extension of their own persons that being denied custody would be like losing a limb or worse. Although it may not be in the child's interest to give custody to a parent whose need for the child is that strong, the point here is simply that feelings often do run high. Even for parents whose identity is less closely bound up with the child, separation is usually traumatic.[2] In divorce, the dispute over custody exacerbates and feeds upon the other conflicts that are cause or consequence of the decision to separate. Important joint decisions about finances and custody have to be made at a moment when the parents are less likely to agree than at any other time. For the child, a divorce can be painful in a number of ways. Whatever the outcome is, it will involve the loss of regular

---

[1] In this chapter I am concerned almost exclusively with custody in divorce cases involving disputes between the two parents. Many similar problems arise in disputes between the biological parents of a child and a welfare agency or foster parents. I occasionally refer to the latter case, which I hope to discuss at length elsewhere.

[2] For a useful review of the psychological literature on the trauma of separation from the child, see Chambers (1984), pp. 541–9.

123

family life, which, however unhappy for the parents, is usually preferred by the child.[3] Unless the parents agree on joint custody, the divorce will also involve severely curtailed contact with one parent. In addition, the process of custody dispute imposes costs of its own on the child, by generating painful uncertainty and conflicts of loyalty.

Custody disputes are also highly traumatic for the third parties called upon to resolve them. Judges and welfare officials regularly report that these are among the most difficult cases to decide.[4] In large part this is so, of course, because the issues are so important to the parties directly involved. But custody decisions are also difficult because they are seldom clear-cut. Indeed, I shall argue that there usually is no rational basis for preferring one parent over another. These two features – the knowledge that the decision will have momentous importance for the parties directly involved and the recognition that it may not be possible to have a rational preference for one parent over the other – conspire to create a psychological tension in decision makers that many will be unable to tolerate. Often, it will be resolved by an irrational belief in the possibility of a rational preference.[5]

There are many issues of this kind in modern societies.[6] The allocation of scarce and vital medical resources, such as organs for transplantation, is characterized by the same two features and gives rise to similar agonizing (II.5). Yet child custody cases are special because there are more of them and, most important, because they

---

[3] In their study of divorced families Wallerstein and Kelly (1980), p. 10, report that 'only a few children in our study thought their parents were happily married, yet the overwhelming majority preferred the unhappy marriage to the divorce'.

[4] Any judge or trial lawyer, any forensic psychiatrist or other mental-health specialist will affirm that child custody is, indeed, the ugliest of all litigation' (Goldzband 1982, p. ix).

[5] Cf. the remarks on hyperrationality or 'pseudorationalism' in I.4 and II.3 and II.8. A preliminary hypothesis, to be explored in future work, is that the need to have and to give reasons for one's decisions generates strong cycles in the weights that courts and welfare agencies assign to criteria for custody and placement. In placement cases, for instance, welfare officials are torn between two opposed considerations. On the one hand, they know that if a child is to be taken away from the family, this should be done as early as possible, to minimize harm and suffering. On the other hand, they also know that the decision, being extremely serious, should not be taken with less than full knowledge about the family situation and that parental rights should be respected. These considerations point against speedy decisions. There is no correct solution to this dilemma. In practice, the ideology of welfare officials and social workers swings from one extreme to the other.

[6] For a general discussion, see Calabresi and Bobbitt (1978).

involve face-to-face confrontation between the claimants.[7] They are among the most important allocative conflicts in society, if we measure importance by the number of people involved and the emotional intensity of their involvement. Yet in another, more traditional sense, custody conflicts are unimportant. They belong to the private life of individuals, not to their public existence. They are highly idiosyncratic, thus lending themselves badly to organized political action. They impinge little on efficiency, liberty, equality, participation and other values that have traditionally been at the center of political debate and philosophy.

The major exception to the lack of political importance of child custody disputes is that to some extent they have been an issue in the women's liberation movement. Yet feminist writers have, by and large, held ambivalent views on the question.[8] On the one hand, it has been argued that in the long run, the disappearance of the maternal presumption rule will lead to desirable changes in sex roles and socialization.[9] On the other hand it has been said[10] that in the short run, giving men an equal chance to obtain custody is an instance of justice according to Saint Matthew: unto every one that hath shall be given (Matt. 25:29).[11] Perhaps as a consequence of these conflicting perspectives, child custody has taken second place, in the feminist movement, to issues of discrimination, oppression and exploitation.

Political philosophers have largely ignored child custody as an issue in distributive justice,[12] perhaps because the problem is inde-

---

[7] Among the tragic choices discussed by Calabresi and Bobbitt (1978), there are none which have this particular feature.

[8] See Gundersen (1984), ch. 4, for a survey of the Norwegian debate before the law of 1981 that replaced maternal presumption with the best interests of the child as the main criterion in custody decisions. She documents that the women's movement was deeply split on the issue.

[9] See Weitzman (1983), pp. 115–20.

[10] See Weitzman (1985).

[11] In the present context this means that the more wealthy parent has a greater chance of getting custody. As Robert Mnookin pointed out to me, the same slogan could be used to characterize the status quo presumption (further discussed in III.2) in custody disputes.

[12] It is not clear how the main views on child custody could be classified in terms of philosophical theories of justice. The basic distinction between rights-based arguments and consequentialist arguments no doubt applies, but with much ambiguity. Nobody to my knowledge has advocated a purely utilitarian position which would place the welfare of the child on a par with that of the parents and of 'society' more generally. The earlier principle that an adulterous party should never get custody is the closest approximation to a purely rights-based criterion. The central argument for the principle that custody should follow the best interests of the child appears to be a mixed one: children have a

terminate (I.1) from the perspective of the major theories.[13] I rely, therefore, mainly on writings by legal scholars. Current legal thinking on custody disputes is dominated by two approaches. On the one hand, Joseph Goldstein, Anna Freud and Albert J. Solnit have had a major impact on the theory and practice of the law through three books that rest on the psychoanalytic theory of child development.[14] They recommend, notably, that custody be decided swiftly, irreversibly and without court-imposed visiting rights to the noncustodial parent, thus enabling the child to have a stable, undisturbed relationship with one adult person. On the other hand, Robert Mnookin has mounted a powerful attack on the principle of 'the best interest of the child', arguing that it is too indeterminate to be helpful in legal decisions.[15] This essay draws upon and extends this attack. I have also been influenced by Mnookin's important work on the incentive effects of custody law.[16]

Two features of child custody disputes render them interesting, even unique, from the point of view of distributive justice: the interests of a third party – the child – and the self-defeating nature of attempts to get custody. On the face of it, custody conflicts seem like other distributive issues. Who gets the house? Who gets the car? Who gets the children? The last case is different, however, because the object to be allocated also has an interest in the allocation. Although the child may to some extent and for some purposes be considered a consumption good for the parents, he is also and predominantly a person in his own right.[17]

right to have their welfare dominate that of other parties. The right, in other words, singles out a certain subset of the consequences that must be considered before any others. That principle allows the welfare (or the rights) of the parents to count only when the interests of the child are indeterminate.

[13] This is clearly true for Rawls's theory, although certain solutions to the custody problem might be said to be roughly Rawlsian in spirit (III.3). Nozick's (1974) principle of first seizure, modified by a Lockean proviso that as good be left for others, has no implications for our problem, although the incentives for kidnapping created by the best-interest standard (III.3) bear a superficial resemblance to that principle.

[14] Goldstein, Freud and Solnit (1979a,b); Goldstein, Freud, Solnit and Goldstein (1986).

[15] Mnookin (1973) and (especially) Mnookin (1975).

[16] Mnookin and Kornhauser (1979); see also Cooter and Marks with Mnookin (1982).

[17] In the introduction to a recently published book on utility and rights, the editor states, 'I shall not bother with the niceties involved in determining who or what is a person; I shall assume that, whatever view of persons one holds, ordinary, *adult* humans are persons' (in Frey, ed., 1985, p. 3; my italics). In one view, which stresses the relation between personhood and the capacity for reflective judgement, children are not 'persons' but rather 'wantons' (Frankfurt 1971). For my purposes here I need not go deeply into this issue.

There is an undeniable tension or paradox here. Before conception, it is easy to think of the child as a consumption good or, to the extent that children work, as a capital good. Parents make decisions about having children by considering them in these perspectives and by making trade-offs between children and other goods.[18] Since the child does not yet exist, one does not think of him as a person with unique qualities, needs and rights. Once the child is born, however, the perspective seems to change. To treat the child as a consumption good for the parents, as one would do in deciding on child custody solely according to the needs or rights of the parents, would violate the principle that persons ought to be treated as ends in themselves, not only as means for other people.

This intuition is probably at the root of the principle, currently accepted in most Western countries, that disputed custody decisions ought to be settled exclusively or almost exclusively according to what is in the child's best interests.[19] The principle is reinforced by the idea that the child is fundamentally *innocent,* in a sense that applies to neither parent, even if one of them has formally been wronged by the adultery of the other. If, as is often asserted, neither party is in a more substantive sense guilty for the break-up, usually neither is innocent either.

Against this I shall argue that following the principle of the child's best interests may in fact be unjust towards the parents. Parental rights and needs could in principle also be relevant in child custody disputes. This is not to say that disputes ought to be settled so as to maximize the total utility of parents and children, assuming that this concept could be made meaningful. Children do have a need for special protection, but their interests do not lexicographically dominate those of all other parties.

The second unique feature of child custody cases is exemplified

---

Policy towards children should enhance and protect their potential for becoming persons in Frankfurt's sense.
[18] Becker (1981), ch. 5.
[19] Undisputed custody settlements, resulting from private bargaining and agreement between the parents, are a different matter. 'There can be few areas of life where the treatment of children as property rather than as persons is better exemplified. And this has been accentuated by the growing trend towards private ordering of divorce.... Outside a slave society commercial contracts are not concerned with the disposal of human beings: bargains about custody and access are' (M. A. Freeman 1983, pp. 192, 198).

by Solomon's original judgement (Kings 3:16–28). The crucial piece of evidence he used for giving the child to one woman rather than the other was the woman's behaviour in the dispute itself. By making certain claims, or by acceding to certain proposals, one can reveal oneself to have a character that has a bearing on the resolution of the dispute. In Solomon's case, the woman who was willing to have the child cut in two thereby revealed herself ineligible for custody. One may wonder whether Solomon would have carried out his announced decision to cut the disputed child in two had both women agreed to that proposal. Should we assume that Solomon, like the God of the Old Testament, had perfect insight into the hearts of men and women so that he knew he would not have to carry it out?[20] Or could it be that he was outguessed by the woman who declared that she would rather give up the child than have it cut in two?[21]

Similar issues arise in modern custody litigation. Thus it has been argued that 'if people are actually litigating for joint custody [i.e., if one parent demands joint custody against the wish of the other], they are generally not likely to be candidates for it'.[22] Nevertheless, many American states allow one parent to claim joint custody against the wish of the other. When this is coupled with a 'friendly parent' provision, to the effect that custody should preferentially be given to the parent who has demonstrated willingness to share custody or to give extensive visiting rights, the outcome may be that parents who do not want joint custody ipso facto reveal themselves to be not fit for sole custody either. This creates a dangerous incentive for strategic behaviour:

The parent requesting joint custody over the opposition of the other parent is given an unconscionable bargaining lever. A parent who does not believe joint custody would be in his or her child's best interest is put into a negotiating position of either 'accepting' joint custody or risking the loss of custody altogether in a contested trial. Ironically, a parent who is least fit for custody and care of a child benefits the most from this type of statute. A parent opposed to joint custody might be more willing to risk loss of sole custody if she or he feels that the other parent is capable of providing sufficient care for the child. However, the parent opposed to joint custody cannot, and probably will not, take the risk when an

[20] See Brams (1980), pp. 118–23. An interesting reference to the 'Solomon syndrome' occurs in *Garska v. McCoy*, W.Va., 278 S.E.2d 357.

[21] Farrell (1987), p. 118.

[22] Gardner (1984), p. 70.

award of custody to the other parent would not provide minimally sufficient care for the child. Thus the more 'unfit' the parent requesting joint custody, the more bargaining leverage the parent gains under this type of statute.[23]

In addition, a Solomon-like judge might deny custody to a parent whose tactics involve procrastination or derogation of the other parent. Since both tactics can be expected to impose additional pain on the child, the conscious use of them shows a lack of concern for the child that disqualifies the parent for custody. Thus, Solomon's method – the use of behaviour in custody decisions to decide custody – can result in a Catch-22. The more forcefully a parent presses a custody claim, the more he or she is proved unfit for custody.

On reflection, this simple decision rule must, of course, be rejected. Derogation, if successful, detracts from the fitness of the derogated parent, not only from that of the derogating one. As long as appeals and adjournments are allowed by the law, presumably because they can serve the cause of justice, it would be perverse to punish a party for making use of them. Yet there is a core of truth in the argument. How, indeed, can a parent claim to represent the child's best interests if the institutional machinery for making the claim works against those very interests? I argue below that the paradox should be resolved by changing child custody legislation, not by allowing the judge to infer character from litigation behaviour.

In this chapter I examine the current decision-making rule governing child custody disputes: custody should be determined according to the best interests of the child. Section III.2 offers a brief overview of past and present principles of child custody legislation in some Western countries. Section III.3 argues against the principle that custody ought to be decided solely by considering what is in the best interest of the child. I argue that the principle is indeterminate, unjust, self-defeating and liable to be overridden by more general policy considerations. Section III.4 surveys, in a somewhat speculative vein, some tactics used by courts in order to circumvent these undesirable features of the principle. In section III.5 I consider various alternatives to the best-interest

---

[23] Schulmann and Pitt (1984), p. 213.

principle and a number of criteria for evaluating them. Section III.6 offers a brief conclusion.

III.2 TOWARDS THE BEST INTERESTS OF THE CHILD

Historically, the laws regulating child custody in divorce cases have reflected concerns for the rights and needs of both parents and children.[24] The absolute *paternal preference rule* that dominated British legislation up to the end of the nineteenth century derived from the father's dominant right in all family matters. Although an abusive father might lose his legal rights to custody, courts could not adjudicate a custody dispute in favour of a wife. The protection of children was kept separate from the settlement of private custody disputes.[25] One writer describes as 'the highpoint of the "sacred rights of the father" ' the decision in *Re Agar-Ellis* (1883): 'When by birth a child is subject to a father, it is for the general interest of families, and for the general interest of children, and really for the interest of the particular infant, that the Court should not except in very extreme cases, interfere with the discretion of the father.'[26] Although in this passage the right of the father is grounded in broader utilitarian considerations, it was in general conceived as a natural right grounded in the inherent superiority of men over women.[27] We may note in the cited passage the distinction, which will concern us later, between what is in the interest of children generally and what is in the interest of the particular child under consideration.

In nineteenth-century America the paternal preference rule did not take hold. Instead a *fault-based presumption* emerged: 'The children will be best taken care of and instructed by the innocent party' to a divorce.[28] Like the paternal preference rule, the principle is justified by the best interests of the child; however, there is little doubt that overtones of compensatory and retributive reasoning were also present. While the fault-based principle never had a cen-

---

[24] For a useful survey of British legislative history, see Maidment (1984), chs. 4 and 5. For brief remarks on the American development, see Mnookin (1975), pp. 233–7.

[25] Mnookin (1975), p. 234, n. 33.

[26] Cited after Maidment (1984), p. 98.

[27] Ibid., pp. 108–10.

[28] Cited after Mnookin (1975), p. 234.

tral status in Britain, it always had some force.[29] As late as 1962, 'the Court of Appeal allowed a father's appeal against a care and control order to the adulterous mother "as a matter of simple justice. . . . Whilst the welfare of the children is first and paramount, the claims of justice cannot be overlooked" ' (Lord Denning).[30]

In this century the *maternal preference rule* gradually emerged as the dominant doctrine in most Western countries, often with the proviso that it applied especially or only to young children.[31] The maternal preference or presumption rule has, like the other rules discussed, been justified on the grounds of the interests of the child. This appears, moreover, to have been virtually the only justification, unlike the other rules, which have also appealed to parental rights as an independent argument.

Like any presumption that of maternal preference is rebuttable. How much it takes to rebut it varies from country to country and from court to court. In the United States rebuttal often required a showing of maternal unfitness in some absolute sense, sometimes shading, however, into a contest of relative fitness.[32] In Norway the law stipulated fairly explicitly that the presumption applied only when there was absolute uncertainty as to which parent was the more fit, but lower courts frequently (and the Supreme Court occasionally) understood the presumption so that it could offset some preponderance of probability, well short of certainty, that the father was best suited.[33] Another possibility is that the presumption could be rebutted by demonstration that the father was clearly and certainly more fit, even assuming that the mother passed the threshold of absolute fitness.[34]

The maternal preference rule contained within itself the seeds of its own destruction. By resting exclusively on considerations of the child's best interests, it invited lawmakers to turn these interests into the explicit criterion for custody adjudication in every

---

[29] Maidment (1984), pp. 154–5.
[30] Ibid., p. 15.
[31] Mnookin (1975), p. 235; Maidment (1984), p. 156.
[32] Mnookin (1975), p. 235, n.41.
[33] Smith (1980), pp. 368–79.
[34] For a discussion of presumptions of various strengths, see Ullmann-Margalit (1983), pp. 152–4. Chambers (1984), pp. 562–4, discusses how a primary-caretaker presumption could similarly be understood as requiring, for its rebuttal, (a) a show of unfitness, (b) 'clear and convincing evidence' that the other parent was more fit or (c) a preponderance of the evidence pointing to the other parent as the more fit.

case. Why rest content with the rule of thumb that the interests of children are in general best served by maternal custody when fine-tuned ways of serving the interests of each particular child are available? Why not judge each case on its merits? Moreover, the incorporation of the best interests of the child as a principle for adjudication, not simply for legislation, has desirable incentive effects. Under the maternal preference rule, the spectre of divorce did not give either parent an incentive to take good care of the child during the marriage.[35] Usually the mother could count on getting custody unless she behaved very badly, and the father knew that no efforts on his part would give him a chance. Under the best-interest rule, it is no longer true that caring for the child is superfluous for the mother and pointless for the father.

The demise of maternal presumption, and its replacement by the principle that custody ought to be decided according to what is *in the best interests of the child,* occurred in several countries some time in the 1970s. The best-interest principle is often formulated in a way that allows some scope for other criteria.[36] In Britain, the child's welfare should be the 'first and paramount' consideration.[37] In Norway, the decision shall 'mainly' consider the interests of the child.[38] It would appear that the other criteria, whatever they are, are not simply intended to function as tiebreakers when the interests of the child are equally well served with either parent. In principle, a slight difference with respect to what serves the child can be offset by large differences in other respects. But the laws are rarely explicit on the nature of the trade-off and on the nature of the other criteria.

The demise of maternal preference must also be seen in the broader perspective of the feminist movement. The idea of equality between the sexes was difficult to reconcile with the survival of a maternal presumption. Several arguments seem to have been at work here. First, there was the view that when women claim the abolition of male privilege, they must also, to be consistent, accept the abolition of any female privileges. Against this idea, but point-

---

[35] For this statement to be false, two conditions have to obtain: the presumption must be taken in a very weak sense and the courts must very seldom find themselves in a state of absolute uncertainty.

[36] For a survey of U.S. legislation, see Mnookin (1975), pp. 235–7.

[37] Maidment (1984), p. 14.

[38] 'Lov av 8 april 1981 nr 7 om barn og foreldre', 34.

ing to the same conclusion, it was argued that maternal presumption was a burden rather than a privilege.[39] Although formally the rule involved nothing more than the right to custody, it went together with and reinforced the view that taking care of children is a woman's job. More generally, the presumption was part of a network of sex roles that has prevented women from forming autonomous career plans and professional expectations.

The interpretation and implementation of the best-interest principle have been governed by various hypotheses that have sometimes acquired the status of informal presumptions. Certain psychological theories, in particular, have come to be seen as 'legislative facts' that can be used to guide decisions without any need to consider the circumstances of each case.[40] The psychological theories of John Bowlby on the importance of the mother–child relationship, which formerly served to justify maternal preference legislation, are no doubt occasionally still used as legislative facts in adjudication.[41] The present conventional wisdom, however, is to rely on the psychoanalytic views of Goldstein, Freud and Solnit, for whom continuity of the relationship is all-important. This doctrine creates what almost amounts to a *presumption for the status quo* – to award custody to a parent with whom the child is living (and has been living for some time) at the time of dispute.[42] It also seems to underlie the *primary-care-taker (or -caregiver) assumption* which is emerging in some American states (West Virginia and Oregon).[43] Thus in actual adjudica-

---

[39] See Weitzman (1983), p. 115; Weitzman (1985), p. 231.

[40] For the notion of 'legislative facts', see Ellis (1984), pp. 605–9. See also Goldstein, Freud and Solnit (1979a), p. 60.

[41] For the role of 'Bowlbyism' in English custody cases, see Maidment (1984), pp. 182–4. She also offers a 'sociological explanation for Bowlby's reception, [namely] that it served economic and political interests in the post-war world to remove women from the labour market, and the maternal deprivation theory thus coincided with a political desire to get women back into the home' (ibid., p. 8). In the absence of a demonstration that the persons with labour-market-oriented reasons to diffuse Bowlby's doctrine also had the intellectual and academic power and opportunity to do so, I remain unconvinced by this functional explanation. For a survey of the literature on maternal deprivation, see Chambers (1984), pp. 515–23.

[42] For a critical discussion of the doctrine of developmental connectedness, see Kagan (1984), ch. 3. For a similarly critical discussion of the status quo principle in custody decisions, see Maidment (1984), ch. 8.

[43] See notably *Garska v. McCoy*, W. Va., 278 S.E.2d 357. For favourable comments, see Goldstein, Freud, Solnit and Goldstein (1986), pp. 24, 63–7, and (especially) Chambers (1984), pp. 527–37.

tions the best-interest principle is not always implemented on a
case-by-case, unstructured and discretionary basis.

III.3   AGAINST THE BEST INTERESTS OF THE
CHILD

This section presents arguments against the principle that the
best interests of the child ought to be the sole, main or paramount considerations in custody decisions. First, following Robert Mnookin, I emphasize the indeterminacy of the principle: in
many, perhaps most, cases it simply does not yield a decision.
Second, I argue that even when determinate the principle is
liable to yield unjust decisions, since it neglects the rights and
needs of the parents. Third, I argue that the principle is self-
defeating, in that fine-tuned considerations of the best interest of
each child is likely to impose 'process costs' that on balance tend
to make children worse off. Finally, in a somewhat different
vein, I point to cases in which the best interests of the child must
take second place to more general considerations of public policy. These arguments are wholly negative. The positive argument for an alternative principle is developed in III.5.

The principle is indeterminate

For the sake of simplicity, I here compare only two custody options: paternal and maternal custody. The arguments developed
in this section also apply, however, to other options (joint custody
or splitting of siblings). The question is whether a court can decide
which of the two options corresponds to the child's best interests.
As in any decision problem, a determinate answer will in general
require that the following conditions be satisfied:[44]

All the options must be known.
All the possible outcomes of each option must be known.
The probabilities of each outcome must be known.
The value attached to each outcome must be known.

---

[44] In special cases they need not all be satisfied. Thus if the comparison yields the same
outcome for any set of probabilities attached to the outcomes, or for any (reasonable)
value ordering, the indeterminacy of fact or value need not bother us.

The first condition is satisfied ex hypothesi. Mnookin argues that we cannot expect any of the others to be.[45]

Consider first the set of possible outcomes. If, say, custody is given to the mother, a great number of things could happen to her, and she could *do* a great number of things, as could the father, that would have an impact on the welfare of the child: so great, in fact, that we cannot even begin to list them. Hence the expected utility calculus cannot be carried out. This objection, while valid, is in a sense too strong. In many, indeed most, decision problems there are associated with each of the options a number of unknown and essentially unknowable possibilities whose materialization depends on the future development of the universe. When trying to make up one's mind, one has to assume that those and other unknowable factors on each side cancel out, so that one can concentrate on the knowable ones. Even among the latter, one has to focus mainly on the known ones, because of the direct costs and opportunity costs of collecting and processing information. The ensuing decision, although not ideally rational from the point of view of an omniscient observer, will at least be as rational as can be expected. Similarly, the custody judge should not let himself be paralysed by all the things that might conceivably happen and that would be relevant if they did happen. He is justified in fixing his attention on a small number of things that might plausibly happen.

Consider next the objection from indeterminacy of probability. It might appear as if the reasoning against Mnookin's first objection (i.e., the indeterminacy of possible outcomes) automatically provides a reply to this one, since in order to decide that something is 'plausible' one must know something about how probable it is. I believe, however, that the plausible can be identified in other ways. If a consequence is predicted by a partial theory, that is, one which is valid ceteris paribus, we may regard it as plausible even if we do not have a more general theory that would allow us to assess its probability.[46] Once the plausible outcomes have been

---

[45] Mnookin (1975), pp. 257–61.
[46] Also, if we can tell a smooth scenario, that is, one that does not rest on accidents and coincidences, about how X could lead to Y, then Y is a plausible outcome of X even if we cannot say anything about how probable it is that X will lead to Y (Kahneman and Tversky 1982c).

identified, we can go on to ask whether their probabilities can be assessed. If they can, and if values can confidently be attached to the outcomes, the expected utility calculus can be carried out and one option singled out as the best, except in the special case in which several options have the same expected utility. If values but not probabilities can be attached to outcomes, we have a problem of decision making under uncertainty (in the technical sense in which it differs from decision making under risk with known probabilities). In such problems a natural response is to play safe, which in the present case means giving custody to the parent with whom the child's worst plausible future will be best. The criterion would tend to reward emotional and financial stability. It is consistent with the axioms of rational decision making under uncertainty (I.3), but so are other criteria that would point in different directions. It is just as rational, for instance, to choose the option under which the child's best plausible future is as good as possible.

Even if one were able to attach probabilities to outcomes or to argue for a specific criterion of decision making under uncertainty, a third objection remains: the difficulty of attaching values to outcomes. Even if the child were as fully capable as an adult of expressing an informed preference over possible futures, the ranking might be partially indeterminate. Having complete preferences, that is, being able to compare and rank all pairs of outcomes, is not part of what it means to be rational. As argued in I.3, comparability may fail when the outcomes are large chunks of a life rather than small, isolated events. Since the extent to which preference orderings approach completeness increases with one's experience and exposure to a large and varied set of alternatives, the early choices that lead to that exposure are less likely to stem from complete preferences. The child, having very little experience, can be expected to have large gaps in his preference ordering.

In trying to make an informed choice on behalf of the child, a judge or psychologist would in general have to add some preferences of his own. Although he might be justified in correcting for the child's tendency to seek immediate gratification, he would in addition have to engage in morally objectionable paternalism. His decisions would often amount to telling one of the parents, 'Because I don't like your life style, you don't get the child'. It would not help much to instruct the judge to make a decision that the child would approve later on the basis of more fully developed preferences, assuming such prediction to be possible.[47] Since those preferences would depend largely on the decision made, the instruction might not discriminate sufficiently between the options.[48] In any case, it is not realistic to assume that judges are able to predict the future preferences of a child.

There is, however, a different and, I believe, superior way of approaching the problem of the child's best interests. Instead of being guided by substantive preferences and choices that are imputed to the child, one could be led by the more formal goal of protecting the child's opportunity and ability to make choices. On this view, a child should be allowed, as far as possible, to reach maturity with a maximum of potentialities and the autonomy needed to choose which of them to develop. Once that point is reached, what he chooses to make of his life is up to him, but one should not knowingly preempt the choice. From this follows the need of the child for physical health and material well-being (to ensure survival and the development of potentialities) and emotional care (as a condition for autonomous choice). Whatever the interests of the child ultimately turn out to be, he has a prior interest in being able to choose without material or psychological constraints.[49]

In most cases, this liberal, pluralist criterion will not yield a determinate preference for one parent. It can, however, serve to exclude some parents as unfit in an absolute sense. To be unfit for custody, parents must be shown to have neglected the physical needs of the child, to have physically or sexually abused the child, to be financially unable to provide for the child, or to have character traits that render them emotionally inadequate. The meaning of the last clause is, of course, controversial.[50] I submit that it should be interpreted narrowly, so as to include little beyond clini-

---

[47] As proposed by Chambers (1984), pp. 493–5.

[48] This is also recognized by Chambers (1984), p. 495; see also Elster (1984), p. 47.

[49] The idea is similar to and partially inspired by John Rawls's notion of 'primary goods' (Rawls 1971, pp. 90–5 and passim). Chambers (1984), pp. 497–9, offers a similar proposal, with emphasis on children's competence to act rather than their autonomy to choose. I suggest, however, that autonomy is the more basic value, since it ensures competence without being required for it.

[50] 'A hot-tempered, emotional, difficult, incompetent wife may be a more suitable person to leave custody than a cold, unsympathetic, self-righteous and very able husband' (from an Irish court, cited after Smith 1980, p. 430). Cf. Elster (1985a).

cally demonstrable psychic disorders. Psychology is an undeveloped and controversial discipline even at the best of times; and the context of a custody dispute is far from the best time to study the dispositions of children and parents.

Although I shall adopt this liberal principle in the following, it does pose certain problems. It counts, for instance, against a parent who intends to give the child a very strict religious upbringing which, for all practical purposes, preempts the child's later choice of religion. This implication may seem unacceptable, since married parents have the right to raise their children as strictly as they want. I believe, however, that this right rests on an essentially rule-utilitarian argument that does not apply to divorced families. Were it possible, within the undivorced family, to ensure the child's autonomy in religious (or political) matters without interfering unduly with family life, I believe one ought to do so. We do not do so, however, because the degree of state control and intervention required would be very harmful to family life and, ultimately, to children's autonomy. The remedy would be worse than the disease. In disputed custody cases, by contrast, judicial intervention is already a fact, and application of the liberal principle adds no disruption to a family which has already broken up.[51]

My conclusion, then, is that the best-interest principle is usually indeterminate when both parents pass the threshold of absolute fitness. This does not imply that a highly qualified expert, if allowed to observe the family before dissolution, would be unable to predict which parent would be more fit for custody. It implies, more weakly, that courts would not be able to make this prediction on the basis of the behaviour of the parents in an exceptionally stressful period and of evidence by expert witnesses whose qualifications they could not judge. Yet I do not exclude that sometimes the evidence is sufficiently clear-cut for one to conclude that one of two fit parents is fitter than the other. I do not believe these cases are frequent, but I might be wrong. Hence in what follows I sometimes assume, contrary to what I have argued so far, that differences in parental fitness can be routinely ascertained by the

---

[51] This point is overlooked by Nanacakos (1984, p. 23), who writes that 'since the state's right to interfere with [parental] rights within the family is limited by a principle far more restrictive than "the best interest of the child", it is hard to see why state interference should become any less restricted after divorce'.

court, to argue that even on this assumption the best-interest principle should be rejected.

The principle is unjust

Barring siblings, a custody case involves three persons, all of whom have a strong interest in the decision. Yet under the best-interest principle the child's welfare is the dominant consideration. The law does not take any account of the needs and rights of the parents, except to the extent that it states that the child's interest is to be the 'first and paramount' rather than the 'sole' criterion. One might think, given the argument from indeterminacy, that there is a wide scope for considering parental interests. Yet, as I argue in III.4, this is not how the law works. Judges make an effort to wring determinate results from the best-interest principle. Although in doing so they might be sensitive to parental interests, they usually do not cite them as independent arguments, but smuggle them in under the guise of the best interests of the child.

Even when (or assuming that) the best-interest principle yields a determinate preference, parental interests ought to be considered. Some of these derive from the rights of parents, others from their needs.

One example of a rights-based claim is Lord Denning's admonition that in cases of adultery one must consider the 'claims of justice' in addition to the welfare of the child. In general, this is a dubious argument. For one thing, relations between spouses are usually so complex that an act of adultery does not in itself create one guilty and one innocent party.[52] For another, adultery, when blamable, is more properly punished through the financial settlement than by the loss of custody. Unlike other forms of behaviour, discussed later, which one might want to reward by custody or punish by the denial of it, adultery is not a child-related action. There is, nevertheless, the incentive argument that a predictable loss of custody will be a more potent deterrent to adultery than mere financial loss. The main thrust of this argument, as usually deployed, is the stabilizing impact on family life in

---

[52] Lord Justice Ormrod, cited in Maidment (1984), p. 15.

general and on the welfare of children in particular. Although the welfare of a given child may be best promoted if custody is given to an adulterous parent, the welfare of children in general may require a presumption, which could be more or less strong, against this practice.

Other rights-based considerations are more compelling. Thus if one parent, usually the mother, has devoted crucial years to child care and perhaps given up her career to do so, it seems prima facie right that she should get custody. Note that in this case the rights-creating behaviour is directly related to the child. It would be odd to give custody to one parent on the ground that he or she had behaved meritoriously in matters unrelated to the child, for example, by taking care of elderly relatives. To use child care as an argument for child custody seems more relevant. By linking expected custody to care, the quality of the latter – and consequently of the former, should the case arise – will be enhanced. In addition to this argument, which appeals to the general interests of children, there is an independent reason in terms of fairness to the primary caretaker (when there is one). To award custody to the other parent would often be justice according to Saint Matthew.

Another rights-based argument is that custody should not be given to a parent who has used illegal tactics of abduction or procrastination to create a fait accompli in order to benefit from the status quo presumption. This principle is like the adultery argument in that it refuses custody to a wrongdoing parent and like the child care argument in that the behaviour in question is related to the child. Against this principle, however, it has been argued that the proper punishment for such behaviour should not be denial of custody, since this would also, given the status quo presumption, be a punishment of the child.[53] Disregarding the difficulty that other ways of punishing the parent may also hurt the child, I believe there is an argument for making the punishment fit the crime. Other things being equal, the punishment ought to be chosen so as to render the illegal action fruitless, that is, to nullify its immediate purpose of gaining custody and not simply to nullify any net gain to the offender by imposing costs at

---

[53] Goldstein, Freud and Solnit (1979b), p. 235; see also Goldstein, Freud, Solnit and Goldstein (1986), pp. 174, n.2, and 175, n.4.

least as large as the immediate gains.[54] Among the other things
that may not be equal are, of course, the costs that punishment or
reward may impose on the child.

The preceding considerations were based on the rights of parents or the violation of these rights. Considerations of parental
needs or welfare may also be relevant.[55] Imagine a case in which
the best interests of the child create a slight but detectable preference for paternal custody, whereas the welfare loss for the mother
from not getting custody would be much larger than what would
be suffered by the father if he were denied custody. Imagine also
that the absolute welfare level of the mother would be very low
were she to be denied custody. In that case, strong welfarist arguments support maternal custody.

In general, however, welfare-based arguments face formidable
difficulties. In principle, parental welfare should count for more
than parental rights. The latter have little weight unless backed by
the former. Consider a mother who (a) in the past has sacrificed
some of her own welfare to take care of the child but (b) would not
suffer much in the present if she did not get custody and (c) has a
welfare level in the present no lower than what she could be expected to have had in the absence of those past sacrifices. Her
rights-based claims, although not totally invalidated by the lack of
links to the present, are, it seems to me, weakened.[56] If her husband, who, let us assume, did not make any sacrifices in the past,

---

[54] In arguing for this view, one cannot simply appeal to the principle that 'no man may
profit from his own wrong' (Dworkin 1978, p. 23), since this does not distinguish between immediate profits and net profits. Rather one must point to the difficulty for
courts of ascertaining the subjective value of the illegal action and, hence, of imposing a
cost equivalent to it. The only way to be *certain* that the offender does not profit from the
offence is to undo it. There is a similar argument for fitting the reward to the deed. One
could in principle let the caretaking parent choose between custody and a suitable
financial compensation, i.e., to waive the right for a fee, were it not for the incentives this
would create to exaggerate the burden of not getting custody.

[55] The distinction between rights and welfare is not absolute, since the belief that one's
rights have been violated may contribute to the misery of not getting custody. The denial
of a right may cause more suffering than the nonexercise of the right following from its
voluntary waiving.

[56] Both the second and the third conditions are needed to weaken the present rights-
creating force of past sacrifice. If condition (b) is not satisfied, one might still want to
award custody to the mother to offset the present welfare losses from past sacrifices. To
accord custody to the father on the grounds that he would benefit more would, once
again, be justice according to Saint Matthew. If condition (c) is not satisfied, maternal
custody could be justified as compensation for past sacrifices.

would suffer greatly in the present from not getting custody, his claim should take precedence. A fatal objection to this reasoning, however, is the tendency, known to every divorce lawyer, towards strategic misrepresentation of preferences.[57] Whereas rights-based arguments build on verifiable statements about past behaviour, needs-based arguments rest on less verifiable, strategically manipulable statements about future welfare.

It seems best, therefore, to use rights as a proxy for needs, even if on first-best principles one would want to discount rights not backed by needs. If, as is frequently the case, the parent most in need of the child is also the primary caretaker, rights-based arguments can serve as proxy for the needs-based ones, but otherwise it may be difficult to give legal force to the latter. As another reason against giving great weight to this factor, one could also cite the well-known tendency of the human mind to lessen its affections when their object falls out of reach. This, however, is a dangerous argument, to be used, if at all, with much circumspection.[58]

The child's welfare, the rights of the parents and the needs of the parents all give rise to prima facie claims that must be balanced against each other. In balancing the child's welfare against that of the parents, I believe we can draw some useful lessons from more general theories of distributive justice. Two well-known extreme views are the utilitarian principle that one ought to maximize the sum total of welfare[59] and Rawls's principle that one ought to maximize the welfare of the worst-off group in society.[60] Each of these principles seems intuitively unacceptable. Utilitarianism has the unpalatable consequence that one might be justified in sacrificing individuals for the sake of the general good. The maximin principle has the equally counterintuitive implication that one would be justified in reducing almost everybody's welfare a great deal for the sake of a slight increase in the welfare

---

[57] Mnookin and Kornhauser (1979); Weitzman (1985); Neely (1986).
[58] I have argued elsewhere (Elster 1983a, p. 113; 1984, pp. 82–3) against a policy maker using the predictable preference changes of the citizens to justify measures which ex ante they do not want.
[59] Harsanyi (1955).
[60] Actually Rawls refers to primary goods, not to welfare, but since there are several primary goods it is hard to see how one could avoid some welfarist considerations when it comes to comparing two bundles of primary goods each of which dominates the other with respect to one good.

of the worst off. Roughly speaking, utilitarianism offers too little protection to the vulnerable while maximin justice offers too much. The commonsensical attitude, to which most nonphilosophers seem to subscribe, is to protect the disadvantaged at the expense of the well off, but not if the gains are unreasonably small compared with the costs. Common sense, of course, has no theory to explain what 'unreasonably' means here, which is why philosophers would dismiss the view as ad hoc and unprincipled. Yet I submit that in making actual allocative decisions we are constantly forced to make intuitive evaluations of what is and what is not an acceptable cost–benefit trade-off.

Applied to child custody, the reasoning suggests that one should avoid two extremes. The child custody decision should not be made on utilitarian principles with the goal of maximizing the total welfare of the family members.[61] The child needs special protection. That protection should not, however, extend to small gains in the child's welfare achieved at the expense of large losses in parental welfare. Assume, for instance, that the parents are equally fit[62] except for the fact that one of them earns 20 per cent more than the other. The child can be expected to be somewhat better off with the parent with the higher income, yet one might feel justified in giving custody to the other parent if having custody means much more to him or to her. The decision would have to be left to judicial discretion. Let me repeat, however, that I am arguing about a case that I really do not believe will arise, since I do not believe it is possible to make such fine-tuned comparisons of parental fitness.

The principle is self-defeating

Another argument against the best interests of the child principle is that by promoting the interests of the child in a particular case, one may work against the interests of children in general. This

---

[61] For an explicit proposal that custody ought to follow 'the best interests of the family', see Gardner (1982), p. 218. He does not, however, specify this criterion. Moreover, the force of the disagreement with the best-interest principle is reduced when he goes on to say that 'a recommendation that might be significantly deleterious to a parent might ultimately be to the detriment of the child' (ibid.).

[62] Note that this is a much stronger statement than saying that we cannot tell whether one is more fit than the other.

perverse result can come about in two ways: if legislators neglect the distinction between act-oriented and rule-oriented principles, and if they neglect the costs of legal decision making.

Act and rule. The distinction between act-utilitarianism and rule-utilitarianism – between searching on each occasion for the act that maximizes utility and searching for a rule that if followed on all occasions will maximize utility – is a familiar one. The two principles suggest different courses of action because they have different expectation and incentive effects.[63] In particular, if one seeks the best decision in each case, more cases may arise. Given that a house has been destroyed by a flood, social welfare may be maximized by society's providing the owner with a cheap loan to rebuild it at the same site, yet it might be better if society announced that it would never do this, for then fewer houses would be built in these areas.

In the present case, we must consider restricted versions of act- and rule-utilitarianism that take account only of the welfare of children. A decision rule that is in the best interests of each particular child whose custody is contested might create parental incentives or expectations that are detrimental to the interests of children in general. The Victorian argument against giving custody to an adulterous parent is one example of this reasoning. The argument against giving custody to a parent who has used illegal tactics to exploit the status quo presumption is another. In general, it is better for children if one removes parental incentives to create such faits accomplis.

A third example concerns the argument for family autonomy and freedom from state intervention. This problem is more relevant to child placement law than to divorce law, but is mentioned here because of its fundamental importance. If the best interests of the child really are the value guiding the law, one might wonder why courts or welfare agencies are not allowed to remove a child from perfectly fit biological parents when other parents are available who would provide even more for the child.[64] To escape

---

[63] Harsanyi (1977b).
[64] Mnookin (1975), p. 268, describes a hypothetical example of this sort. In his further discussion of the example, however, he seems to confuse the inappropriateness of the act-oriented application of the best-interest principle with its indeterminacy.

this conclusion, it is not necessary to embrace the view that there is a fundamental, natural right to family autonomy.[65] It is sufficient to point out that in this context an act-oriented interpretation of the best-interest principle would create so much uncertainty among parents, with subsequent lack of emotional attachment to their children, that the net effect would be to harm children in general. In addition, there would be a strong disincentive to having children at all.[66]

Decision costs. Decision making is a costly process. It requires time, energy and other scarce resources with alternative uses. Rational decision making that does not take account of this fact runs the risk of being self-defeating. If the goal is to arrive at the decision that would have been best if found instantaneously and costlessly, the occasion for acting may no longer be present by the time one finds out what it would have been optimal to do. Forecasting tomorrow's weather became a practical science only when the calculations took less than twenty-four hours. Predicting the outcome of the roulette wheel was pointless before the advent of a technology that allowed one to collect data and process them in less time than it took for the wheel to come to a halt.

Even if there still is an occasion to act when the abstractly optimal solution has been found, the outcome may on balance be worse than if a less than optimal decision had been acted upon earlier. A rational decision maker will strive for the decision that yields the best outcome all things considered, including the costs of decision making themselves. A doctor who is brought a severely

---

[65] Guggenheim (1984) fails to recognize this point when he assumes (pp. 110–16) that if the courts do not recognize a fundamental right to family autonomy, but offer instead 'a utilitarian justification for family autonomy', there might follow 'a dramatic expansion of state power in the area of child development'. He cites with approval a statement that 'if all that matters is what is most advantageous to a *particular child*, perhaps state intervention in parent–child relationships should be more readily allowed than it is under existing law and practices' (italics added). But if what matters is what is most advantageous to *children*, courts would be very reluctant to interfere with family autonomy because of the uncertainty such practices would create.

[66] It has been argued that there was less emotional attachment to children in earlier centuries, when few of them could be expected to reach adulthood. (For a brief survey of the literature, see M. A. Freeman 1983, pp. 8–13.) By an ironic compensating mechanism, the poor state of medical knowledge which was responsible for the low survival rates also prevented family planning: if the looser emotional ties created disincentives to having children, the technology needed to act on them was absent.

injured patient must sometimes make a snap decision about what to do, knowing that with more time he could have made the correct diagnosis but also knowing that he does not now have that time at his disposal.

Because legal decisions differ from medical ones, the costs of litigation are not a reason for the judge to make snap decisions. If the law calls for fine-tuned determination of what is in the best interests of the child, the judge's task is to arrive at the decision which would have been best if found costlessly and instantaneously.[67] The fact that it will be neither costless nor instantaneous is of less concern to him than arriving at the 'correct' decision. He will call expert witnesses to the extent necessary; he will allow the parties to call character witnesses; he will have to allow postponements and appeals within the limits of the law. Although he may resist attempts at strategic procrastination, if he can distinguish them from bona fide moves that just happen to be time-consuming, he cannot object to the latter.

Parties have several incentives to procrastinate in custody litigation. A party may want to procrastinate if it has more resources than the other, so as to force the other to a more favourable private settlement.[68] In addition, the longer the case drags on, the better the chance of the party with temporary custody of gaining custody in a legal settlement. These incentives provide an additional argument, in terms of justice to the parents, against the best-interest principle. By virtue of its fine-tuned character the principle invites protracted litigation.

The main cost of a protracted litigation, however, is to the child. A custody battle places the child in many difficult roles: mediator, weapon, pawn, bargaining chip, trophy or even spy.[69] The use of expert and character witnesses can be especially harmful. 'The parents will call each other crazy, and the children will begin to wonder about themselves as well as their parents.'[70] Also, the 'ef-

---

[67] This is a rather gross simplification, since what is in the best interest of the child may not be the same when the case is decided as it was when it was brought. The mere passing of time may give an edge to the parent with temporary custody. Time thus has a double effect here: by allowing the judge to gather more information it makes it easier for him to reach the best solution, but it can also affect what *is* the best solution.

[68] See Cooter and Marks with Mnookin (1982).

[69] Musetto (1982), p. 75.

[70] Goldzband (1982), p. 55.

forts of attorneys, working in an adversary spirit, can escalate conflict between parents and draw children into divorce arguments'.[71] Divorce seems to be more harmful to the mental health of children when dispute is contested than when it is not.[72] The best-interest principle increases costs to children in two ways. First, more cases will be brought than if there existed a strong presumption rule or an automatic decision procedure, because both parties may persuade themselves that they stand a chance of getting custody. Second, for any given case that is brought, the legal process will be more protracted because it is not simply a case of deciding whether one parent is unfit.

The best-interest principle may, however, yield decisions which are better for the child than are decisions based on mechanical criteria, in the abstract sense that disregards the harm done to the child by the decision-making process itself. At least I shall proceed on this assumption, setting aside for the time being the objection from indeterminacy. The question, then, is whether children are on the whole better off with fine-tuning than with the cruder principles to be discussed in III.5. I shall use as a representative of these cruder principles a strong form of the maternal preference rule: unless the mother is clearly unfit, she will get custody.

Assuming that some children will be better off with the father and others with the mother, but that before a legal and psychological examination is conducted we do not know which children fall in which category, there are three cases to be considered.[73] In the first are children who would in any case be better off with the mother and thus can only benefit from a presumption rule that spares them the cost of litigation. The second contains those children who would be better off with the father, but will be better off with the mother if spared these costs. Finally, there may be children who, even with a legal conflict, would be better off with the

---

[71] Hess and Camara (1979), p. 95.

[72] Wallerstein (1985), p. 177; Eekelaar (1982), pp. 73–6. No difference between the two groups of children is found by Elton (1979), p. 131. As the author notes, however, parental reports may not be the most reliable way to measure the mental health of the child. In any case, statistical studies of this problem must confront, as they usually do not, the problem of distinguishing between correlation and causation. Even if children suffer to a greater extent when custody is contested, one cannot conclude without further argument that their suffering is caused by the dispute.

[73] The following draws upon a characteristically helpful clarification by Aanund Hylland.

father than they would be if the mother were given custody following the presumption.

Since cases in which the mother is unfit are automatically decided
in the father's favour under both regimes, the third category may
be quite small. If it is empty, the coarse-grained maternal presumption is better *for all children* than the fine-tuned principle of the
child's best interests. If – as is probable – it is not empty, is the
crude principle likely to be better for children *on the average?* The
answer depends on one's belief about the ability of the court to
assess differences in parental fitness and about the size distribution
of these differences. Even if there are detectable degrees of parental fitness, these may not offset the pain to the child from being the
object of a custody litigation. Also, intellectual honesty should force
one to recognize that there is a great deal of uncertainty surrounding the assessment of degrees of fitness, whereas the damage done
to children by litigation is hardly open to doubt. Against the conjectural long-term effects on the child of being with the mother or the
father one must set the known short-term pain and damage created
by custody disputes.[74] If it is *often* the case that the court can say *with
high probability* that the benefit for the child from being with one
parent rather than the other is *substantially greater* than the pain
created by litigation, fine-tuning may be justified. But even those
who are not fully persuaded by the arguments presented earlier
may perhaps agree that the ability of courts to make such judgements is not great.

The principle can be overridden by the public interest

This final consideration has a somewhat different status than the
ones presented in the preceding sections. It will probably be accepted by most defenders of the best-interest standard, as the kind
of exception that can arise to the best-grounded principles. It is
presented to show only that the best-interest principle cannot be an
absolute one. Sometimes courts, knowingly and deliberately, must
refuse to follow what they take to be the child's best interests on the
ground that more general policy considerations take precedence.

---

[74] On the latter side, there are also the (equally conjectural) long-term effects of the
custody struggle. The child's capacity to receive affection and accord trust can be permanently stultified by this traumatic experience.

I shall consider two ways in which the public interest might override the principle. Imagine, first, that one parent (I shall assume the mother) has a life situation or life style which is generally disapproved of by the local community. The child, living with the mother, would be stigmatized in a very painful way. Living with the father would, but only for this reason, be better for the child. Yet the public policy is to promote equal concern and respect for the way of life in question. To recognize popular prejudice and stigma as a factor in custody decisions is therefore objectionable.[75] The child's welfare must, to put it crudely, be sacrificed for the greater good.

The sacrificing of a child's best interests for public policy reasons is best illustrated by the case of *Palmore v. Sidoti*. In that case, the U.S. Supreme Court overturned a lower court decision which had denied custody to a mother who had recently married a person of different race. The lower court had argued 'despite the strides that have been made in bettering relations between the races in this country, it is inevitable that Melanie will, if allowed to remain in her present situation and attains school age and thus more vulnerable to peer pressure, suffer from the social stigmatization that is sure to come'.[76] The Supreme Court found the reasoning of this statement no less dubious than the syntax: 'The effects of racial prejudice, however real, cannot justify a racial classification removing an infant child from the custody of its natural mother. The Constitution cannot control such prejudices, but neither can it tolerate them. Private biases may be outside the reach of the law, but the law cannot, directly or indirectly, give them effect.'[77]

Along similar lines is a British case in which a mother lost custody because she was a lesbian.[78] In so holding, the court referred to 'the risk of children, at critical ages, being exposed or introduced to ways of life which, as this case illustrates, may lead to severance from normal society, to psychological stresses and unhappiness and possibly even to physical experiences which may

---

[75] Chambers (1984), p. 543, n. 252, makes the related point that stigma to a mother caused by not getting custody should not be allowed to count as a determinant of her welfare.

[76] Florida District Court of Appeal 426 So2d 34.

[77] *Palmore v. Sidoti*, 104 S. Ct.1879 (1984).

[78] S v S (1980) 1 *Family Law Reports* 143.

scar them for life'. It is not clear whether this language refers to direct effects of the mother's sexual deviation or to indirect effects from stigma. Yet the following summary suggests that the latter were intended:

> The welfare report had recommended custody to the mother on the grounds that the sexual identity of both children was well established, both children expressed wishes to be with their mother, and the mother would provide better material care than the father. Both sides had called expert witnesses: for the mother it was said that 'there was no danger in this case of the children being led into deviant sexual ways'; for the father the consultant psychiatrist agreed as regards sexual deviation, but considered that the 'social embarrassment and hurt' resulting from local knowledge of their mother's lesbianism would be very harmful to the children.[79]

Like the state court's decision in *Palmore v. Sidoti*, the decision to deny custody to the mother appears unjustified. Once society has accepted the rights of homosexuals to equal concern and respect, bias and stigma arising from slowness of diffusion of this attitude should not be allowed to have effect.

A second example of an overriding public interest that may affect custody decisions is the financial status of the parents. This interest can be seen at work in Norway, where the parents' financial status is not allowed to count in the custody decision, as long as both parents are above some (unspecified) minimal level.[80] This principle could be seen as expressing the somewhat idealistic view that beyond a certain level of wealth the child's interests are unaffected by the resources of the parents. Given that a basic interest of the child is to reach maturity with as many potentialities as possible, however, a parent has to be very affluent before further wealth makes no difference in this respect. It is more plausible to understand the principle as a policy statement that beyond a certain level the financial situation of the parents, while relevant for the child's best interests, should not be allowed to count. A society committed to the value of equality must often treat its citizens as if they were equal when in fact they are not. Also, courts must not give the impression that custody can be bought.

---

[79] Maidment (1984), p. 181.

[80] The principle is stated not in the law, but in the deliberations of the committee which prepared the reform that led to the current law (NOU 1977:35, p. 64). Courts are to some extent bound by these deliberations.

III.4   CIRCUMVENTING THE BEST INTERESTS OF
THE CHILD

If the preceding objections to the best-interest principle are accepted, one might expect courts to find it difficult to apply literally. Consequently, one would not be surprised to see courts using
a lexicographic principle of decision making: when the best interests of the child are indifferent or silent,[81] give custody to the
parent with the strongest rights-based or needs-based claim. Or
they might give some weight to the interests of children in general, when the interest of the child in question is indeterminate.

These lines of reasoning, however, have not been extensively
followed by the courts. Where the best interests of the child are
the dominant principle of the law, courts award custody by finding, however tortuously, a difference between the parents in this
respect. The main reason for this is probably that courts are inherently reluctant to conclude that a principle laid down in the law
can be indeterminate in its application.[82] In an important article
on compromise – or rather its absence – in the law John Coons
has discussed various cases in which an indeterminacy of fact or of
law would seem to justify a compromise between the parties,
rather than the usual winner-takes-all practice of the courts.[83]
Among the reasons he offers to explain why compromises nevertheless occur so rarely, one is also relevant here. Judges might
take their task less seriously if they did not have to come up with a
clear-cut and definite interpretation of the law, or a clear and
unambiguous statement of the facts.[84] A judge is not paid to throw

---

[81] By 'indifferent' I mean that both parents are deemed equally good; by 'silent' that
neither is deemed better than the other. In the document cited in note 80 it was suggested that courts might consider the needs of parents in cases of indifference. In the
later parliamentary report (Inst. O. nr. 30 [1980–1], p. 14) parental needs are allowed to
count in cases of silence. The change must be taken to imply a tacit recognition that the
best-interest standard is too finely tuned.

[82] In addition, courts sometimes confuse indifference and silence. Assume that a court is
unable to compare the parents with respect to the more important dimensions of caring,
but that it can detect a clear difference in some minor respect. If the court neglects the
conceptual distinction between silence and indifference, it can then easily use this difference as the basis for awarding custody, thus seeking precision in the second decimal
while ignoring the first.

[83] Coons (1964).

[84] Ibid., p. 770. For a similar argument against allowing nonunanimous jury decisions see
the dissent by Justice Douglas in *Apodaca v. Oregon* 406 U.S. 404 (1972).

up his hands and say that since the law offers no guide to the decision, he will impose a compromise or, as in the present case, take account of such other considerations that seem relevant.

Courts, therefore, seem to follow a different strategy.[85] Instead of arguing that parental interests or the interests of children in general come into play when the child's interests are indeterminate, they take account of the former interests by making them part of the child's interests. I am not suggesting that judges consciously reason in this manner, only that their reasoning may be influenced by interests other than the particular child's that are irrelevant under existing law but that they feel to be morally pertinent. Judges, no less than others, are vulnerable to self-deception, wishful thinking and other forms of motivated irrationality. Although they are somewhat subject to reality control, since their claims can be appealed and reversed, their mistakes are less strongly sanctioned than those of a soldier or manager.

I shall discuss four ways in which judges can distort the best-interest principle.

Guilt and innocence

The idea that the 'innocent' (nonadulterous) party in a divorce has a special right to custody and the closely related notion that the guilty party should be punished by being denied custody have largely been eliminated from the law, but are sure to live on in the minds of many judges. They may then appear explicitly in a decision, in the guise that it is not in the best interest of the child to live with a parent of loose morals. More frequently, perhaps, they contribute to the decision by making the judge weigh other parts of the evidence in a way that favours the innocent party.

Caretaking

Devoting time to child care during marriage, perhaps at great costs to personal and professional development, would seem to

---

[85] The argument in the rest of this section is largely speculative. In a later essay I hope to substantiate it by a study of actual cases. From a preliminary look at some material from Norway, it would appear that lower courts are more likely to engage in these circumventing tactics.

create a prima facie right to custody. Custody would be a just reward for past devotion and sacrifice. The 'primary-caretaker criterion', when used in modern decisions, is not explicitly justified on these grounds. Rather the argument is that the primary caretaker can be expected to have the strongest emotional bonds to the child and for that reason to be better fit for custody.[86] In his exhaustive survey of the relevant psychological literature, David Chambers finds that on balance the support for this view is very slight.[87] Concluding he writes:

> I have shared earlier drafts of this Article with a substantial number of persons with training in psychology or psychiatry. Nearly all acknowledge the absence of a firm empirical foundation for the conclusion that preserving the bond of children to primary caretakers is more critical than preserving the bond to secondary caretakers and yet nearly all believe that there is something special in that relationship worthy of weight in making decisions about placement.

He then adds in a footnote, 'In conversation, I am never fully certain whether the psychologists are reflecting an unspoken, and perhaps unconscious, concern for the primary caretakers as well'. Judges, no less than psychologists, may be vulnerable to such bias. They might adopt the primary-caretaker principle because the rights of the caretaking parent hover in the back of their mind.

Creating a fait accompli

The parent with temporary custody may deliberately drag out the legal process, by appeals and various legal subterfuges, so that when the decision is finally made, he or she can truthfully say that it would not be in the best interest of the child to have custody given to the other parent who, in the meantime, has become a psychological stranger. Illegal means such as abduction or obstructing visitation rights can be used to the same end. In both cases, especially the latter, it seems unfair to give custody to the parent who has created the fait accompli. In addition, the decision

---

[86] *Garska v. McCoy*, W.Va., 278 S.E.2d 357; Goldstein, Freud, Solnit and Golstein (1986), pp. 24, 63–6. Chambers (1984), p. 501, objects to the use of the rights of the primary caretaker as an argument in custody decisions. He is more sympathetic to the argument that the primary caretaker would be more distressed if he or she did not get custody (even when discounting distress created by stigma).

[87] Chambers (1984), pp. 527–38. The cited passage occurs on p. 537.

would be counter to the interests of children in general, because it would render future procrastination, abduction and obstruction more likely. Courts may, in such cases, rely on the general principle that no one should profit from wrongdoing. However, they also can (and do) justify their reluctance to reward such behaviour by appealing to the best interests of the child: a parent who behaves in this way ipso facto reveals himself or herself to be unfit for custody.[88]

Parental needs

In some cases a court might want to accord custody to the parent most in need of the child but feel that the decision has to be justified by the best-interest principle. This could take the form of arguing that if one parent would be very unhappy if not given custody, the child would suffer too. This is plausible simply by virtue of the interdependence of utility functions within the family.[89] In addition the child might suffer from believing, however irrationally, that his causal involvement in the unhappiness of the parent also confers some moral responsibility.

The stratagems that have been described here are not necessarily disingenuous. Adultery can be one indication, among others, of moral character; primary caretaking can create a bond that ought not to be broken; a parent who kidnaps a child to get custody certainly reveals something about his or her character; the welfare of the parent may be a strong determinant of the child's welfare. Rather my claim is that these arguments are easily exaggerated and made to support conclusions beyond what they can justify. The interests of parents not infrequently point in a different direction from those of a particular child. When one believes that the latter interests are overridden, it ought to be possible to offer direct arguments for that conclusion instead of being compelled to dress them up as arguments about the best interests of the child. Similarly, the concern for the fate of children in general ought to be embodied in legislation rather than represented as concern for a particular child. The law might state,

---

[88] Some Norwegian cases are cited in Smith (1980), pp. 396, 418.
[89] Becker (1976), p. 270.

for instance, that illegal abduction of the child is a direct argument against giving custody to the abducting parent, whereas at present it is merely an indirect argument that the judge can use if he finds that such behaviour is evidence of lack of fitness for custody.

III.5 ALTERNATIVES TO THE BEST INTERESTS OF THE CHILD

It remains to be seen whether any other principle is superior, on balance, to the best-interest standard. I shall first discuss the criteria to be used in evaluating and comparing alternative principles. As will be clear from the earlier discussion, I believe that in addition to the interests of the child in any given decision, one must take account of the interests of parents and of children in general. In addition to the quality of the legal decision, one must consider the bargaining and incentive effects of the principles, as well as procedural values and the broader educative effects of the law.

Let me first, however, eliminate political feasibility as a possible criterion. One may ask, with respect to any given principle, if it corresponds to the *Zeitgeist,* popular opinion or the views of Congress, and refuse to consider proposals which go against these powerful forces. Against this, I consider only the intrinsic merit of the proposals. In doing so I follow the fundamental principle of intellectual argument that in discussions of economic and legal reforms, scholars should not try to preempt the decision of politicians of endogenizing their reactions. If they do so, they deprive politicians of the chance to form their own considered opinion on the basis of the best available evidence and argument.[90] Although in any given case the goal to be attained may be promoted by preemption and self-censorship, the long-term effect of this practice can only be to reduce the influence of professionals, intellectuals and academics. The fact that some of the proposals discussed later – return to maternal preference or custody by the toss of a coin – are likely to meet wide opposition is not *in itself* a reason for refusing to consider them.

[90] A similar argument is made in Goldstein, Freud, Solnit and Goldstein (1986), pp. 70–9, who argue that psychologists and social workers should not anticipate and internalize the judge's reasoning, but present their views to him without self-censorship.

Criteria for custody rules

In addition to the arguments that concern the quality of the legal decision, as it affects the interests of children and parents in the particular case, one may consider a number of other criteria.

Bargaining effects arise because the law serves as what is known as the 'threat point' in private settlements.[91] By defining the outcome for the parties in the case that bargaining breaks down, the law creates a baseline with which to compare the gains from private settlement. It can make a big difference to the bargaining power of the parties whether the legal baseline for custody is a presumption rule, a form of compromise or the strict best-interest principle. One might think that with presumption rules bargaining is simply eliminated. If maternal preference prevails, why should the mother give up in bargaining what she is sure to get in court? For one thing, the degree of her certainty depends on the strength of the presumption and, if the presumption is weak, on the likelihood that the judge will be unable to declare one parent fitter than the other. For another, bargaining over custody is usually coupled with a financial settlement. A mother may be willing to give up custody in return for a good settlement.[92]

Incentive effects of custody rules can arise at various stages. After the dissolution of a marriage, a strict best-interest standard supported by a status quo presumption creates incentives for procrastination and abduction. During marriage, a fault-based presumption may create a deterrence against adultery. A primary-caretaker presumption creates incentives for the parents to spend time with the child, whereas the maternal preference presumption creates disincentives to do so. The incentive effects might even reach back to earlier stages, before marriage and childbirth. In the unlikely event that a paternal preference rule was reintroduced today, one might expect to see more childless marriages and more unwed mothers. Some women might be unwilling to marry and have children if they knew that the husband would get custody in case of divorce. Other criteria which increase the probability of paternal custody can be expected to have similar, although weaker, effects.

[91] Mnookin and Kornhauser (1979). See also Cooter and Marks with Mnookin (1982) and, more generally, Galanter (1981).
[92] This coupling is emphasized by Mnookin and Kornhauser (1979) and by Weitzman (1985), ch. 8.

Some of these bargaining and incentive effects are fairly plausible, others more speculative. The conclusion that a maternal preference rule is more favourable to the mother in financial settlements than the best-interest principle seems robust, as does the view that the status quo presumption creates an incentive for strategic procrastination. When a marriage is dissolved, instrumental rationality easily becomes predominant. The idea that custody rules also create incentives during the marriage itself, before it is threatened by dissolution, is more tenuous. It is far from clear that married people make a rational assessment of the probability of divorce and adjust their behaviour accordingly. At the very least it seems clear that it is not in their interest to do so (I.2). From this observation one cannot conclude, of course, that people tend to have the irrationally optimistic beliefs having which is good for them. But there is other evidence (I.2) that this tends to be true. Thus one should probably not place much emphasis on the incentive and deterrence effects of divorce rules in a marriage in which divorce is not threatening.

Educative and socialization effects are even more tenuous. These effects have been used to justify a statutory presumption for joint custody[93] and to argue against the maternal presumption. The latter argument claims that the maternal presumption forms one link in a vast network of formal and informal rules which tend to preempt women's choices by shaping their self-image and career expectations. The maternal presumption, while superficially a right and therefore an asset, easily becomes a duty and a burden.[94] On the one hand, these assertions sound plausible and may well be true. On the other hand, there is in general very little

[93] 'One of the most noble functions of the law is to serve as a model of expected behavior' (Folberg 1984, p. 10).

[94] The concern over whether the maternal presumption rule is in women's interest is similar to the debate regarding other laws challenged on sex discrimination grounds. Sometimes the Supreme Court has struck down laws that classify or use generalizations about women on the ground that such laws perpetuate stereotypical sex roles. See *Orr v. Orr*, 440 U.S. 268 (1979) (striking down ban on alimony awards against women, noting that sex-based statutes designed to mitigate past discrimination carry 'inherent risk of reinforcing stereotypes about the proper role of women'; *Califano v. Goldfarb*, 430 U.S. 199 (1977); *Mississippi University for Women v. Hogan*, 458 U.S.718 (1982). Sometimes, however, the Court has upheld sex-based laws on the ground that they compensate women for real differences. See, e.g., *Califano v. Webster*, 430 U.S. 313 (1977) (upholding a social security act provision treating women more favourably); see also *Heckler v. Mathews* 465 U.S. 728 (1984) (upholding gender-based classification of the pension offset exception of the Social Security Act).

knowledge about the alleged educative effects of the law.[95] This criterion, therefore, cannot be assigned great weight.

Process values (II.8) form another criterion for choosing among custody principles. These values have been taken to include, among others, the following principles. For justice not only to be done but to be seen to be done, the parties must be allowed to select and present the information they deem relevant.[96] Where a decision affects the 'moral worth' of an individual, 'adjudication . . . on the basis of documents submitted largely by third parties and by adjudicators who have never confronted the claimant seems inappropriate'.[97] Commenting on the proposal that child custody might be decided by the toss of a coin, Robert Mnookin argues that this procedure 'would deprive the parents of a process and a forum where their angers and aspirations might be expressed' and that 'symbolic and participatory values of adjudication would be lost by a random process'.[98]

I return to Mnookin's argument later. Here I only make a distinction between cases in which the substantive decision is likely to be affected if one takes account of process values and those in which essentially the same decision would be reached by a more circuitous and expensive route. In the latter case the advocacy of process values amounts to arguing that justice should be both done and seen to be done. But in the former it comes dangerously close to arguing that it is better for something else than justice to be done and seen to be done than for justice to be done but not seen.

Evaluating the alternatives

In the light of these criteria – the child's interests, the interests of children, parental interests, bargaining and incentive effects, educative effects and process values – the following surveys the main alternatives to the best-interest principle. These are (a) a return to the maternal presumption rule, (b) a primary-caretaker presumption and (c) some form of compromise between the parents. I shall

---

[95] See Melton and Saks (1985), esp. pp. 251–68.
[96] Thibaut and Walker (1978).
[97] Mashaw (1977).
[98] Mnookin (1975), p. 290.

consider several forms of compromise, but only one of them – the choice of a custodial parent by the flip of a coin – will be discussed in detail.

Return to maternal presumption. A number of arguments against this proposal come to mind. Children would be widely perceived to suffer if the best-interest standard were abandoned. Men would oppose being deprived of a fair chance of custody. Many women would object to the presumption on the grounds that it in fact burdens women, either in the actual cases to which it is applied or through the effects on future socialization. Other women, however, would favour it because it would shift the balance of bargaining power towards the weaker part, and because it would offer women fair compensation for child care. Needless to say, the mother is not always the weaker part in divorce bargaining, nor is she invariably the primary caretaker. Nevertheless, one might argue, these statements hold sufficiently true to justify a return to maternal preference.

A widespread response to the last set of arguments would be that the interests of the parents are at best a secondary consideration, and that the interests of children are not served by a return to maternal presumption. It is not clear, however, that the last statement is true if the interests of children are taken to include, as they should, their interest in being spared the pain of custody litigation. The statement becomes even less plausible if one admits that the question of which parent is most fit for custody does not, in most cases, have a determinate answer. The paramount consideration then becomes the swiftness of the decision, an end to which the maternal presumption rule is well suited.

In sum, maternal preference yields on the whole better decisions for currently living parents (if we disregard the tenuous argument that the right to custody could turn into a duty) and for children than the best-interest principle. It can be argued, however, that it presupposes and tends to perpetuate sex roles which it is in the interest of future men, women and children to have abolished.

A primary-caretaker assumption. Two arguments are usually advanced for this principle: it confers justice on the parents while also producing substantively good decisions for the child. It is just that the parent who has devoted the most time to the child should get custody, and it is good for the child to be with the parent who has devoted the most time to him.[99]

The principle could be implemented in several ways. It could be used in a very rough and ready manner, so that it applied to all and only those parents who do not work and to those who work part time and have a full-time working spouse. Like the maternal presumption rule, the principle thus interpreted would be easy to implement and hence would minimize the damage done to the child by protracted litigation. Against the proposal one might argue that it does not tell the court what to do when both parents work full time. In addition, it might have undesirable educative effects, since it signals to women that the surest way of getting custody is to stay away from work.

The simple rule just stated is not, however, how courts and scholars have understood the primary-caretaker principle. They have suggested a much more finely tuned implementation, by proposing detailed criteria for what counts as caretaking. For example, the supreme court of West Virginia, building on Oregon decisions, has laid down ten such criteria, ranging from the preparing and planning of meals to the teaching of reading, writing and arithmetic.[100] The proposal invites a number of remarks.

First, among the criteria, several (the preparing and planning of meals and the purchasing, cleaning and care of clothes) involve doing something *for* the child rather than doing something *with* him.[101] Inclusion of these tasks reflects a (probably unconscious)

---

[99] For a thorough discussion, see Chambers (1984).
[100] *Garska v. McCoy*, W.Va., 278 S.E.2d 357. This decision is somewhat confused. On the one hand, it states that 'intelligent determination of relative degrees of fitness requires a precision of measurement which is not possible given the tools available to the judges'. Thus except when the 'facts demonstrate that care and custody were shared in an entirely equal way', the court should determine in favour of the primary caretaker. Given the court's criteria for primary caretaking, the idea of demonstrating that it has been shared 'in an entirely equal way' is chimerical (see text). Perhaps the court just meant to refer to cases in which there is no detectable difference between the parents, i.e., to cases of silence rather than indifference. Moreover, the court virtually contradicts itself when it goes on to argue that only in the case of equal caretaking must one proceed 'to inquire further into relative degrees of parental competence' – although the impossibility of the latter inquiry was the reason for adopting the caretaking criterion in the first place.
[101] Chambers (1984), p. 538, n.230.

concern for the rights of the primary caretaker, as distinct from the needs of the child. Many fathers would then say that through the income they earn by working they also make a contribution to primary caretaking, in the sense of doing something for the child. To distinguish more clearly between parents, the list of criteria could be redrawn to include only activities that were done with the child and hence either gave rise to a special need of the child for the primary caretaker or a special need of the primary caretaker for the child.[102] David Chambers has shown, however, that the psychological literature gives little if any support to the notion that these needs are more important than the need for and the need of the secondary caretaker.[103]

Second, it will often be difficult to ascertain who is the primary caretaker when both parents are working full time. Although many surveys show that the mother usually performs much more of the housework and child care in such families,[104] this may not be easy to demonstrate in any given, contested case, since each parent has an incentive to magnify his or her own efforts and to diminish those of the other. Finally, even were it possible to establish the facts in an uncontroversial manner, their interpretation might still be contested. It is not just the quantity of time spent with the child which should count: the quality of interaction is also relevant. It is easy to imagine litigation over these issues being almost as protracted, and the outcome almost as indeterminate, as when the issue at stake is the relative fitness of the parents. A fine-tuned implementation of the primary-caretaker criterion might not satisfy the child's interests in a swift decision.

In sum, the primary-caretaking criterion, if implemented in a coarse-grained way, would minimize pain to children from custody litigation but would not be fully determinate and might have undesirable socialization effects. A fine-tuned implementation would not have the latter disadvantages, but neither would it recommend itself on the former grounds. Arguments based on the

[102] One could also insist on *sacrifice* rather than *contribution* as the decisive factor in awarding custody, but this would not support a primary-caretaker presumption. A mother might contribute less and sacrifice more than the father, if her career opportunities were greater to begin with.
[103] Chambers (1984), pp. 527–48.
[104] Berk and Berk (1979), S. F. Berk (1980).

needs of the primary caretaker or on the needs of children for the primary caretaker have a weak empirical foundation.

Compromise solutions. Under this heading I discuss various solutions that depart from the winner-take-all principle usually followed in child custody proceedings. Solomon's first, announced judgement represented a perverse but not infrequent form of compromise: when there is conflict over the allocation of some indivisible object, resolve it by destroying the good or, slightly less drastically, by withholding it from everyone (II.5). Less perverse forms of compromise include splitting of siblings, joint custody and random selection of the custodial parent.

One can achieve compromise by splitting siblings between the parents if each parent prefers this allocation to the other parent's getting custody of all the children.[105] Not infrequently, this arrangement, when privately agreed upon, takes the form of letting boys stay with the father and girls with the mother.[106] It accommodates two important parental concerns: to remain a full-time parent and to share the burden of being a parent. It will often be against the interests of the children, however, to split them in this way, especially if the proposal leads to one or both parents having custody of only one child. Children's moral development, and especially their sense of fairness and reciprocity, are greatly enhanced by their growing up with siblings.[107] If splitting the siblings is the outcome of private bargaining, as in the example discussed later, such considerations may not receive the weight they deserve.

[105] If this condition is not satisfied, a situation can arise in which each parent ranks the alternatives in the following order. First, I have custody of all children; second, the other parent has custody of all; third, custody is split. This corresponds to the strategic game 'The Battle of the Sexes' (see Luce and Raiffa 1957, pp. 90–4). The child custody conflict could also take the form of a game of 'Chicken' (see Rapoport 1966, pp. 137–44.) Assume, for this case, that there is one child and that each parent ranks the options in the following order. First, the other parent gets custody; second, I get custody; third, the state gets custody. (I assume, following Goldstein, Freud and Solnit 1979b, pp. 33–7, that the parents can abdicate responsibility for the child, since otherwise they would have an incentive to abuse the child so as to have it taken away from them.) This situation may become increasingly frequent in one-child families with both parents working.
[106] For a survey of the psychological literature on the importance of matching children with a parent of the same sex, see Chambers (1984), pp. 524–6.
[107] Eckhoff (1974), pp. 356–7.

The form of compromise most frequently advocated is joint custody.[108] This arrangement can reconcile the interests of both parents and children – when it works. Unlike the other solutions discussed here, it is not very plausible as a court-imposed compromise. If the parents cannot agree on joint custody, there is a grave risk that the child will suffer if the court forces them to cooperate. Nevertheless, current American legislation tends to view parental agreement as neither sufficient nor necessary for joint custody awards. The nonsufficiency is justified by the risk that parents may use joint custody as a way of avoiding their responsibilities, each of them thinking that the other will bear the main burden. The non-necessity is more paradoxical. It may be true that 'we have no data on the outcome of joint custody for families in which parents have come to joint custody (at least initially) involuntarily or as a result of pressure from the legal system',[109] but it seems clear that a parent who is strongly opposed to a court-imposed joint custody will usually be able to sabotage it. Perhaps having a presumption for joint custody could have useful educative effects, but courts would in any case need supplementary rules about what to do when joint custody does not work.

The last alternative I shall consider is also the most controversial: flipping a coin (or, more generally, using a randomizing device) when neither parent is unfit for custody. The proposal has been discussed,[110] but to my knowledge never applied. I shall first discuss randomization as an outcome of private bargaining over custody and then consider court-imposed randomization.[111]

As argued in II.5, both parties may prefer a probabilistic compromise to physical compromise such as splitting siblings, time sharing or joint custody.[112] Sometimes physical compromise is not

[108] Joint custody can take many forms, both de facto and de jure. For an exhaustive survey, see the essays in Folberg, ed. (1984).
[109] Steinman (1984), p. 117.
[110] Goldstein, Freud and Solnit (1979a), p. 175, n.12; Goldstein, Freud, Solnit and Goldstein (1986), p. 24; Mnookin (1975), pp. 289–91; Mnookin and Kornhauser (1979), pp. 970–1; Chambers (1984), p. 485.
[111] Mnookin and Kornhauser (1979), p. 975, argue that when physical split of custody is impossible, there is 'no middle ground' on which a compromise can be reached. While recognizing the possibility of court-imposed randomization, they neglect that of private randomizing.
[112] Here preference refers to expected utility, in which elements of risk aversion are also included (Luce and Raiffa 1957, ch. 2).

feasible if the parents live a long distance apart or are unable to get along. Even when a physical compromise is feasible, random selection of one custodial parent may be preferable. For some parents, there is increasing marginal utility in being with the child. They view time sharing as qualitatively different from, and much inferior to, a life which is fully shared with the child. For others custody of one sibling could be worse than no custody at all if they care about the welfare of their children and believe this requires them to be raised together. In the more complicated case discussed later, a probabilistic compromise over two options, one of which involves splitting the siblings one way, is superior to splitting them the other way.

In most divorces, bargaining over custody takes place simultaneously with bargaining over the financial settlement. The two negotiations tend to be coupled, so that the parents try to extract financial advantages by offering custody and vice versa. In the following, I consider bargaining over custody that is uncontaminated by the parties' other negotiations. The spouses may have no property worth bargaining over, or they may want to keep custody negotiations separate from other conflicts.

I shall nevertheless begin by considering bargaining over money, since it illustrates the standard bargaining case with which I shall later contrast bargaining over custody. Consider, then, a childless couple who try to agree on how to divide a joint property valued at $100 000. If they do not agree and go to court, each of them will incur legal fees of $20 000. In light of the circumstances of the case and of earlier decisions, the court can be expected to award $60 000 to the wife and $40 000 to the husband. The disagreement point (or threat point), in other words, is $40 000 to the wife and $20 000 to the husband. The husband, however, has much greater earning power than the wife. He can thus credibly threaten to go to court, knowing that her need for money is such that she will accept an offer of a private settlement that splits the property equally between them. This 'Matthew effect' – to him that hath shall be given – is standard in bargaining.

The relevant features of this case are the following. (a) There is a continuum of Pareto-optimal divisions of the property, that is, of divisions summing to $100 000. (b) There is a non-Pareto-optimal threat point which defines what happens if no agreement is reached. (c) The parties have differently shaped utility functions over money. We may assume, for instance, that the marginal utility of money is constant for the husband and decreasing for the wife. The wife is not disadvantaged because she 'needs money more' than the husband, in a sense which would require interpersonal comparisons of utility. Strictly speaking, her weak bargaining position is due solely to the fact that for her the importance of any given $10 000 is greater than that of the next $10 000. Yet in standard cases the cause of this fact is indeed that her objective needs are larger than those of her husband.[113]

Bargaining over child custody differs from bargaining over money in one important respect: the object of the bargaining is not infinitely divisible. Solomon's judgement illustrates the point. True, siblings can be split up, but not infinitely. Even with, say, one girl and one boy there are only four possible allocations to the parents. One might argue, perhaps, that by including more or less liberal visitation rights in the settlement, the set of feasible outcomes can be rendered continuous. That argument fails, however, in that it neglects the fact that at the core of custody there is a nondivisible right to make decisions on behalf of the child. Time spent with the child can be divided continuously; control over medical, religious and educational matters cannot. Joint legal custody might seem to offer a way out but is not really a solution to the initial bargaining problem. Rather it replaces one big bargaining problem – who shall get sole legal custody? – by many small ones, as the parents will have to negotiate solutions whenever they disagree on some aspect of the child's upbringing.

Bargaining theory cannot get off the ground without a continuum of possible outcomes. In the absence of a wide (not necessarily continuous) range of possible allocations it may not be possible to achieve any kind of compromise. If the only possible outcomes are 'I get the child' and 'He gets the child', there is no scope for conces-

---

[113] For an exposition of the theory of bargaining invoked in this paragraph, see Roth (1979). As explained in Kalai (1985), pp. 88–90, interpersonal comparisons of welfare are probably quite important in bargaining. He shows how the notoriously intractable problem of making such comparisons can be partially finessed by choosing a reference situation in which we have strong intuitions about what the outcome will be.

sions, compromise or agreement. There will be no bargaining and *a fortiori* no theory of bargaining. Also, the formal mathematical analysis becomes intractable without a continuity assumption.

There are two ways of introducing continuity. The first and most general is through the notion of a jointly mixed strategy. Assume that in some noncooperative game each agent has the choice between two pure strategies, A and B, which for each of them give rise to an infinite number of individually mixed strategies of the following general form: Strategy A is chosen with probability p, B with probability $1 - p$. If A is driving on the left side of the road and B is driving on the right, the combinations AB and BA could be disastrous. Yet there is no way in which rational players deciding in isolation from each other can make sure that neither outcome will occur. If each tosses a coin about what to do, there is a 50 per cent chance that one of the disastrous combinations will come about. If, however, they are able to communicate and to enter into enforceable agreements with each other, they can use the jointly mixed strategy of tossing a coin between AA and BB. If one of the parties has a preference for AA and the other for BB, while both prefer each of these to AB and to BA, they might agree to use a lottery device with probabilities differing from fifty–fifty, reflecting, besides their different preferences, their relative bargaining powers. In addition to the pure cases AA and BB there is an infinitely divisible set of lotteries between AA and BB.

Jointly mixed strategies are not the only device available to create a continuous set of options. The same goal can be achieved by permitting side payments, that is, by letting a typical agreement take the form 'Person I gets the indivisible object and pays $X to person II'. This device is not as general as that of jointly mixed strategies, since it can be employed only when the parties have some means of payment and side payments are perceived as appropriate. In some marriages, both spouses might be propertyless. In others, they might insist on decoupling custody bargaining from bargaining over property, out of a belief that children should not be bought and sold. Jointly mixed strategies may then be the main avenue to compromise. Let us apply this idea to child custody conflicts.

With two children there are, as I said, four ways of allocating

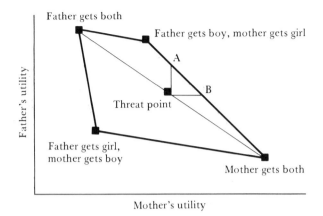

Fig. III.1

custody. The utilities of these to the mother and the father are indicated by the four vertices in Fig. III.1. For the mother, it is very important to get both children, and relatively unimportant which of them she gets if she gets only one. For the father, what matters most is to get the boy.

The parents might agree on one of these four allocations. They might also, however, decide to use a jointly mixed strategy. They might decide, that is, to use a lottery in which the various allocations are assigned definite probabilities, adding up to 1. To each such lottery corresponds a point within the quadrangle defined by the four allocations. The utility of a lottery is simply the sum of the utilities of the allocations weighed by their probability. Thus the points on a line between two vertices correspond to lotteries in which the allocations underlying these vertices are assigned probabilities p and $1 - p$, with p taking on all values between 0 and 1. In this way, the set of feasible outcomes is rendered continuous, so that bargaining theory can be applied.

To predict the outcome of the bargaining, we must first make an assumption about the threat point. We can stipulate, as in the diagram, that the parents believe that in a legal dispute each of them has a 50 per cent chance of getting custody of both children. This belief could be brought about in several ways. If the legal rule is to give custody according to what is in the best interests of the child, the parents might well believe that there is no detectable difference in fitness between them, so that, for all they know, each has as good a chance as the other of getting custody. Or – and this is the possibility to be explored later – the legal rule might actually be to use a fair coin to settle the issue. Whatever the grounds for the fifty–fifty expectation, it follows that the expected utility of the parents in the case of a legal dispute is midway on the line between the vertices corresponding to maternal custody of both children and paternal custody of both. Both parents know that by going to court they can achieve at least this level of expected utility; hence they will reject any proposed solution which offers them less. (For simplicity, I ignore the costs of litigation.) If, moreover, we assume that they will not accept any solution which is worse for both than some other feasible outcome, we see that if they reach an agreement, it will be somewhere on the line AB. Each point on AB assigns a probability p that the mother gets custody of both children and a probability $1 - p$ that the father gets the boy and the mother gets the girl. By inspecting Fig. III.1 we can see that p ranges between .22 and .45 (approximate values).

I now want to make the following negative claim. When parents bargain over custody, they will never choose a point on AB. Indeed, I think lotteries are virtually never used to settle private, nontrivial disputes. I have no systematic empirical evidence to back this claim, only casual observation, together with some general theoretical arguments. First, of course, the conditions under which lotteries or probabilistic compromises are superior to physical compromises may not often be realized. In particular, when side payments are available and acceptable, they provide a much more robust form of compromise.

Second, even when a lottery would seem to be called for, as in the present case, lack of enforceability might prevent it from being used. As far as I know, no country has a public official or public institution with the power to carry out and enforce lotteries privately agreed upon by the parties. Each party might agree to a lottery in the hope that the outcome would be his or her preferred alternative, and then renege if it turned out differently. The knowledge that this may happen could easily prevent a lottery from being attempted in the first place.

Third, even if an enforcing institution were created, I doubt whether it would be much used. To see why, observe that the parties would have to agree on the probabilities to be fed into the lottery device. These probabilities could be derived on the basis of (a) the threat point, (b) the utilities associated with the pure outcomes and (c) the particular solution concept adopted. Each of these, however, would lend itself to strategic or nonstrategic posturing or misrepresentation. The parties might have excessively optimistic beliefs about the outcome of a legal dispute, or they might represent themselves as having such beliefs. They might exaggerate the extent to which they would suffer if their preferred outcome were not chosen. Given the plurality of approaches to bargaining theory, they might even engage in bargaining over the proper solution concept. For all of these reasons, it seems very unlikely that the parties would be able to agree on a point on *AB*. Indeed, as many readers will have been thinking for some time, the whole proposal of a lottery solution has an unreal and bizarre air.

There is one possible exception to the claim that lotteries are never used to settle private, nontrivial disputes such as custody decisions. I would not want to exclude the possibility that some parents privately decide to toss a coin over custody and then manage to respect the outcome. Note, however, that a coin toss is the simplest possible lottery: that of two alternatives with a fifty–fifty chance each. The fairness, simplicity and apparent nonmanipulability of this procedure may well make it sufficiently robust to survive the obstacles cited above. With respect to the specific example illustrated in Fig. III.1, one should note, nevertheless, the following points. First, here there are four alternatives, not two. I would regard it as highly unlikely that parents would use a lottery assigning a 25 per cent chance to each of these. Why, indeed, would they want to include among the lottery prizes an outcome which was worse for both than the expected outcome of a legal settlement and, moreover, worse for both than one of the other pure outcomes? Second, a fifty–fifty lottery between maternal custody of both children and the outcome in which the father got the boy and the mother the girl would also be unlikely. For one thing, these alternatives lack symmetry and simplicity; for another, the outcome is not in the bargaining set (i.e., it is not individually rational for both parties). Third, a fifty–fifty lottery between maternal custody of both children and paternal custody of both represents no improvement on the legal settlement, except for the costs of litigation. It is, moreover, worse for both parents than points on *AB*. Nevertheless, because of its Schelling-point quality I believe this is the only lottery with some likelihood of occurring, because the costs of litigation may be quite substantial.

As will be clear by now, the prominence of a fifty–fifty lottery cannot be predicted by formal bargaining theory. Whether its prominence is due to its appearance of fairness or to its uniquely simple character is hard to tell. There is some evidence that in allocative conflicts the parties first look for some aspect – *any* aspect – of the situation which allows for equal division and then rationalize it as required on grounds of fairness.[114] Be that as it may, I am fairly confident – although once again I have no hard evidence – that equal probabilistic division occurs much more rarely than equal physical division. Equality ex post has a much more robust appeal than equality ex ante. Once the coin is tossed, the winner takes all and the loser's knowledge that he or she had an equal chance of being the winner is meagre consolation. In the absence of an enforcement mechanism, the temptation to defect from the agreement will be great. To give people a chance to precommit themselves against temptation, one might consider creating a 'notary of lotteries' whose sole function would be to enforce private agreements to resolve conflicts by probabilistic devices. I predict that in the overwhelming majority of cases, he would be asked simply to use a fair coin.

The notary of lotteries would be subject to the agreement of the parties to decide custody by the toss of a coin. A more radical proposal would be to make randomization obligatory when the parties could not reach agreement. There are two main arguments for this proposal. First, the procedure has the virtue of being simple and automatic, thus sparing the child the pain of custody litigation. The point of litigating would largely disappear, and as a result the number of cases brought would be drastically reduced. When a case was brought, it would be decided as soon as the judge found that neither parent was unfit. Using simple, robust criteria for unfitness (physical neglect, physical abuse, sexual

---

[114] For an experiment throwing some doubts on the distinction between salience and fairness, see Harris and Joyce (1980).

abuse, psychic disorders), courts would be able to make swift rulings. Less damage would be imposed on fewer children. Second, awarding custody by the flip of a coin would be fair to the parents, since the procedure would safeguard the important values of equal treatment and equal opportunity.

The main counterarguments are the following. First, one might argue that the principle is unfair to the parents, if one's conception of justice emphasizes *equity* (to each according to contribution) or *need* (to each according to need) rather than absolute *equality*. I have argued that parental rights (equity) and welfare (need) are relevant values. They would frequently be violated by coin tossing. Next, one might question the bargaining and incentive effects of this mechanism. As under the best-interest principle, mothers would be placed in a weak bargaining situation. The very real chance of losing custody could make them bargain away everything else. Also, more speculatively, the incentive to marry and have children in the first place might be weakened. Finally, the use of a coin to choose the custodial parent would be certain to meet strong objections based on process values. Let me consider the last group of objections in more detail.

Robert Mnookin's argument that coin flipping would deprive the parents of a forum in which their angers and aspirations might be expressed does not seem well-founded. Social psychology does not confirm the view that aggression can be relieved by being expressed, through some form of catharsis. If anything, acting-out leads to more aggression.[115] Nor do I accept his contention that symbolic and participatory values of adjudication would have to be lost in a random-choice mechanism. One may well imagine a coin-tossing procedure coming to symbolize the equal worth of the parents, as well as the child's right to a speedy decision. It may well be true that 'law, after all, is for the happiness of men, and some men will always be happier with the appearance of justice'[116] – happier, presumably, than with the reality of justice. A legal procedure is not viable if it strongly offends the sense of justice of a large part of the population, whatever else might be said for it. Yet if there *is* something to be said for it, one ought to

[115] Aronson (1984), p. 192.
[116] Coons (1964), p. 771.

think seriously about how it could be implemented, perhaps gradually, partially or optionally, in ways that would not give offence. The cart of procedural justice should not be set before the horse of substantive justice (II.8).

Many people consider the proposal inhuman, frivolous or both.[117] A decision with such far-reaching consequences must be made by appeal to reason and argument, not by an arbitrary choice. Coin tossing may be acceptable in trivial decisions, but not in matters of such momentous importance. At the same time, it has been argued that 'random selection is most favoured when the outcome is either of very *small* or very *great* importance to the recipients.'[118] This may well be so. Among the examples of randomly made decisions surveyed in chapter II some are of great importance to the recipients, such as the draft, allocation of kidney machines and the choice of persons to be thrown overboard from an overfull lifeboat or to be eaten by the other passengers.

One central rationale for using lotteries to make these momentous decisions is that random choice is appropriate when the other criteria would force us to compare the intrinsic worth of persons. This argument also applies to custody decisions. Although the best-interest standard asks us to scrutinize the mother and the father only with respect to their fitness for custody, it is easily understood as conferring a judgement on their worth more generally. But the essential point is that randomizing in custody decisions recommends itself because it has good consequences for a person other than the potential recipients – for the child.

In sum, tossing a coin to decide custody shares the advantages of any automatic decision rule, in minimizing the harm done to children by protracted litigation. With regard to parents, it appeals to intuitions about equal treatment and equal worth, although it can violate rights-based and needs-based considerations. It shares a drawback with the best-interest principle in creating uncertainty about the final outcome so that the more risk averse parent, usually the one for whom the child matters most, is punished by loss of bargaining power over other matters.

[117] Chambers (1984), p. 485, characterizes it (without further argument) as 'callous, an evasion of responsibilities both to children and justice'.
[118] Eckhoff (1974), p. 305.

III.6 CONCLUSION

The central premise of this chapter is that the current legal standard governing child custody disputes is indeterminate. In the bulk of divorce cases, there is no basis for saying that the child will be better off with one parent than with the other. Nevertheless, the legal regime can and should incorporate the interests of children in two ways. First, custody should not be given to a parent who is clearly unfit. Second, the pain and stress to the child created by the custody decision itself should be minimized. This second consideration points to the need for a more mechanical and automatic decision procedure than the very finely tuned best-interest standard.

Three alternatives suggest themselves: a strong maternal presumption, a strong primary-caretaker presumption (if interpreted in a suitably coarse-grained way) and random decision. The maternal presumption and primary-caretaker rules are superior to randomization in that they compensate to some extent for the weak economic position of most women in our societies. These rules, however, may create expectations which perpetuate existing sex roles and, along with them, the weak position of women. In comparison, randomizing is inferior in the short run. Compared with the other principles, it increases the bargaining leverage of men over women. But by treating the parents equally it may – like the best-interest standard – promote equality between the sexes in the long run.

The long-term educative effects are, however, largely conjectural. By contrast, the losses suffered by women when no-fault divorce and the best-interest standard were introduced around 1970 are hardly open to doubt. For many, these reforms amounted to a change of the rules in midgame and to the frustration of legitimate expectations about custody and financial security.[119] A maternal presumption or a coarse-grained primary-caretaker presumption could undo the damage. The latter rule is useless, however, for the increasing number of divorces in which both parents work full time.

The common feature of these themes is the all-pervasive pres-

[119] See Weitzman (1985).

ence of *uncertainty about the remote consequences of present decisions.* We cannot tell, in most cases, whether maternal or paternal custody will be best for any given child. Nor can we tell whether the educative and attitude-changing effects of custody law are strong enough to count heavily in legislative reform. By contrast, we do know that custody litigation imposes clear and immediate harm upon children. We also know that women in our societies labour under various disadvantages for which, until recently, divorce and custody legislation offered at least some compensation. While current harm done to children and harm done to currently living women do not in themselves count for more than the future gains to children and the gains to future women, they do so when the latter are discounted for the uncertainty attached to them.

No very satisfactory conclusion emerges. If the conjectural argument about long-term educative effects is accepted, randomization seems to be the best solution. If it is rejected, a return to maternal presumption would seem to be called for. Both proposals are likely to meet strong opposition. More imaginative measures could be envisaged, such as offering marrying couples the option of binding themselves to a specific custody procedure in case they later decided to divorce and found themselves unable to agree on custody. One could even make this precommitment an obligatory feature of the marriage contract. I have neither the space nor the competence to discuss the modalities of custody reform, but I hope that I have made a case for thinking seriously about them.

IV

THE POSSIBILITY OF RATIONAL POLITICS

IV.1 INTRODUCTION

The notion of the 'body politic', suggesting that political action is individual action writ large, is very old. Among its modern guises are the notions of social engineering and economic planning. It can be more precisely stated as the idea that societies can and do form preferences, gather information, make decisions and execute them in ways that are strictly or at least roughly analogous to rational individual choice. This chapter is a critical examination of this view, organized so as to parallel the discussion in chapter I.

Section IV.2 explores the extent to which the formal apparatus in I.2 can be applied to political decisions, with the main emphasis on the differences between individual choice and social choice. The best-known disanalogy arises in the process of preference formation. Arrow's impossibility theorem and subsequent developments have shown that the notion of *social preferences* is in general not well-defined. Another argument, first articulated by Hayek, is that the information which is diffused and dispersed throughout society cannot be gathered at the center to form *social beliefs*. A further argument, associated especially with public choice theorists, is that *social action* is likely to be distorted and deflected by the private interests of the agents and agencies who are to carry them out. I conclude that social decision making bears at best a rough similarity to individual choice.

Section IV.3 emphasizes the large scope for indeterminacy in social decisions. Large-scale social decisions have equilibrium effects that are very difficult to assess theoretically, because the usual ceteris paribus methodology is inapplicable. To an even larger extent than in individual decisions, uncertainty and igno-

rance come to the forefront. Also, the ignorance cannot be overcome by trial-and-error procedures. 'Learning from experience'
proceeds by largely unreliable inferences from small-scale, short-
term, transitional effects to large-scale, long-term, equilibrium effects. In addition, the very notion of 'experimenting with reform'
borders on incoherence, since the agents' knowledge that they are
taking part in an experiment induces them to adopt a short time
horizon that makes it less likely that the experiment will succeed.

Section IV.4 considers weakness of will and excess of will as
forms of political irrationality. I emphasize differences as well as
similarities between individual and political akrasia, the main disanalogy being that societies by definition cannot overcome their
problem by entrusting their will to an external enforcer. Political
excess of will also differs from the individual case, in that the
subject and the target of the excessive will can be different individuals. The temptation to engage in such behaviour is therefore
greater, although the prospects of long-term success are equally
small.

In IV.5 I consider *justice* as an alternative guide to political
action. Given the fragility of instrumental thinking in politics, the
chosen conception of justice cannot be a consequentialist one like
utilitarianism. Rather it must focus on the inherent rights of individuals to equal shares in decision making and in material welfare.
In this subsection I draw heavily on the writings of John Rawls,
Ronald Dworkin and Jürgen Habermas. I give notice, however,
that my goal here is not to propose or even sketch a theory of
justice. I do not know how to derive a theory of democracy from
first principles. Given the existence of democracy, however, and
notably democracy as constrained by rational public discussion, I
believe certain implications for political action and choice can be
drawn out.[1]

IV.2   INDIVIDUAL AND SOCIAL CHOICE

On one conception, politics is like individual choice writ large.
First, political *preferences* – goals, trade-offs and priorities – are defined by the democratic political process. Next, government agen-

---

[1] This is also how I understand some recent writings by Rawls, notably Rawls (1985).

cies gather *information* about factual matters and about ends–means relationships, to form an opinion about which policies will best realize those goals. Finally, other agencies *implement* these optimal policies. Parliament, the Central Bureau of Statistics and government form, on this conception, a unified system for making rational political decisions, closely analogous to the model expressed in Fig. I.1.

My concern is not with those (if any) who believe that this view of the political process is literally true, that is, that political choice can be understood in terms of the desires, beliefs and actions of a supraindividual entity, 'society'. Rather my concern is with those who, while accepting the canons of methodological individualism, assume or argue that we may proceed *as if* the view is correct.[2] They assume, in other words, that little harm is done by treating the polity as a unitary actor, with coherent and stable values, well-grounded beliefs and a capacity to carry out its decisions. The assumption has been most prominent in the study of international relations[3] and in the theory of economic planning.[4] For obvious reasons, it has been less pronounced in the study of domestic politics in pluralist democracies. Yet even here, the temptation to use the convenient actor language can be strong. This section argues that this language, while tempting, can also be treacherous and misleading.

Opportunism provides a general reason for the difference between polities and individuals. It is easier for an individual to deceive others than to deceive himself. When individuals engage in self-serving deception or opportunism, there is no certainty that the aggregate outcome of their behaviour will correspond to the unitary-actor model of political rationality. Let me explain what this means in the three dimensions of choice that concern us here: preferences, information and action.

Let us first define the problem more carefully, as a difficulty for *democratic* politics. We exclude, that is, conceptions of politics corresponding to Napoleon's dictum, 'Tout pour le peuple, rien par le peuple'. Specifically, the method for aggregating individual

---

[2] Similarly, for some purposes cells may be treated as if they were the fundamental units of biological or medical analysis, knowledge about their molecular structure notwithstanding.
[3] For a discussion, see Snidal (1986), especially pp. 29–36.
[4] For a discussion, see Johansen (1977), ch. 2.

preferences should not be dictatorial. In addition, we want the method to be invulnerable to opportunism. The individual should not be able, by misrepresenting his preferences, to bring about an outcome which is better according to his true preferences than the one that would be brought about if he expressed these true preferences. Finally, we want the mechanism to ensure that outcomes are Pareto-optimal. As explained in II.6, the only method satisfying these requirements is some form of lottery voting, which, however, has too many other drawbacks to be seriously considered. Although strategy-proof mechanisms for preference revelation can be devised for special cases,[5] one cannot in general assume that people can be induced to be honest out of self-interest.

The problem of incentive compatibility extends to that of gathering information about factual matters. When economic agents are asked to provide information which is easily available to them, but would be available only at some cost (if at all) to others, one may assume that they will ask themselves whether it is in their interest to do so. It is well known, for instance, that the only nondistorting form of taxation is a lump-sum tax imposed on individuals according to their estimated productive capacity rather than according to their actual production. But it would rarely be in the interests of individuals to give correct information about their capacity. Similarly, it might not be in the interest of individuals to report truthfully how much they would be willing to pay for the provision of public goods. Soviet-type economies are well known for the perverse incentives they create against truthful reporting. Sometimes the fear of being punished as the bearer of bad tidings creates an incentive to present things as better than they really are. At other times, self-interest leads one to present the situation as worse than it actually is, as when a manager underreports production in order to avoid an increase in his quota. Essentially similar problems can be expected to arise in any system that depends on the collection of information from decentralized sources. Again, while the problem may be overcome in special cases, there is no general recipe for inducing truthful reporting.

Finally, incentive problems arise at the level of implementation. For the individual there is usually no distance between making a

---

[5] See, e.g., Ordeshook (1986), chs. 5 and 6.

decision and carrying it out, barring weakness of will or physical inability. In typical cases, the unity of the individual ensures that decisions, once made, will also be executed. The lack of unity of the polity makes this a much more problematic assumption. The agents who are charged with implementing the decisions cannot in general be trusted to disregard their self-interest or their personal conception of the general interest.[6] Nor can their principal always monitor their activities, if only for the reason that the monitoring agents may themselves be corrupt.[7]

One need not, however, rest one's case on the dangers of opportunism. Indeed, one should not. While there is always a risk of self-serving behaviour, the extent to which it is actually present varies widely. Much of the social choice and public choice literature, with its assumption of universally opportunistic behaviour, simply seems out of touch with the real world, in which there is a great deal of honesty and sense of duty. If people always engaged in opportunistic behaviour when they could get away with it, civilization as we know it would not exist.[8] We should not assume that the only task of politics is to devise institutions that can harness opportunistic self-interest to socially useful purposes. An equally important task is to create institutions that embody a valid conception of justice. If people do not feel they are being taken advantage of, the temptation to take advantage of society will be greatly reduced.[9]

We must ask, therefore, whether a just society, with effective norms of honesty and trust, would be a good approximation to the unitary-actor model of rational politics. The short answer is that while it would surely be a better approximation than a society in which opportunism was rampant, serious difficulties would remain. Although the implementation problem would disappear, problems of aggregating preferences and centralizing information would not. Even when preferences are sincerely expressed, the notion of the 'popular will' is incoherent (II.6). Even if individuals tried to report their preferences and abilities as truthfully

---

[6] For a survey of the large literature on budget-maximizing or otherwise corrupt bureaucracies, see Mueller (1979), ch. 8.
[7] See Andvig and Moene (1988) for a model incorporating this possibility.
[8] Elster (1989) offers an extended argument to this effect.
[9] Rawls (1971), pp. 177–83, 567–77.

as possible, and even if we disregard the opportunity costs of writing the reports and the risk that the information might be out of date when finally used, the center would not find it very useful. The individual's knowledge about his mental states and productive capacities is largely tacit, embodied and personal, rather than explicit, verbal and abstract.[10] Firms do not have access to the whole production function on which they are operating. They have to know what they are doing, but they have no incentive to know what they could do, until forced to by circumstances.[11] Consumers may be quite unable to tell what purchases they plan to make over the next year or years. These familiar objections[12] to central planning remain, I believe, irrefutable.

Actual political systems approach the unitary-actor model to various degrees. The more they try to achieve through deliberate planning, that is, the more their self-image is that of a unitary actor, the more they are likely to deviate from that model in practice. Soviet-type economies illustrate this paradox. Conversely, pluralist democracies are likely to achieve more, by virtue of trying to do less. Macroeconomic planning with fiscal and monetary policies as instruments is more likely to achieve its goals than the more ambitious forms of physical planning. Central physical planning requires very detailed information and also tends to generate opportunism. The former problem is inherent in physical planning. The latter, if I am right, derives from lack of legitimacy. If people feel that they are being taken advantage of, why should they not rip off the system in return? By contrast, political systems that leave more decisions to the individual can both economize on information and generate more trust.

In conclusion to this section, we may note that the analogy between individual and social choice could also be made from the converse perspective. Instead of arguing that society is to be understood on the model of the unitary actor, one might argue that the individual should be understood on the model of the fragmented polity.[13] First, there are intrapersonal problems of preference aggregation; second, there is self-deception and other forms

[10] Polanyi (1962).
[11] Nelson and Winter (1982), ch. 4 and passim.
[12] See notably the writings of Friedrich Hayek from Hayek (1937) to Hayek (1982).
[13] The essays collected in Elster, ed. (1986) explore several analogies of this kind.

of cognitive compartmentalization; third, there is weakness of will and other obstacles to the execution of decisions. Individuals, like polities, often do not know what they want; or do not know what they know; or fail to do what they have decided to do. I believe, however, that the analogy breaks down in a crucial respect: individuals, unlike polities, have an organizing centre – variously referred to as the will or the ego – that is constantly trying to integrate these fragmented parts.[14] Societies, by contrast, have no centre.

IV.3   POLITICAL INDETERMINACY

In this section, I make a two-pronged argument against the feasibility of large-scale social engineering. First, I argue that no theories exist that allow us to predict the long-term equilibrium effects of large-scale social reforms. Second, I argue that trial and error cannot substitute for theoretical prediction. Theory is impotent, and we cannot learn from experience and experiments. Consequently, political choices are made under conditions of radical cognitive indeterminacy.[15]

Now, these are very large claims. I will not attempt to demonstrate their validity as general propositions, although I believe that many of my specific arguments can be generalized.[16] Instead, I shall proceed by way of three main examples: the transitions from aristocracy to democracy, from private ownership to cooperative ownership and from a planned economy to a market economy. For the basic framework, here and later, I draw on Tocqueville's analyses of democracy and the ancien régime.[17] For a current and controversial example, I refer to the proposal of replacing private ownership of the means of production by cooperative ownership.[18] Finally, I occasionally refer to the current economic reforms in China.

---

[14] For further comments on this issue see Elster (1985b) and the editorial introduction to Elster, ed. (1986).

[15] These are not the only sources of political indeterminacy. The problem of preference aggregation discussed in IV.2 implies that the polity may not be able to evaluate the consequences of action, even assuming that they can be predicted.

[16] The general theory of the second-best (Lipsey and Lancaster 1956), in particular, provides a more abstract and unified account of many of the claims made below.

[17] Elster (1988b) has a fuller discussion.

[18] Drawing on Elster and Moene (1989).

The first prong of my argument will not, I imagine, provoke strong disagreements. Imagine that society is in a state of (approximate) equilibrium, in the sense that individual endowments, beliefs, social norms, habits and goals are well adjusted to one another as well as to their natural and institutional environment.[19] We want to predict the consequences of a major change in the property rights system or in the political system. As a first approach to the problem, we might consider two basic questions. What will the new equilibrium be like when everything else has adapted to the institutional change? What will the path of transition to the new equilibrium be like?

I shall return to these questions, but first note that they are enormously question-begging. The existence of an equilibrium and the tendency to approach it must be demonstrated, not presupposed. Writing around 1855 about the impact of the French Revolution, Tocqueville remarked that 'I have already heard it said four times in my lifetime that the new society, such as the Revolution had made it, had finally found its natural and permanent state, and then the next events proved this to be mistaken'.[20] In such cases we should consider four possibilities: (a) The process is approaching an equilibrium, but has not yet reached it. (b) At any given time the process is moving towards an equilibrium, which is itself, however, constantly shifting because of changes in the external environment. If the rate of change of the environment exceeds the rate of speed of adaptation to the environment, no equilibrium will ever be reached. (c) The system does not have a fixed equilibrium but converges towards a limit cycle. It has been argued, for instance, that the permanent effect of the French Revolution was to introduce a cyclical change between Orleanism and Bonapartism;[21] that the political systems of Highland Burma were in a 'moving equilibrium' with cycles of 150 years;[22] and that modern societies are condemned to oscillate between two ugly systems – capitalism and socialism – each of which appears attractive when seen from within the other.[23] (d) The

---

[19] Stinchcombe (1983) is a good example of equilibrium analysis in this sense.
[20] Tocqueville (1953), p. 343.
[21] Lévi-Strauss (1960), p. 94; Aron (1967), p. 292.
[22] Leach (1954), p. xi.
[23] Dunn (1985). For a brief discussion of such 'counteradaptive preferences' see also Elster (1983a), pp. 111–12.

system is inherently unstable. Even within a constant environment it would have neither a fixed equilibrium nor a limit cycle. The first question of the preceding paragraph presupposes that (a) offers the proper explanation of Tocqueville's observation.

My central argument, however, is not that the questions are inappropriate. Rather it is that they cannot be answered, even if their presuppositions should happen to be satisfied. In the present state of the social sciences we cannot even imagine what a theory of general social equilibrium would be like – a theory in which *everything was endogenous* so that the usual ceteris paribus methodology would be inapplicable. Social scientists are reasonably good at predicting short-term effects of marginal changes; to assert, for instance, that if the marginal tax rate for married women is reduced by x per cent, the labour supply will go up by y per cent. But the long-term impact of changes in work patterns on religion, marriage, social conflict or criminality remains utterly inaccessible to us. For a more dramatic example, consider the problems facing the Chinese planners. They face the impossibly complex task of assessing the long-term equilibrium effects of market reforms in a mainly agrarian economy which is deeply impregnated by two strongly antimarket ideologies, Confucianism and Marxism. How can they tell in advance whether the ideologies will thwart attempts to introduce a market system or whether the market will corrupt the ideologies?

The framework for discussing the second prong of my argument derives from Tocqueville's discussion of political democracy in America. His argument,[24] addressed mainly to French critics of democracy, takes the form of a refutation of a series of fallacies, four altogether. They consist in making erroneous inferences from the local, partial, short-term or transitional effects of democracy to the global, net, long-term, equilibrium effects. The French critics, observing that the former effects were in many case negative, wrongly inferred that democracy was undesirable. That the inferences are unwarranted does not prove, of course, that their conclusions are false. Tocqueville argued, however, that the equilibrium effects of democracy could be observed in the United

---

[24] Or, rather, my reconstruction of his argument. Although highly sophisticated in his methodology, Tocqueville took a historian's pride in hiding the scaffolding of his argument.

States[25] and that they systematically proved the critics' conclusions to be wrong. In the cases of reforms that are yet to be undertaken or completed, one cannot similarly show that the inferences yield the wrong conclusions, only that there is no reason to believe them to yield the right ones.

Local versus global effects

Tocqueville gives an instructive example of the fallacious tendency to generalize from the effect of an institutional change when implemented on a small scale to its effect when carried out on a large scale. Discussing the effects of marrying for love, a practice which is widespread in democracies, he writes that 'our ancestors conceived a singular opinion with regard to marriage. As they had noticed that the few love matches which took place in their days almost always ended in tragedy, they came to the firm conclusion that in such matters it was very dangerous to rely on one's own heart'.[26] He then points out two reasons to judge this view untenable. The first is negative *discrimination:* to marry for love in a society in which this is the exception is to court disaster, since going against the current tends to create hostility in others and in turn bitterness in oneself. The second is adverse *self-selection:* only very opinionated persons will go against the current in the first place – and this is not a characteristic conducive to happy marriages.

The performance of labour cooperatives may similarly be influenced by (positive or negative) discrimination and by (positive or negative) self-selection. Consider first positive discrimination. It has been argued that cooperatives, to survive in a capitalist economy, need an ideologically motivated support organization.[27] To the extent that such organizations are in place, the good performance of the cooperatives supported by them obviously does not

[25] This is a bit of a simplification. Tocqueville was aware of several tendencies that threatened the stability of American democracy. At various points he argued that the system might evolve into the tyranny of the majority over the minority, into a mild, tutelary despotism or into a plutocracy. This is consistent, however, with the assumption that the American society he observed around 1830 had acquired a relative and temporary stability, unlike the constant flux he found in French political life.
[26] Tocqueville (1969), p. 596.
[27] Gunn (1984), pp. 57–61.

allow us to infer that a system of cooperatives would perform equally well. Negative discrimination has been more widely discussed. It has frequently been alleged that the capitalist environment, and in particular the financial institutions of capitalism, discriminate against cooperatives, so that the bad performance of isolated cooperatives must not be allowed to count as an argument against the cooperative principle.[28] Against this it has been said, first, that in a competitive financial market no institution can afford passing up a profitable opportunity[29] and, second, that because of their ownership structure cooperatives are unsound objects for investment and lending.[30] Neither counterargument, however, is fully compelling.[31]

Positive self-selection can occur if the few cooperatives in an otherwise capitalist environment attract (or only admit) highly motivated and idealistic persons, who are willing to work hard, to endure the costs of participation and if necessary, to take a wage cut. The forest workers' cooperatives in the U.S. Northwest seem to correspond to this description.[32] Similarly, the Mondragon cooperatives in Spain have been able to screen applicants and to admit only those with cooperative value systems.[33] To an even higher degree, positive self-selection occurs in the Israeli kibbutzim.[34] Clearly, the viability of such cooperatives does not imply

---

[28] See, e.g., Bowles and Gintis (1976), p. 62.

[29] Nozick (1974), pp. 252–3.

[30] Miller (1981).

[31] Against Nozick's argument we may cite a letter written by John Stuart Mill in support of a cooperative that was the target of unfair competition by its capitalist counterparts: 'I beg to enclose a subscription of £10 to aid, as far as such a sum can do it, in the struggle which the co-operative platelock makers of Wolverhampton are sustaining against unfair competition on the part of the masters in the trade. Against fair competition I have no desire to shield them, . . . but to carry on business at a loss, in order to ruin competitors, is not fair competition. In such a contest, if prolonged, the competitors who have the smallest means, though they may have every other element of success, must necessarily be crushed through no fault of their own. . . . I am now convinced that they ought to be supported against the attempt to ruin them' (cited after Jones 1894, p. 438). Against Miller's argument, we may note that the cooperative would to some extent be kept in line by the knowledge that it may need to attract more capital in the future. Unless outside (nonvoting) shareholders are paid satisfactory dividends, future sharebuyers will not be forthcoming. Knowing this, present sharebuyers might not be deterred by the fact that the cooperative is formally free to reduce the dividend to zero (Jay 1980, pp. 14–15).

[32] Gunn (1984), ch. 3.

[33] Bradley and Gelb (1982).

[34] See Ben-Ner and Neuberger (1982).

that the model would be easily transferred elsewhere. The situation is somewhat analogous to that of private, ideologically motivated schools versus municipal schools. Since private schools are often able to attract exceptionally motivated teachers, they produce results that one could never expect to duplicate in a larger system in which teachers form a more or less average cross-section of the population. Adverse self-selection could also occur, as in Tocqueville's example: 'These reform experiments might attract unstable individuals, excessive risktakers, and people lacking in pragmatic orientation'.[35]

The divergence of local and global effects can also arise without selection and discrimination if a positive or negative externality is operating. If an isolated cooperative can take a free ride on capitalist enterprises, it will perform better than it would do as part of a cooperative system. If cooperatives are bad at innovating but good at imitating, they can do well as long as there are some dynamic capitalist firms to imitate. More conjecturally, the motivation to participate in self-managed firms could depend on a feeling of moral superiority which presupposes that most firms are capitalist.

Conversely, isolated cooperatives could be disadvantaged (a) by negative externalities created by capitalist firms or (b) by their failure to internalize positive externalities generated by themselves. An example of (a) is the 'ideological externality' created by the presence of wage labour in the economy. In a largely capitalist environment, successful cooperatives will be tempted to employ some workers on a wage basis, to increase their ability to adjust flexibly to changes in market conditions.[36] In so doing, however, they may end up losing both the intangible productivity benefits and the tangible benefits that arise from the intangible ones. Another example of (a) is the 'collective bargaining externality' identified as follows by Peter Jay: 'Insofar as the crucial advantage urged for the labour-managed economy is that it would cause collective bargaining . . . to wither away, so dissolving the catastrophic dilemma of high unemployment or accelerating inflation, that cannot be tested by examining the experience of individual

---

[35] Putterman (1982), p. 152.
[36] Jones (1894) contains numerous examples of such 'failures by success'.

co-operatives in a capital-managed economy where the general need for trade union organization and collective bargaining is bound to be strongly felt'.[37]

An example of (b) is the 'entrepreneurial externality' created by cooperatives. In a democratically run enterprise, entrepreneurially gifted individuals will not just make good decisions: they will also educate their fellow workers. The Mondragon workers, for instance, have their own technical school. If the workers who have benefited from the education leave the firm and take a job in a capitalist enterprise, the education is in fact made available to other firms free of charge. Even if the cooperative is driven out of business because the private return to its activities is below that of the typical capitalist firm, the social return may be higher for the cooperative than for the capitalist firm. Another suggested example of (b) is the 'political externality' created by cooperatives. If members of cooperatives make better political citizens and if civic spirit is a public good, cooperatives generate diffuse benefits not captured by the price mechanism.[38] Against this one may object, first, that for many people economic participation will reduce rather than enhance their participation in political affairs. Paraphrasing Oscar Wilde, there are only so many evenings to go around. Second, it is doubtful that participation in economic decision making will have these positive effects in other arenas unless it is regarded as valuable in its own right. The spillover effects of participation are essentially by-products.[39]

Partial versus net effects

An amusing example in Tocqueville is the following. 'As there is no precautionary organization in the United States, there are more fires than in Europe, but generally they are put out more speedily, because the neighbors never fail to come quickly to the danger spot'.[40] The structure of the argument is as follows. We want to examine the effect of an independent variable (political

[37] Jay (1980), p. 40.
[38] Pateman (1970); see also Krouse and McPherson (1986).
[39] For this notion see Elster (1983a), ch. 2, sec. 9.
[40] Tocqueville (1969), p. 723.

regime) on a dependent variable (the number of houses destroyed by fire). Between cause and effect there are two intermediate variables which interact multiplicatively: the number of houses that catch fire and the proportion of fires that are not quickly extinguished. One can easily imagine adversaries of American democracy to focus on the first partial effect and its advocates to emphasize the second. The real issue, however, is whether the net effect is positive or negative. In the absence of more precise information about the strength of the opposing tendencies it may not be possible to answer this question.

A closely related form of argument is the following. Tocqueville first has the occasion to observe that democracy tends to increase people's opportunities in a potentially dangerous way and then goes on to point out that it also tends to reduce their desire to make use of them. He notes that the American constitution 'gave the president much power, but took away from him the will to use it'.[41] The power stems from his prerogatives and veto, the lack of will from the constant preoccupation with reelection. A similar reasoning is applied to religion, as can be seen by juxtaposing two passages: 'While the law allows the American people to do everything, there are things which religion prevents them from imagining and forbids them to dare'.[42] And 'I doubt whether man can support complete religious independence and entire political liberty at the same time. I am led to think that if he has no faith he must obey, and if he is free he must believe'.[43] The thrust of the second passage is that religion is endogenous to democracies, while the first argues that it tends to restrict the potentially dangerous freedom that is also part and parcel of democratic society. Opponents of democracy will naturally focus on what people *can* do in that regime, and its defenders on the endogenously generated limits on what they will *want* to do.

Similar causal structures can be expected to arise in the case of market socialism. Indeed, the dual character of that system is obvious, since *market* and *socialism* have quite different connotations and may be expected to lead in quite opposite directions.

[41] Tocqueville (1969), p. 138.
[42] Ibid., p. 292
[43] Ibid., p. 444.

Thus the socialist aspect of the system, that is, the workers' owner-ship of their means of production, might be expected to promote a spirit of cooperation and solidarity, while the market aspect would tend to work in the direction of competitiveness and even hostility. It is hard to say *a priori* whether personal relations in a market socialist society would be shaped mainly by the former or mainly by the latter.

The impact on the distribution of income is similarly ambigu-ous. On the one hand, one would expect the within-firm distribu-tion of income among workers of different skill levels to be rela-tively egalitarian. On the other hand, there could well be durable inequalities among workers of similar skills in different firms. Since there is no labour market in a market socialist economy, there is no natural tendency for wages to reach a uniform level. Successful firms, moreover, have no tendency to expand and thus to absorb other workers.[44] And even if they do invite other work-ers to join them, the latecomers might get a lower return on their equity than the pioneers if they have to pay the market value for a share in the firm.[45] One might hope that in a very profitable line of activity the creation of new firms would achieve what expansion of existing firms does in capitalism. The creation of new firms takes more time, however, than the expansion of old ones, and in the meantime the activity may have become less profitable. Focus-ing on partial effects, one can argue both that the distribution of income will be more equal under market socialism than under capitalism and that it will be less equal.

Short-term versus long-term effects

This distinction is a special case of the preceding one, but suffi-ciently important to be singled out for separate consideration. On this point, Tocqueville writes that 'in the long run government by democracy should increase the real forces of a society, but it can-not immediately assemble, at one point and at a given time, forces as great as those at the disposal of an aristocratic government or

---

[44] For a simple and lucid exposition of the reasons for the difference in the behaviour of labour cooperatives and capitalist firms in this respect, see Meade (1972).

[45] Meade (1980). This practice is followed in the plywood cooperatives in the United States (see Gunn 1984), but not, for instance, in the Mondragon cooperatives.

an absolute monarchy'.[46] Applied to warfare the argument says
that 'an aristocratic people which, fighting against a democracy,
does not succeed in bringing it to ruin in the first campaign always
runs a great risk of being defeated by it'.[47] Applied to taxation it
says that 'liberty engenders thousandfold more goods than it de-
stroys, and in nations where it is understood, the people's resources always increase faster than the taxes'.[48]

Later, Schumpeter independently (or so I assume) made the
same point in his famous observation that 'a system – any system,
economic or other – that at *every* given point of time fully utilizes
its possibilities to the best advantage may yet in the long run be
inferior to a system that does so at *no* given point of time, because
the latter's failure to do may be a condition for the level or speed
of long-run performance'.[49] In assessing efficiency, one must take
account of the system's ability to create new resources and not
simply of its ability to allocate existing resources optimally.

A similar argument applies to cooperative ownership. 'While
static economizing on scarce decision-making capabilities, which characterizes hierarchical organizations, may be advantageous in the
short run, this same characteristic may have an associated property of retarding such multiplication of capabilities as might be
brought about by a more participatory system, and which might,
in fact, prove widely beneficial'.[50] This is Tocqueville's argument
for political democracy transferred to economic democracy. Note
that the point here is not that short-term sacrifices may be a necessary causal condition for long-term growth, as exemplified by the
need for investment (short-term sacrifice of consumption) as a
means to future increases in consumption. Rather it is that short-
term inefficiency (and the concomitant loss of consumption) may
be an inevitable by-product of the system with the best long-term
performance. The short-term sacrifice is correlated with the long-
term performance, but does not cause it.

---

[46] Tocqueville (1969), p. 224.
[47] Ibid., p. 658.
[48] Ibid., p. 209.
[49] Schumpeter (1961), p. 83. As we might expect, the point had been made even earlier by
Leibniz: 'On pourrait dire que toute la suite des choses à l'infini peut être la meilleure
qui soit possible, quoique ce qui existe par tout l'univers dans chaque partie du temps ne
soit pas le meilleur' (Leibniz 1875–90, vol. 6, p. 237; see also vol. 3, pp. 582–3).
[50] Putterman (1982), p. 149. Italics in original.

Transitional versus steady-state effects

Tocqueville writes that 'one must be careful not to confuse the fact of equality with the revolution which succeeds in introducing it into the state of society and into the laws'.[51] The endogenous equilibrium products of democracy must not be confused with the temporary products of democratization. The latter may be undesirable, and yet the former very desirable, as Tocqueville shows in a number of examples. For instance, 'while equality favors sound morals, the social upheaval leading to it has a very damaging influence on them'.[52] Also, 'although high ambitions swell while conditions are in process of equalization, that characteristic is lost when equality is a fact'.[53] Conversely, in his notes for the second volume on the French Revolution Tocqueville argues against the view that politically unfree regimes are especially favourable to literary creation because they leave more time to individuals for their private pursuits. Rather it is the transition from freedom to lack of freedom which tends to stimulate the arts.[54] Once tyranny becomes entrenched, the creative spirit withers.

The argument has very wide application. To evaluate an economic, social or political system one must not look at its performance immediately after it has been introduced, but wait until its equilibrium properties have had time to emerge.[55] Whether the transitional system performs better or worse than the new equilibrium, it will certainly differ from it in important respects. 'Hence to compare the efficiency of a participatory institution having hierarchically adapted members with that of a hierarchical institution having such members is likely to be a biased procedure, since the participatory institution composed of such personnel may not be a fully appropriate proxy for the appropriately endowed participatory organization that might evolve under more ideal conditions'.[56] Conversely, in a successfully organized cooperative econ-

[51] Tocqueville (1969), p. 688,
[52] Ibid., p. 599.
[53] Ibid., p. 629.
[54] Tocqueville (1953), pp. 345–6.
[55] Note that the distinction between transitional and steady-state effects does not coincide with that between short-term and long-term effects, since we may distinguish among different temporal perspectives within the steady state.
[56] Putterman (1982), p. 149.

omy there might be transitional gains to be realized from reversal to hierarchy, since for a while it might be possible to enjoy both the capabilities generated by the cooperatives and the efficient utilization of them made possible by hierarchy.

In addition to these four Tocquevillian reasons that learning from experience and from experiments cannot substitute for theory, I want to consider a futher argument, also somewhat Tocquevillian in spirit. Like some of the arguments discussed earlier, it concerns the temporal dimension of political change. Unlike those arguments, however, it concerns time both from the point of view of the actors and from the perspective of the external observer. Generally speaking, and other things being equal, a system that encourages long-term planning will in the long run outperform a system that induces the actors to adopt very short time horizons. Other things may, of course, not be equal. Tocqueville argued that American democracy, while inducing very short time horizons in the actors, is also very productive in the long run. In democracies, people 'are afraid of themselves, dreading that, their taste having changed, they will come to regret not being able to drop what once had formed the object of their lust'.[57] In consequence, 'they carry through many undertakings quickly in preference to erecting long-lasting monuments'.[58] Nevertheless, their long-run performance is better than those of people capable of seeing further ahead. Each achievement is less impressive, but their 'restless activity, superabundant energy and force'[59] enable them to achieve many more things.

The stability of consumer taste, however, is only one determinant of long-term planning. Another and more important is the stability of the institutional environment. Economic agents will be reluctant to engage in investments that take a long time to bear fruit if they fear the imposition of new taxes or changes in the basic system of property rights. The current Chinese reforms illustrate this point. The reformers explicitly consider what they are doing to be a gigantic experiment. In an often-used phrase they liken the reform process to 'feeling the stones with one's feet in crossing the river', implying that a retreat to an earlier position may be neces-

[57] Tocqueville (1969), p. 582.
[58] Ibid., p. 631.
[59] Ibid., p. 243.

sary if a particular line of advance leads into deep water. This attitude cannot fail to induce a very short time horizon in the economic agents. Knowing that the reform will be quickly abandoned if it fails, they adopt a cautiously prudent attitude, which in turn increases the likelihood of failure. This tendency is reinforced by the strong political pressures to achieve quick results, partly because the agrarian reforms of 1978 were so immediately and strikingly successful that workers now expect the industrial reforms to be equally successful and partly because conservative groups will use any short-term costs and losses as a pretext to reverse the reform process.

In practice, this implies that the emerging entrepreneurs are willing to invest only if there are prospects of superprofits, sufficient for their investment to be paid back in two or three years. In an economy in transition from central planning to market exchange, there are in fact many imbalances and disequilibria to be exploited by entrepreneurs who want to get rich in a hurry.[60] There is much less incentive to undertake long-term productive investments. Also, successful entrepreneurs tend not to plough the profits back into the business, preferring to invest in private residences which are less vulnerable to confiscation by the state. Peasants, likewise, invest their earnings in housing rather than in improving their land, since they do not fully believe the government's promise to respect the fifteen-year leases on the land.

Hence the planners are in a fix. Ideally, they would like to present each new reform as a definitive and irreversible commitment, since the efficacy and benefits of a reform depend strongly on people's belief that it will last long enough to make long-term investment worth while. In practice, of course, such statements are not credible, in the absence of irreversible precommitment devices. I argue in IV.4 that the Chinese planners may not be able to bind themselves. Moreover, it is not clear that they would want

---

[60] For instance, private banks are emerging whose shareholders get a return of more than 30% on their investment. Normally, one would expect this to generate competition. Some banks would offer lower rates of interest on loans, while simultaneously raising the rate of interest on deposits to attract the capital to finance the loans. This does not happen, however, as the state sets an upper limit to the rate of interest on deposits. The limit is made necessary by the artificially low and politically determined rate of interest on loans from state banks to state enterprises. Since the state banks have to finance interest on deposits out of the interest they earn on loans, the low level of the latter constrains the former to be low.

to do so even if they could. If market reforms turn out to create widespread unemployment and starvation, the planners would not want to be unable to unbind themselves.[61] I conclude, therefore, that the very notion of 'experimenting with reform' is close to meaningless, unless the planners can successfully fool the economic agents into believing that the reform is definitive and irrevocable. They may be able to do this once or twice, but they will almost certainly not be able to fool all of the people all the time. Each reversal causes a loss of confidence; each retreat in crossing the river overturns some stepping stones and makes the next attempted crossing more difficult.

IV.4   POLITICAL IRRATIONALITY

In the model of individual rational action (I.2), irrationality can arise by weakness of will, excess of will and distortions in the formation of beliefs or preferences. I will not here discuss the political analogues of the last class of phenomena. For reasons explained in IV.2, there is no canonical model of *rational* beliefs and preferences in the political realm; hence there can be no clear notion of what irrational beliefs and preferences mean either. By contrast, I believe that weakness of will and excess of will do arise in political action, the former because the polity may be unable to stick to past decisions, being bound by no superior authority to do so; the latter because the polity, even more than an individual, is constantly tempted to deploy means the knowledge of which renders them inefficacious. The analogy between the individual and the political cases is, not surprisingly, far from perfect. Indeed, the comparison is valuable largely because of the numerous disanalogies, which help us understand exactly what is involved in the two varieties of irrationality.

In the individual, weakness of will can arise either because one is overwhelmed by passion or because one finds oneself unable to

---

[61] F. Bates, writing in *The Economist* of 21 March 1981, makes a similar argument: 'Can a democratic government credibly commit itself to adhere to a policy no matter what its consequences – to guarantee that the monetary base will not be allowed to grow faster than $x\%$, even if the optimists should turn out to be wrong, and the policy leads to massive unemployment and idle capacity quickly, and slows down inflation only very gradually? Catch 22: maybe the theory is right, but the only way to test it is to convince people that the government would persist even if it is wrong'.

stick to a past decision. The former case is illustrated by the man who leaves his wife because of an infatuation with another woman, the latter by the man who always tells himself that he will start exercising tomorrow. There are rough political analogues to both cases. Democratic societies can yield to undemocratic impulses, under the sway of irrational fears or demagoguery. Taxes introduced as temporary measures tend to become permanent, in spite of firm intentions to abolish them as soon as the occasion for them disappears. More generally, dumping problems on the future is a constant temptation for politicians concerned with reelection.

In the individual case, the generic responses to weakness of will are precommitment[62] and bunching.[63] For a man, marriage is a precommitment to one woman that makes divorce less likely even when it is legally possible. The machinery of divorce, being time-consuming, creates a chance for passion to cool and for better judgement to resume its place. I can force myself to start exercising by entering into an enforceable contract to pay a large amount of money to a charitable cause in case I do not. The latter problem, unlike the former, can also be resolved by bunching: if I do not start jogging today, will I ever do so? In the following I shall disregard bunching, which does not seem to be an important mechanism in the political case, and concentrate on precommitment as a solution to political weakness of will.

In an early discussion of the problem, Spinoza made an explicit analogy between individual and political precommitment:

[It] is by no means contrary to practice for laws to be so firmly established that even the king himself cannot repeal them. The Persians, for example, used to worship their kings as gods, yet even their kings had no power to repeal laws that had once been established, as is clear from Daniel, Chapter 6, and nowhere, as far as I know, is a king appointed unconditionally, without any explicit terms. This, in fact, is contrary neither to reason nor to the absolute obedience due to a king; for the fundamental laws of the state must be regarded as the king's permanent decrees, so that his ministers render him complete obedience in refusing to execute any command of his which contravenes them. We may clarify this point by reference to Ulysses, whose comrades did execute his command in refusing, in spite of all his orders and threats, to untie him from his ship's mast while he was enchanted by the Siren's song: and it is put down to his good sense that he thanked them afterwards for carrying out his original intention so obediently. Even kings have followed the example of Ulysses; they usually instruct

[62] Elster (1984); Schelling (1984), chs. 3, 4, and 6.
[63] Ainslie (1982, 1984, 1986).

their judges to have no respect for persons in administering justice, not even the king himself, if by some odd mischance he commands something which they know to contravene established laws. For kings are not gods, but men, who are often enhanced by the Siren's song. Accordingly, if everything depended on the inconstant will of one man, nothing would be stable.[64]

Similar considerations apply to democracies.[65] If all issues were subject to simple majority voting, society would lack stability and predictability. A small majority might easily be reversed, by accidents of participation or by a few individuals changing their minds. More important, if the majority followed short-lived passions or short-term expediency, it might act rashly and override individual rights granted by earlier decisions. All democracies, whether direct or indirect, have had some stabilizing devices to prevent all issues from being up for grabs by simple majority voting all the time (see II.6 for some examples from Athens and Florence). In modern representative democracies self-binding can take several forms.[66] Democratic abdication of power occurs when the assembly irrevocably delegates certain power to independent bodies, like the Federal Reserve Board or the International Monetary Fund. Political constitutions also embody limitations on democratic power, through a combination of substantive rules protecting privacy, property and civil liberties and procedural rules requiring more than a simple majority for any change in the constitution.

Yet the analogy between individual and political self-binding is severely limited. An individual can bind himself to certain actions, or at least make deviations from them more costly and hence less likely, by having recourse to a legal framework that is external to and independent of himself. *But nothing is external to society.* With the exception of a few special cases, like the abdication of powers to the International Monetary Fund, societies cannot deposit their will in structures outside their control: they can always undo their ties should they want to. The problem is not to explain why many constitutions fail to bind their creators and never become more than pieces of paper. Rather it is to understand how many constitutions come to acquire this mysterious binding force.[67]

---

[64] *Tractatus Politicus*, VII.1.
[65] For a discussion of the changing function of the Rule of Law, from a protection against absolute monarchy to a protection against absolute democracy, see Sejersted (1988).
[66] See the essays in Elster and Slagstad, eds. (1988).
[67] I am indebted to Adam Przeworski for this way of phrasing the question.

To illustrate this problem, I return to the current reform process in China. In addition to the problems created by the experimental attitude towards the reforms, a major obstacle to progress and success is the absence of the principle of legality, defined as follows. (a) An individual action is permitted unless there exists a law that expressly and unambiguously forbids it. (b) State interference is forbidden unless there exists a law that expressly and unambiguously authorizes it. Instead, the Chinese traditionally have a positive conception of the law: (a) An individual action is permitted if there exists a law that expressly authorizes it. (b) The state has the right to interfere in all unauthorized activities, even if they are not expressly forbidden.[68] If an activity is not authorized by the law, individuals may or may not be allowed to engage in it – they can never know. For example, there was a period when there was a law authorizing mural posters. Later, when that law was withdrawn, it was interpreted as forbidding posters, even though no law expressly forbidding them was passed. Similarly, 'until 1980, the size of private enterprise was limited to seven workers. This restriction was lifted, but no explicit laws enacted *permitting* the employment of more than seven workers until 1987. Thus, the mere lifting of the limitation to seven was not sufficient to create the climate for the formation of private enterprise. . . . Unless a state authority has explicitly delineated in the regulations a certain practice, it may be, arbitrarily, found to be illegal'.[69]

In this kind of system, political signals are more important than laws in indicating to individuals what they can and cannot do. Janos Kornai says that there are limits to economic reform in any socialist economy as long as 'the bureaucracy is unwilling to observe a voluntary restraint from its interference'.[70] But this seems to be the wrong way of phrasing the question. The problem is whether the bureaucracy is *able and willing to make itself unable* to interfere, since the temptation to do so will always be there. There

---

[68] 'The 1979 Chinese Criminal Law does not recognize the principle of "no punishment without preexisting law making the act a crime" (nullum crimen, nulla poena sine lege). Article 79 of the Law provides that: "A person who commits a crime not explicitly defined in the specific parts of the Criminal Law may be convicted and sentenced, after obtaining the approval of the Supreme People's Court, according to the most similar article in the Law"' (Chiu 1987). In the West, by contrast, reasoning by analogy is allowed only in civil law.

[69] Roemer (1988).

[70] Cited after Dernberger (1987).

is a need for new constitutional measures, including measures that take the interpretation of the constitution out of the hands of those whom it is supposed to keep in line. Today, 'the National People's Congress can enact any law it wishes in disregard of the spirit and the letter of the Constitution. This is because the Constitution has given the power to interpret the Constitution to the NPC's Standing Committee. . . . It is beyond imagination that this subordinate organ would interpret a law enacted by its parent organ, i.e. the NPC, as unconstitutional'.[71]

I have been saying two things about the Chinese reforms. First, the lack of standing and stable rules makes it difficult for economic agents to make the long-term investments that are necessary if the reforms are to succeed. In the current situation, this is probably inevitable. If the planners were to commit themselves definitely and irreversibly to a particular system of ownership, taxation and transfers, the result could be disastrous, creating unemployment and starvation on a vast scale. Precommitment can create more problems than it solves if the environment is sufficiently uncertain and unpredictable.[72] Ideally, we would like to be able to distinguish between bad and good motives for breaking rules, the former being the reason for creating the rules in the first place and the latter being legitimate exceptions due to unforeseen circumstances. (After all, sometimes we do have good reasons for cancelling an appointment with the dentist.) Individuals use a variety of devices to make this distinction, but they are always fragile and vulnerable to self-deception.[73] It would seem even more difficult for a political system to have built into itself not only first-order safeguards against impulsiveness but also second-order safe-

[71] Chiu (1987). As Tang Tsou has pointed out to me, this legalistic description is misleading. In reality, the standing committee is the superior instance and the 'parent organ' the subordinate one.
[72] Consider again the story of Daniel in the den of lions. Here it is told how King Darius was trapped by Daniel's enemies into issuing a decree 'that whosoever shall ask a petition of any God or man for thirty days, save of thee, O king, he shall be cast into the den of lions'. When Daniel then proceeded to make his prayers to God, his enemies denounced him to Darius and demanded that he be cast in the den. Darius tried to get out of this predicament, but they confronted him with the law that 'no decree nor statute which the king establishes may be changed', upon which he had to yield. As we know, the lions did not touch Daniel, but the story nevertheless illustrates the risks of precommitment. By rigidly binding oneself to certain rules of procedure, one may be prevented from making the right choice in unforeseen circumstances.
[73] Ainslie (1986).

guards against unreasonably strict adherence to the first-order safeguards. It is not a question of guarding the guardians, but of making them lay down their guard in cases of force majeure.[74]

My second observation about the Chinese practice, concerning the absence of the principle of legality, is more critical. Accepting the need for experiment and the dangers of rigid commitments is one thing. Allowing retroactive legislation and invoking a positive conception of the law is another. These practices encourage passivity and reluctance to stick one's neck out in any way. In this respect the current regime is perpetuating the ways of the turbulent years from 1957 to 1976, which created a deeply seated tendency in people to live in the future perfect tense, constantly asking themselves how their current actions would be interpreted and penalized if 'the other side' got back into power. The first step in constitutional reform must therefore be to introduce the principle of legality.

Finally, there is a deeper question: can the planners implement constitutional reform without a normative commitment to the principle of legality and to individual rights? If they introduce a constitutional system and abdicate some of their powers simply to get the economy going, the economic agents will always fear that the rights will be abolished if the economy gets into trouble. Even if the planners abdicated the power to interpret the constitution, they would for a long time be able to act outside the law. In the short and medium term the Chinese Communist Party will not be able to make itself *effectively* unable to reverse the reform. It has many sorts of power, *but not the power to make itself powerless.* Ulysses was lucky in that he had the requisite technology for self-binding at hand. Central planners have no ways of tying their hands and

---

[74] Cass Sunstein has pointed out to me two interesting American cases that bring out the ambiguity of exceptions to constitutional rules. In *Korematsu v. United States,* 323 U.S. 214 (1944), confining measures imposed on American citizens of Japanese ancestry were deemed constitutional. In *New York Times Co. v. United States; United States v. Washington Post Co.,* 404 U.S. 713 (1971), the attempt to stop publication of the 'Pentagon Papers' was deemed unconstitutional. In both cases, those who defended the restrictive measures argued that the Constitution must not be a straightjacket on governmental action when the military security of the nation is at stake. 'The Constitution is not a suicide pact'. It is unclear to me, however, whether those views represented (a) the kind of temptation that the Constitution was set up to prevent in the first place, (b) a legitimate concern that the Constitution might impose excessively tight bonds on the government or (c) an argument that the First Amendment can sometimes be overridden by other parts of the Constitution.

preventing their underlings from untying them. As a result the economic agents will adopt a short time horizon, and the system will indeed get into trouble. Only if and when rights become adopted on noninstrumental grounds will they acquire the desired instrumental efficacy, because only then will the government be able credibly to say that rights violations will not be tolerated.

In suggesting that the beneficial effects of freedom are essentially by-products, I am once again following Tocqueville:

> Nor do I think that a genuine love of freedom is ever quickened by the prospect of material rewards; indeed, that prospect is often dubious, anyhow as regards the immediate future. True, in the long run freedom always brings to those who know how to retain it comfort and well-being, and often great prosperity. Nevertheless, for the moment it sometimes tells against amenities of this nature, and there are times, indeed, when despotism can best ensure a brief enjoyment of them. In fact, those who prize freedom only for the material benefits it offers have never kept it long.[75]

Nor, presumably, have those who prize freedom only for the material benefits it offers retained those benefits themselves. The deliberate attempt to create political freedom as a means of achieving material prosperity is a form of excess of will (I.2). For freedom to be instrumentally valuable it must be known to have a noninstrumental base, because otherwise it will not induce the security and peace of mind by which its good consequences arise. The knowledge that the freedoms have been granted for merely instrumental purposes detracts from their instrumental efficacy, because the citizens can never be confident that the government will not curtail the freedoms if it appears expedient in the short run to do so.

A related problem underlies many government programs for work relief.[76] Among the frequently cited benefits of these programs is the effect on the self-respect of the persons provided with work. It is indeed true that being unemployed and living on unemployment benefits can be detrimental to one's self-respect, but it is far from clear that work which has the creation of self-respect as its sole or main purpose will have the intended effect.[77] To generate self-respect, work must have as its immediate purpose the

---

[75] Tocqueville (1952), p. 217.
[76] The following draws heavily on Elster (1988a).
[77] Similarly, political movements that justify themselves by the self-respect they provide to the participants are not likely to succeed even in that respect (Elster 1983a), pp. 98–100.

production of socially valuable goods and services. The noninstrumental value of self-respect can be realized only as the by-product of the instrumental value of producing goods and services. Experience from the work relief programs of the 1930s offers some support for this view:

> The political economy of work relief placed a web of constraints on the productive factors, the technology, the organization, and the type of products. These constraints affected the social value of the output. Not only was the efficiency of work relief operations forced below that of comparable contract projects, but the political forces of a private enterprise economy restricted projects to being noncompetitive. The restriction of project types was probably the more serious factor in reducing the value of output. *The non-pecuniary benefits to be derived from work relief – maintenance of morale, skills and work habits – themselves hinged crucially on the value of output.*[78]

Policies that for similar reasons risk being self-defeating include attempts to keep young people in schools (or universities) in order to prevent them from making trouble rather than to impart useful knowledge; the widespread emphasis on participation, process values and dignitary values (II.8) as goals in themselves rather than as means for improving outcomes; and the practice in centrally planned economies of deliberately setting unfeasible targets in order to force the agents to exert themselves to the limit. Such policies are somewhat more likely to succeed (and therefore all the more tempting) in the political than in the individual case, because in the former case the subject and the object of the excessive will are distinct agents. When the government promotes freedom to stimulate the initiative of the citizens or creates jobs to sustain the self-respect of the workers, the target groups need not be aware of these intentions. By contrast, an individual can hardly fail to be aware of his intention to defeat insomnia or to achieve spontaneity.

Yet democratic societies are built on the premise that the government should not mislead its citizens, be it for their own good. The *condition of publicity* promulgated by Kant and Rawls[79] rules out the kind of deception that would allow the government to carry out policies that cannot stand the light of day, like make-believe work, education or participation. Even in nondemocratic societies and in formally democratic societies in which the condi-

---

[78] Kesselman (1978), p. 215, emphasis added.
[79] For references and further discussion see Elster (1983a), pp. 92–3.

tion is violated, governments are usually unable to carry out the deception for long. Hypocrisy is contagious. Make-believe teaching and jobs create make-believe students and workers. The simulated enthusiasm with which the factory manager announces the plan target for next year betrays him.

IV.5 ALTERNATIVES TO RATIONALISM IN POLITICS

If the unitary-actor conception of rationality is unable to guide or explain political action, what are the alternatives? The explanatory issue reduces to an analysis of individual behaviour, once the need to disaggregate the political process has been recognized. Here I focus on the normative problem: what kind of arguments for action are consistent with the cognitive limits on rationality that I have been concerned to bring out? One answer, which would be that of Michael Oakeshott or Friedrich Hayek, is that the frailty of human reasoning excludes conscious, deliberate reform altogether. In their view, attempts to change society in a specific direction embody what they call 'rationalism' and what Otto Neurath referred to as 'pseudorationalism', the failure of reason to define and respect its own boundaries. I shall argue, however, that their ultraskeptical conclusion does not follow, because not all arguments for reform are consequentialist in nature.

Within the decision-theoretic paradigm several alternatives to consequentialism have been proposed. Isaac Levi suggests, for instance, that *security* and *deferability* can supplement instrumental rationality as criteria for choice under uncertainty.[80] Clearly, both are relevant to political action. In the choice of energy form – fossil versus nuclear – the long-term costs and risks are often hard to assess.[81] One line of argument is to assume that the worst will happen and to prefer, for instance, the local risks of nuclear accidents against the global risk created by the greenhouse effect. Another line is to emphasize the need for gaining time and for keeping one's options open until one knows more about the hazards involved.

---

[80] Levi (1974).
[81] Elster (1983b), app. 1.

Here I want to go outside the decision-theoretic approach and argue that *justice* provides an alternative motivation for political reform. I do not believe that the main political reforms of the past century have been supported mainly by instrumental considerations. Rather they have been carried by social movements anchored in a conception of justice. I shall illustrate this proposition by two main examples: the extension of suffrage and the rise of the welfare state. Later I shall apply the same idea to some current proposals for economic reform. The conception of justice on which I shall rely is the noninstrumental *right to equal concern and respect* that in various guises underlies the writings of John Rawls and Ronald Dworkin. This includes, notably, the right to share equally in the making of political decisions and the right to equal material welfare. Under this conception, inequalities are justified only under a narrowly confined set of conditions. Exclusion from suffrage can be justified only on grounds of severe mental incompetence. Deviations from full equality of welfare can be justified only by two criteria of 'nonperversity'. First, compensation and redistribution should not take place if the benefits to the compensated are small compared with the costs to others.[82] Second, compensation should not occur if it involves treating the compensated as not responsible for their own mental states.

The thrust of my argument is that to the extent that the principle underlying reforms is perceived as fundamentally just, in the sense just indicated, people will be willing and motivated to put up with the costs of transition and of experimenting with different modes of implementing it. Those who find this statement excessively idealistic may be more attracted by an alternative formulation: if a reform is widely perceived as fundamentally just, it is difficult to oppose it in more than a half-hearted way. It is usually easy to distinguish real opposition to reform from rearguard actions which are designed mainly to delay the inevitable.

Consider first the extension of the electorate. In democracies,

---

[82] This includes, as a special case, transfers that make the recipients worse off. The deliberately vague formulation ('The bucket may leak, but it should not leak too much') is compatible both with Rawls's theory and with utilitarianism, as well as with the 'common-sense' theory of justice documented in Frohlich, Oppenheimer and Eavey (1987). I am also being deliberately vague about the nature of the distribuendum, since the arguments set out below apply equally to welfare, primary goods, basic capabilities or opportunities for welfare.

suffrage is of necessity restricted by age and citizenship (or residence). Beyond these, no restrictions are inherently necessary, and in most democracies there are today very few other limitations. In the past, however, restrictions have been numerous and strong. They can be distinguished according to their substantive content or, more usefully, according to the underlying motivation.

Economic restrictions, such as ownership of property or payment of taxes, have been justified in at least four ways.[83] First, before the introduction of the secret ballot, economic well-being was often seen to be a guarantee of *integrity*, which in turn was thought to be necessary to prevent voters from being bribed.[84] Next, ownership of property has frequently been seen to provide the owners with special *competence* to take part in politics, because ownership is seen as a proxy for education (hence property owners have often been exempted from literacy tests), because it is thought to ensure the indispensable free time or because it is thought to induce in the owners an interest in the long-term welfare of society, as distinct from a desire for immediate gain. Landowners, in particular, have been favoured on this ground. Furthermore, poll taxes have been advocated on the grounds that the willingness to pay them demonstrates a higher *motivation* and concern for political matters.[85] The main argument for poll taxes, however, has been that they indicate that a citizen is competent to deliberate. Finally, economic restrictions have been justified on grounds of *commutative justice:* no taxation without representation and vice versa. Of these arguments, the first three are clearly instrumental, in the sense that they aim at bringing about substantively good decisions. They would pass the 'rational basis' test and might even pass the 'special scrutiny test' of what constitutes an admissible classification.[86] The last argument is grounded in con-

---

[83] The following draws heavily on Seymour and Frary (1918); McGovney (1949); C. Williamson (1960); Kay(1986).

[84] Actually, the argument shows only that bribing rich voters is more costly, which may be offset by the fact that when suffrage is restricted to the rich there are fewer voters to be bribed.

[85] Stephen Holmes has pointed out to me that the Romans imposed economic conditions on the right to vote in order to elicit information from the citizens about their taxable property. In theory, this rule could also serve the purpose of sorting out the citizens who were sufficiently concerned with the *res publica* to risk bringing their wealth to the attention of the authorities.

[86] Ely (1980), pp. 31, 120–4, 146–8.

siderations of justice, but of a very special and restricted kind, as I argue below.

Most other restrictions fall in one of these categories. The exclusion of live-in sons without a room of their own, as was the practice in Britain before 1914, was justified by an argument from integrity. No political opinion could be properly and independently formed by someone who did not have the minimal privacy of his own room in the family. The link between universal suffrage and universal military service is grounded in considerations of commutative justice.[87] Disenfranchisement of serving soldiers, by contrast, has been justified on the grounds that they are transient members of the community with no interest in its long-term welfare.[88] This argument has also been used against student representation on the governing bodies of universities and to support stringent residence requirements for the right to vote in local elections. Literacy tests are supposed to sort out competent voters from the less qualified. Disenfranchisement of the mentally ill has similarly been justified on grounds of competence. Disenfranchisement of felons, during the period of confinement or beyond, may be justified on grounds of commutative justice, but legislators have probably also been influenced by the idea that the political opinions of convicted criminals tend to be twisted or unsound, and hence should not be represented.[89] The exclusion of women, finally, has been justified on grounds of competence or on grounds of commutative justice (because women do not do military service).

The arguments from commutative justice rest on a vision of society as a joint-stock company, with the citizens cooperating for mutual advantage. Although taxpayers may be willing to have some of their taxes spent on nontaxpayers, they usually insist on taking part in the decision to spend the money that way and, crucially, on excluding nontaxpayers from the decision.[90] 'No representation without taxation'. I later consider an ambiguity in the term 'nontaxpayers', which may include those who are perma-

---

[87] Athenian citizens were disfranchised for cowardice in war and for unpaid debts to the state (MacDowell 1978, pp. 160, 165).

[88] Ely (1980), p. 120.

[89] Thus Aiskhines in the speech *Against Timarkhos:* 'The legislator considered it impossible for the same man to be bad privately and good publicly' (cited after MacDowell 1978, p. 174).

[90] This is, of course, how rich countries today decide on aid to poor countries.

nently unable to work and thus to pay taxes as well as those who are temporarily out of work. For the time being, it is sufficient to note that in either acceptation, the denial of the right to vote to nontaxpayers (or, for that matter, to those who do not or cannot perform military service) rests on a very narrow conception of justice. It is a vision of the well-ordered society as emerging from a bargain among self-interested individuals, in which those who have nothing to contribute and hence no bargaining power cannot expect to receive anything either, except from charity.[91]

Universal adult suffrage rests on a simpler and more compelling conception, transcending both instrumental considerations and commutative justice. Society is indeed a joint venture, but the bond between members is not simply one of mutual advantage, but also one of mutual respect and tolerance. If the first step in the development of democracy was the idea that no group of persons could be assumed to be inherently superior to others,[92] the second was that no group could be assumed to be inherently inferior. The (reconstructed) argument goes as follows. (a) There is no independently defined group (the rich, the noble, landed property owners, males, the old, the educated or the intelligent) all of whose members are inherently better suited than nonmembers to make political decisions. (b) Since assertions of group superiority or inferiority can at most have statistical validity, individuals would be justifiably offended and degraded by being excluded under a generalization which would inevitably have many exceptions. (c) The choice of experts to verify assertions of superiority and inferiority is a conflictual matter from which no potentially inferior group should be excluded. (d) If members of some group were to be shown to lack the necessary competence and motivation, there would be a strong presumption that the cause was their lack of occasions to participate and not any inborn deficit of reason. Moreover, excluded individuals would have good reasons to doubt that the decisions taken by the enfranchised were guided by the concern of eventually incorporating them.[93] (e) Specifically, there is no reason for believing that integrity – arguably the most important qualification for political participation – is more frequently found in any of the

---

[91] Gauthier (1986) offers the most recent and systematic exposition of this view.
[92] Barry (1979b).
[93] Ely (1980), pp. 120–1.

groups just mentioned, or in any other group for that matter. Government by the smart, rich and well-educated tends to become and to remain government for the smart, rich and well-educated. (f) Those who are shut off from voting are rarely shut off from arguing that they should be given the vote. As a consequence, privileged groups face a dilemma. If they refuse to give reasons, they undermine their position as the possessors of superior wisdom. If they do argue, they implicitly recognize the excluded groups as their equals in reason.[94] Once some form of democracy has been created, the defence of partial privilege becomes unstable; there are no half-way houses; democracy must expand or disappear. The condition of publicity ensures that equality will be promoted by the very attempt to argue against it.

It is often argued that the extension of suffrage must be understood in terms of legitimacy requirements.[95] Governments and ruling classes have successively removed restrictions on suffrage because they were forced to do so in order to retain their legitimacy. If universal adult suffrage had not eventually been granted, there would have been massive discontent and social unrest; hence governments elected by a smaller electorate chose the lesser evil, that is, acted instrumentally rationally, in extending the suffrage. This conception may be true as far as it goes, but it falls well short of a full explanation. Arguments from legitimacy presuppose other arguments. Unless the extension of suffrage were desired by the population at large on other grounds, governments would not lose legitimacy by not granting it. My claim is that among these other grounds, arguments from justice have been important. The granting of voting rights to women may provide the clearest example. This was not carried out by a political party or movement with the purpose of using the vote to promote women's social or economic interests. Rather the unenfranchisement of women was seen as inherently insufferable and degrading.[96] In the case of the working

---

[94] This crucial insight derives from the work of Habermas, as interpreted in Elster (1983a), ch. 1, sec. 5.

[95] See, e.g., Freeman and Snidal (1982).

[96] In Britain, there was also an element of commutative justice. In light of the vital tasks performed by women during the First World War, it became impossible to argue that women had nothing to offer in return for the suffrage. The provision by women of a crucial collective good – the children who would ensure the continuation of society – could equally well have been used as an argument (and probably was).

class, this motivation was intertwined, sometimes inextricably, with the struggle for economic interests. It should be clear, however, to any reader of E. P. Thompson's *The Making of the English Working Class* that the struggle for manhood suffrage was motivated largely by arguments from simple justice.[97]

The rise of the welfare state is analogous to and intertwined with the extension of suffrage. First, let me distinguish between two aspects of the welfare state. On the one hand, some activities take the form of compulsory saving or compulsory risk pooling, with no redistributive elements. On the other hand, some activities are essentially redistributive. Although most welfare services combine elements of both, it will nevertheless be useful to distinguish them.

The welfare-state element in the first activities derives from their compulsory character. Individuals can and do save privately for their old age and take out private insurance against illness or accidents. Increasingly, however, payments of insurance are removed from the free choice of individuals and become a matter of compulsory payroll deductions.[98] Sometimes compulsory compensation schemes retain the actuarial basis of private schemes. In that case, the arguments for having them can only be paternalist or self-paternalist ones. Through their politicians, people may bind themselves to measures they would want to take as private citizens were it not for their predictable weakness of will. Usually, however, compulsory schemes deviate from private insurance in two ways: they are neither actuarially correct at the individual level nor self-financing at the collective level.

Compulsory insurance is often accompanied by redistributive measures. Usually people do not get back in old age the actuarial equivalent of what they have paid over the years. True, redistributive features also characterize most private insurance schemes: 'Because no risk class is completely homogeneous, there always

---

[97] One might also consider a purely instrumental-utilitarian argument for extension of the suffrage, by arguing that the removal of this degrading discrimination ipso facto represented a gain in welfare. Yet again this instrumental consideration would be parasitic on a noninstrumental one, namely the perceived injustice inherent in the unequal treatment.

[98] Formally, these are often presented as contributions by the employer. Economists agree, however, that these are de facto payroll deductions, in the sense that without compulsory employer contributions the salaries of employees would be higher by the same amount (Page 1983, p. 28).

appears to be some subsidy of the slightly higher risks within a class by the slightly lower risks'.[99] The redistributive aspects of social insurance deliberately go beyond these effects, usually in an equalizing direction. This is increasingly true also of private insurance companies, when they are prohibited by law from using certain classifications to distinguish between risk classes. For instance, if sex classifications were disallowed, 'males would subsidize female pension rates, and females subsidize male life insurance rates'.[100] Such policies can lead to absurdities. For example, 'it seems inappropriate to ask disability insureds to bear the full costs of subsidies to hemophiliacs'.[101] Similarly, as soon as society decides to use compulsory insurance for redistributive purposes, it becomes inappropriate to require each separate program to be self-financing. In fact, there is no point in requiring even the whole set of programs to be self-supporting, since there is no reason to keep this form of redistribution neatly separate from redistribution through taxation. The upshot is 'the welfare state', a system in which the original correlation between premiums and benefits has largely disappeared.

Although compulsory risk pooling and redistribution often go together in the modern welfare state, the distinction is not useless. On the one hand, the system covers many disabilities against which one could never get private insurance. People with congenital blindness or genetic defects cannot insure themselves against these accidents of fortune, since one cannot insure against an event that has already taken place. It is difficult to insure privately against unemployment, since the risks for different individuals are not statistically uncorrelated, as is required for a sound insurance scheme. At the other end of the spectrum, some parts of social insurance still obey approximately actuarial principles.[102] In between, some services have a larger element of redistribution, others of risk pooling. The element of risk pooling reflects the idea of society as a joint venture for mutual advantage, whereas the redistributive component reflects a more fundamental principle of simple justice.

[99] Abraham (1986), p. 84.
[100] Ibid., p. 92.
[101] Ibid., p. 99.
[102] Page (1983), pp. 67, 75.

We may explore the distinction further by introducing the notion of a 'veil of ignorance'. Many theories of distributive justice agree on the formal point that a just distribution of resources is that which would be chosen by rational agents behind the veil of ignorance, although they are in substantive disagreement as concerns the 'thickness' of that veil. In different but essentially equivalent terminology, the theories may agree that the distribution of goods or welfare should not be affected by 'morally arbitrary' features of persons, while differing over what is arbitrary and what is relevant. Risk pooling takes place behind a very thin veil, which allows people to know their actual skills, preferences and wealth, but not their future earning power and earning opportunities. Under these circumstances, rational individuals will agree to insure against risk, that is, to pay a premium into a common pool out of which compensation can be made. Redistribution takes place behind a thicker veil, which denies people knowledge of many, perhaps all, of their personal qualities and endowments. Behind a thick veil of ignorance people will ask themselves how they would want society to be organized if they did not know what assets or preferences they would turn out to have. Rational individuals might want to protect themselves against the risk of being born poor, or poorly endowed with productive skills, or endowed with expensive tastes.

The notion of a thin veil of ignorance can be understood quite literally. Because we do not know what the future will bring, it makes sense to take precautions. The thick veil, by contrast, cannot be taken literally, since we do know our skills, preferences and wealth. The thick veils are only literary devices to express the idea that the welfare of individuals ought not to be affected by certain morally arbitrary properties – those, precisely, from which abstraction is made behind the veil in question. The thinnest of these thicker veils corresponds to a meritocratic conception of justice, according to which people are entitled to the fruits of their skill and effort but not to the fruits of inherited property. A somewhat thicker veil is that proposed by Ronald Dworkin, who argues that distribution of welfare should be 'ambition-sensitive' but not 'endowment-sensitive'.[103] The most impenetrable veil is that pro-

---

[103] Dworkin (1981), pt. 2.

posed by John Rawls, who claims that ambitions and preferences, including time preferences, preference for leisure and risk aversion, are no less morally arbitrary than skills. Utilitarianism rests on a similar idea, but reaches different conclusions because of a different notion of what constitutes rational choice behind the veil of ignorance.

The redistributive component of the welfare state rests on a premise that some qualities of individuals are morally arbitrary. Minimally, these include inborn abilities and disabilities. The welfare state corresponds to a widespread belief that it would be unfair to let individuals suffer from genetic accidents outside their control. In this perspective, the meritocratic conception appears inconsistent. If social luck is to be eliminated as a determinant of welfare, why should genetic luck be respected? Yet Dworkin's position can also be criticized as inconsistent.[104] How can one defend the view that a low level of ambition and a high rate of time discounting are not also the products of social and genetic luck? If they are, why do they not provide grounds for compensation? This seems to be the central philosophical question in current controversies over the welfare state.[105]

The beginning of an answer is provided by the fact that the modern welfare state is inserted into a political democracy, based among other things on the condition of publicity. To tell a citizen that he is entitled to welfare because he is not responsible for his preferences is pragmatically incoherent.[106] One cannot at one and the same time treat the preferences of an individual as a handicap that justifies compensation *and* treat them as a legitimate input to

---

[104] See notably Roemer (1985).

[105] To avoid ambiguity, we may note that there are two aspects to ambition. On the one hand, one may want to encourage ambition for everybody's sake. Any theory of justice must take account of the need to pay people more when this is necessary to elicit socially useful work. On the other hand, one may (with Dworkin) or may not (with Rawls) think that ambition is a morally relevant ground for higher rewards. Consider three equally skilled workers, A, B and C, who choose to work, respectively, 4, 8, and 12 hours per day at a given wage per hour. One may believe (with Rawls and utilitarianism) that it is morally justified to tax C (and perhaps B), and use the proceeds to subsidize A, and yet stop short of the tax rate that would make the three equally well off, namely if this rate were to make A worse off (Rawls) or reduce total welfare (utilitarianism) compared with a lower tax rate. Dworkin, however, would not accept any taxation on earning differentials due to ambition rather than skills.

[106] Dworkin (1981), pt. 1 refers to the similarly manifest absurdity of a policy that would compensate individuals for unhappiness caused by their religious beliefs.

212 Solomonic judgements

the political process; not in one and the same breath treat him as moved by psychic forces outside his control *and* treat him as rational and open to arguments. Perhaps one might justify such practices to a third party, on the grounds that it is better to let irresponsible individuals have access to the political process than to cause political turmoil by excluding them. In a democratic society, however, a policy must be rejected if it cannot coherently be explained to the individuals in question. By withholding material benefits one protects the crucial values of concern and respect. Those who are able but unwilling to work should not receive support, nor should those who are able but unwilling to save be compensated for their incontinence. There *is* an element of commutative justice or quid pro quo in political democracy: not that the citizens should be unconditionally required to do certain things (pay taxes or fight wars), but that they should be required to do certain things *if they can do them.*

Yet, as I said, this austere principle is only the beginning of an answer. Applied to most contemporary societies, it would be widely and correctly perceived as unfair, because the economic means to form autonomous preferences are massively unequally distributed. In any society there will be individuals who for idiosyncratic reasons are deaf to incentives and, in more serious cases, have to be supported by the state. In a society with fair background conditions the support would, however, not be offered as compensation; and the supported individuals would, like the mentally ill, be more or less randomly distributed across all social groups. Most contemporary societies do not approach this condition. They contain large groups whose members are systematically prevented, by poverty and lack of employment opportunities, from developing the mental attitude of holding themselves responsible for their actions.[107] To treat them as if the background conditions were just, telling them that they have only themselves to blame for their failure, would be a massive piece of bad faith.

---

[107] Some groups have a more ambiguous status. Consider the attitude of the welfare state towards gypsies in an affluent society like Norway. The only thing that prevents them from a life of regular work and schooling is their own attitude towards such things. They like to be free, to travel and not to have to make plans for the future. Should society bail them out of trouble and more generally support their life style, at the expense of other citizens? I return to a similar problem when discussing the proposal for a social dividend.

As long as the influence of genuinely arbitrary features such as wealth has not been eliminated, justice may require us to count as morally arbitrary some features which would be considered non-arbitrary in the absence of the former.

The extension of the suffrage and of the welfare state was carried out against many instrumentally minded objections. The propertyless classes would abuse their electoral power, confiscate the wealth of the rich and eventually impoverish everybody, themselves included. The shift from risk pooling to redistribution would create a new class of parasites, who would exploit the hardworking core of the population until eventually they, too, would become losers from reform. On the other side, advocates of the reforms also put forward arguments based on expected instrumental benefits. The political process would gain from the larger diversity of viewpoints and perspectives which would follow upon an extension of the suffrage. The provision of welfare benefits would reduce morbidity and mortality not only among the propertyless but also, by reducing the incidence of contagious diseases, among the propertied classes. And so on, down a long list of conjectural risks and benefits.

If the reasoning in IV.3 and IV.4 is accepted, such arguments are misguided, the positive arguments sometimes doubly so. It is virtually impossible to anticipate the long-term net equilibrium effects of major reforms of this kind. Also, some of the positive arguments for reform do not stand the light of day. The publicity condition precludes one from advocating measures whose sole or main justification lies in their expected impact on the character of the citizens, whom they are supposed to make more enthusiastic, more public-spirited or more quiescent. By contrast, the norm of equality is transparent and compelling. It is an inescapable feature of a democratic society which rests on rational, public discussion. To oppose it is, as I said, already to recognize it. To ignore it is to refuse the democratic framework of discussion and justification.

I conclude by making some comments on three recent proposals for economic reform. These are (a) James Meade's proposal for a property-owning democracy, elaborated by Richard Krouse and Michael McPherson;[108] (b) proposals for a 'social dividend'

---

[108] Meade (1964); Krouse and McPherson (1986); see also the comments in Elster (1986b).

or guaranteed income at a level sufficient to provide a decent living without any obligation to work in return;[109] and (c) economic democracy at the enterprise level, with full workers' ownership at the immediate or ultimate goal.[110] All of these would involve major changes in the capitalist organization of production as it currently exists. I shall argue that the first two proposals are nonstarters, because they do not rest on a simple conception of justice, rooted in equality and capable of inspiring a mass movement. They are engineering blueprints for utopias – technocratic dreams or nightmares without the potential for animating a social movement. Attempts to implement them would meet with massive resistance because people would feel, correctly, that they were being asked to participate in a large-scale experiment of no intrinsic value and highly uncertain extrinsic value.

Consider first Meade's proposal for property-owning democracy, which rests on a combination of a progressive property tax and a radical reform of the inheritance tax. The latter is intended to induce large holders of property to bequeath their wealth to a large number of relatively poor individuals. This goal could be achieved in two ways: either by taxing 'each individual gift or bequest not solely according to the size of the individual gift or bequest, but also according to the existing wealth of the beneficiary' or by taxing the beneficiary 'when he received any gift or bequest neither according to the size of that gift or bequest nor according to his total property at the time of the receipt of that gift or bequest, but according to the size of the total amount which he had received over the whole of his life by way of gift or inheritance'.[111] According to Krouse and McPherson, this scheme would ensure that 'everyone would start out in life with substantial property income'. It would also create psychological attitudes importantly different from current experience, as 'workers of one firm would be part owners of others: under the authority of managers in one firm they will help oversee managers in others'. Finally, income generated by the scheme would create the material means for workers to form cooperatives, without any need to impose this as the compulsory mode of ownership.

---

[109] Van Parijs and van der Veen (1986); see also the comments in Elster (1986c).
[110] For discussion and further references, see Elster and Moene, eds. (1989).
[111] Meade (1964), pp. 56–7.

The alleged consequences of the scheme are highly doubtful. The inheritance scheme would have perverse incentive effects and mind-boggling problems of implementation.[112] Moreover, there is no reason to expect that everyone would be chosen by someone as the recipient of a gift or bequest. One can easily imagine the negative impact on the self-respect of those to whom nobody had chosen to give or bequeath property. Furthermore, the suggestion that owning shares in other firms could somehow offer a power which would compensate for being subject to managerial authority in one's own work place is absurd.[113] Hence the proposal fails on two counts. The alleged benefits are highly conjectural. Also, the scheme does not have any inherent virtues which might make people willing to suffer the costs of trial and error during a period of experimentation.

Consider next proposals for a negative income tax, social dividends, universal grants and the like. There are obvious objections to the economic feasibility of a guaranteed, substantial and unconditional income for everybody. Here I shall simply argue that any such proposal would fail because it would be perceived as unfair, indeed as exploitative.[114] People who chose to work for an income rather than to live in a commune on the universal grant would have to pay higher taxes in order to support those who took the other option. They would think, correctly in my opinion, that they were being exploited by the other group. Against this objection, the following counterargument has been made.[115] By assumption, everyone would be free to choose the unconditional grant. If some people chose not to do that, they could hardly complain if others did. Their preference for consumption over leisure would provide no reason for preventing others from acting on different preferences. To this I have two replies. First, some people might remain in the work force simply because they believed someone had to be in the work force. When contemplating the happy commune members, they might mutter, angrily, 'What if everyone did that?' Next, even if they did in fact prefer to work because they

---

[112] Elster (1986b) enumerates some of the difficulties.
[113] Here Meade (1964), p. 40, is more realistic when he argues that 'investments [would have to be] chosen by specialists on behalf of the man in the street'.
[114] For a similar argument see Frank (1985), pp. 256–7.
[115] Van Parijs and van der Veen (1986b).

valued consumption, there would be no reason to tax them more heavily. They might well prefer the forty-hour week over the fifty-hour week they had to work because of the high taxes imposed on them by those who chose to live on the grant. Hence the argument from freedom of choice fails, because the workers would be forced by the nonworkers to work harder than they wished.

Consider finally proposals for worker ownership, market socialism and the like. As explained in IV.3, it is hard to predict what the consequences would be of a cooperative regime. Much would depend on the particular arrangements chosen. There would be a choice between direct and representative democracy. Managers could be subject to instant recall or be appointed for longer periods. They could have wide discretionary powers or be obliged to consult the general assembly on all important issues. The economic rights and obligations associated with entry, membership and exit could be shaped in many different ways. There would be a choice between debt financing and equity financing, including the possibility of outside, nonvoting shares. Given all these dimensions of variation, the odds are that a workable arrangement could be found, given patience and willingness to endure experiments. Unlike the other proposals discussed here, the idea of cooperative ownership is rooted in a conception of justice that can provide the necessary motivation. The extension of equality from the political and social realms to the economic domain is bound to come up against many vested interests that will slow down the rate of progress. Owners will offer pseudosolutions and rituals of participation to buy time. Labour unions will resist this encroachment on their authority. If I am right, however, these will increasingly be seen as rearguard actions. At the very least, it *makes sense* to argue for cooperative ownership. It aims at doing away with the most important remnants of authority and hierarchy in society. It is the stuff that social movements are built of.[116]

[116] See, e.g., Jones (1894).

REFERENCES

Abraham, K. (1986). *Distributing risk*. New Haven, Conn.: Yale University Press.
Ackerman, B. (1980). *Social justice in the liberal state*. New Haven, Conn.: Yale University Press.
Ainslie, G. (1975). Specious reward. *Psychological Bulletin* 82: 463–96.
   (1982). A behavioral economic approach to the defense mechanisms: Freud's energy theory revisited. *Social Science Information* 21: 735–79.
   (1984). Behavioral economics II: Motivated involuntary behavior. *Social Science Information* 23: 247–74.
   (1986). Beyond microeconomics. In J. Elster (ed.), *The multiple self*, pp. 133–76. Cambridge University Press.
Akerlof, G. and Dickens, W. T. (1982). The economic consequences of cognitive dissonance. *American Economic Review* 72: 307–19.
Allen, F. (1964). Comments [on Coons (1964)]. *Northwestern University Law Review* 58: 798–805.
Alloy, L. and Abrahamson, L. (1979). Judgment of contingency in depressed and non-depressed students: Sadder but wiser? *Journal of Experimental Psychology: General* 108: 441–85.
Amar, A. (1984). Choosing representatives by lottery voting. *Yale Law Journal* 93: 1283–1308.
Andvig, J. and Moene, K. O. (1988). How corruption corrupts (unpublished manuscript).
Aron, R. (1967). *Les étapes de la pensée sociologique*. Paris: Gallimard.
Aronson, E. (1984). *The social animal*, 4th ed. New York: Freeman.
Arrow, K. (1982). Risk perception in psychology and economics. *Economic Inquiry* 20: 1–9.
Arrow, K. and Hurwicz, L. (1971). An optimality criterion for decision-making under uncertainty. In C. F. Carter and J. L. Ford (eds.), *Uncertainty and expectation in economics*, pp. 1–11. Clifton, N.J.: Kelley.
Aubert, V. (1980). Chance in social affairs. In J. Dowie and P. Lefrere (eds.), *Risk and chance*. Milton Keynes: The Open University.
Badeau, A. (1882). *Le village sous l'ancien régime*. Paris: Didier.
Barry, B. (1978). Comment. In S. Benn et al., *Political participation*, pp. 37–48. Canberra: Australian National University Press.
   (1979a). *Sociologists, economists and democracy*, 2d ed. University of Chicago Press.
   (1979b). Is democracy special? In P. Laslett and J. Fishkin (eds.), *Philosophy, politics and society*, 5th ser., pp. 155–96. Oxford: Blackwell Publisher.

(1986). Lady Chatterley's lover and doctor Fischer's bomb party. In J. Elster and A. Hylland (eds.), *Foundations of social choice theory*, pp. 11–44. Cambridge University Press.

Bartlett, R. (1986). *Trial by fire and water*. New York: Oxford University Press.

Barzel, Y. (1974). A theory of rationing by waiting. *Journal of Law and Economics* 17: 73–95.

Bass, J. (1981). *Unlikely heroes*. New York: Simon & Schuster.

Basson, M. (1979). Choosing among candidates for scarce medical resources. *Journal of Medicine and Philosophy* 4: 313–33.

Becker, G. (1976). *The economic approach to human behavior*. University of Chicago Press.

(1981). *A treatise on the family*. Cambridge, Mass.: Harvard University Press.

Beecher, H. K. (1969). Scarce medical resources and medical advancement. *Daedalus* 98: 275–313.

Begg, D. K. H. (1982). *The rational expectations revolution in macroeconomics*. Oxford: Allan.

Belliotti, R. A. (1980). Moral assessment and the allocation of scarce medical resources. *Man and Medicine* 5: 251–62.

Ben-Ner, A. and Neuberger, E. (1982). The kibbutz. In F. Stephen (ed.), *The performance of labour-managed firms*, pp. 186–213. New York: St. Martin's Press.

Berk, R. A. and Berk, S. F. (1979). *Labor and leisure at home*. Beverly Hills, Calif.: Sage.

Berk, S. F. (1980). *Women and household labor*. Beverly Hills, Calif.: Sage.

Binmore, K. (1987). Remodeled rational players. *Economics and Philosophy* 3: 179–214.

Bloch, S. and Reddaway, P. (1978). *Russia's political hospitals*. London: Futura Books.

Bohigas, N. de (1968). Some opinions on exemption from military service in nineteenth-century Europe. *Comparative Studies in Society and History* 10:261–88.

Bowles, S. and Gintis, H. (1976). *Schooling in capitalist America*. London: Routledge & Kegan Paul.

Bradley, K. and Gelb, A. (1982). The Mondragon cooperatives. In D. C. Jones and J. Svejnar (eds.), *Participatory and self-managed firms*, pp. 153–72. Lexington, Mass.: Lexington Books.

Brams, S. (1980). *Biblical games*. Cambridge, Mass.: MIT Press.

Brehm, J. (1956). Postdecision changes in the desirability of alternatives. *Journal of Abnormal and Social Psychology* 52: 384–9.

Broome, J. (1984a). Uncertainty and fairness. *Economic Journal* 94: 624–32.

(1984b). Selecting people randomly. *Ethics* 95: 38–55.

(1987). Fairness and the random distribution of goods (unpublished manuscript).

Burkert, W. (1985). *Greek religion*. Cambridge, Mass.: Harvard University Press.

Burnheim, J. (1985). *Is democracy possible?* Oxford: Polity Press.

Calabresi, G. and Bobbit, P. (1978). *Tragic choices*. New York: Norton.

Campbell, R. and Sowden L. (eds.) (1985). *Paradoxes of rationality and cooperation*. Vancouver: University of British Columbia Press.

Capron, A. M. (1975). Social experimentation and the law. In A. O. Rivlin and P. M. Timbane (eds.), *Ethical and legal issues of social experimentation*, pp. 127–64. Washington, D.C.: Brookings Institution.

Carrère, C. (1967). *Barcelone centre économique à l'époque des difficultés, 1380–1462.* Paris: Mouton.

Chaitin, G. C. (1975). Randomness and mathematical proof. *Scientific American* 232: 437–52.

Chambers, D. (1984). Rethinking the substantive rules for custody disputes in divorce. *Michigan Law Review* 83: 480–569.

Charms, R. de (1968). *Personal causation.* New York: Academic Press.

Chiu, H. (1987). Institutionalizing a new legal system in Deng's China. Prepared for the International Conference on a Decade of Reform under Deng Xiaoping, Brown University, Providence, R.I., November 4–7.

Choisel, F. (1981). Du tirage au sort au service universel. *Revue Historique des Armées* 37: 43–60.

Cole, J. (1989). The paradox of individual particularism and institutional universalism. *Social Science Information* 28: 51–76.

Cole, S., Cole J. and Simon, G. A. (1981). Chance and consensus in peer review. *Science* 214: 881–6.

Cook, J. T. (1987). Deciding to believe without self-deception. *Journal of Philosophy* 84: 441–6.

Coons, J. E. (1964). Approaches to court-imposed compromises: The uses of doubt and reason. *Northwestern University Law Review* 58: 750–94.

(1987). Consistency. *California Law Review* 75, 59–113.

Cooter, R. and Marks, S. with Mnookin, R. (1982). Bargaining in the shadow of the law: A testable model of strategic behavior. *Journal of Legal Studies* 11: 225–51.

Czwartosz, Z. (1988). On queuing. *Archives Européennes de Sociologie* 29, 3–11.

Dale, E. E. (1983). Oklahoma's great land lottery. *Great Plains Journal* 22: 2–41.

Dasgupta, P. and Stiglitz, J. (1980). Uncertainty, industrial structure, and the speed of R&D. *Bell Journal of Economics* 11: 1–28.

Davidson, D. (1980). *Essays on actions and events.* New York: Oxford University Press.

Davis, K. C. (1971). *Discretionary justice.* Urbana: University of Illinois Press.

Dernberger, R. F. (1987). The drive for economic modernization and growth: Performance and trends. Prepared for the International Conference on a Decade of Reform under Deng Xiaoping, Brown University, Providence, R.I. November 4–7.

Descartes, R. (1897–1910). *Oeuvres complètes,* ed. C. Adam and P. Tannery. Paris: Vrin.

Deutsch, M. (1975). Equity, equality and need. *Journal of Social Issues* 31: 137–49.

Divine, T. M. (1976). Women in the academy: Sex discrimination in university faculty hiring and promotion. *Journal of Law and Education* 5: 429–51.

Donagan, B. (1983). Godly choice: Puritan decision-making in seventeenth-century England. *Harvard Theological Review* 76: 307–34.

Dunn, J. (1985). *The politics of socialism.* Cambridge University Press.

Dworkin, R. (1978). *Taking rights seriously.* London: Duckworth.

(1981). What is equality? Part 1: Equality of welfare. *Philosophy and Public Affairs* 10: 185–246. Part 2: Equality of resources. Ibid., 283–345.

Eckhoff, T. (1974). *Justice: Its determinants in social interaction.* Rotterdam University Press.

Edgerton, R. B. (1985). *Rules, exceptions and social order.* Berkeley and Los Angeles: University of California Press.

Eekelaar, J. (1982). Children in divorce: Some further data. *Oxford Journal of Legal Studies* 2: 63–85.

Ellis, J. W. (1984). Evaluating the expert: Judicial expectations of expert opinion evidence in child placement adjudication. *Cardozo Law Review* 5: 587–634.

Ellsberg, D. (1961). Risk, ambiguity and the Savage axioms. *Quarterly Journal of Economics* 75: 643–69.

Elster, J. (1975). *Leibniz et la formation de l'esprit capitaliste*. Paris: Montaigne-Aubier.

(1983a). *Sour grapes*. Cambridge University Press.

(1983b). *Explaining technical change*. Cambridge University Press.

(1984). *Ulysses and the sirens*, rev. ed. Cambridge University Press.

(1985a). Sadder but wiser? Rationality and the emotions. *Social Science Information* 24: 375–406.

(1985b). Weakness of will and the free-rider problem. *Economics and Philosophy* 1: 231–65.

(1986a). Introduction to J. Elster (ed.), *Rational choice*, pp. 1–33. Oxford: Blackwell Publisher.

(1986b). Comments on Krouse and McPherson. *Ethics* 97, 146–53.

(1986c). Comments on van Parijs and van der Veen. *Theory and Society* 15, 709–22.

(ed.) (1986). *The multiple self*. Cambridge University Press.

(1988a). Is there (or should there be) a right to work? In A. Guttman (ed.), *Democracy and the welfare state*, pp. 53–78. Princeton, N.J.: Princeton University Press.

(1988b). Consequences of constitutional choice: Reflections on Tocqueville. In J. Elster and R. Slagstad (eds.), *Constitutionalism and democracy*, pp. 81–102. Cambridge University Press.

(1989). *The cement of society*. Cambridge University Press.

(forthcoming). Local justice and interpersonal comparisons. In J. Elster and J. Roemer (eds.), *Interpersonal comparisons of welfare*.

Elster, J. and Moene, K. O. (eds.) (1989). Introduction to *Alternatives to capitalism*, pp. 1–35. Cambridge University Press.

Elster, J. and Slagstad, R. (eds.) (1988). *Constitutionalism and democracy*. Cambridge University Press.

Elton, J. A. (1979). Parental reports of children's post-divorce adjustment. *Journal of Social Issues* 35: 126–39.

Ely, J. H. (1980). *Democracy and distrust*. Cambridge, Mass.: Harvard University Press.

Farber, H. (1980). An analysis of final-offer arbitration. *Journal of Conflict Resolution* 24: 683–705.

Farber, L.(1976). *Lying, despair, jealousy, envy, sex, suicide, drugs, and the good life*. New York: Basic Books.

Farrell, J. (1987). Information and the Coase theorem. *Journal of Economic Perspectives* 1(2): 113–30.

Federal jury selection, Wednesday, 20 March 1967, U.S. Senate Subcommittee on Improvements in the Judicial Machinery of the Committee of the Judiciary.

Feinberg, J. (1980). Noncomparative justice. In *Rights, justice and the bounds of liberty*, pp. 265–306. Princeton, N.J.: Princeton University Press.

Feller, W. (1968). *An introduction to probability theory and its applications*, 3d ed., vol. 1, New York: Wiley.

Festinger, L. (1957). *A theory of cognitive dissonance.* Stanford, Calif.: Stanford University Press.

(1964). *Conflict, decision and dissonance.* Stanford, Calif.: Stanford University Press.

Fienberg, S. (1971). Randomization and social affairs: The 1970 draft lottery. *Science* 171: 255–61.

Finlay, R. (1980). *Politics in Renaissance Venice.* London: Benn.

Fischhoff, B. (1983). Predicting frames. *Journal of Experimental Psychology: Learning, Memory and Cognition* 9: 103–16.

Fishburn, P. (1972). Even-chance lotteries in social choice. *Theory and Decision* 3: 18–40.

(1978). Acceptable social-choice lotteries. In H. W. Gottinger and W. Leinfellner (eds.), *Decision theory and social ethics,* pp. 133–52. Dordrecht: Reidel.

Fishkin, J. (1983). *Justice, equal opportunity and the family.* New Haven, Conn.: Yale University Press.

Folberg, J. (1984). Custody overview. In J. Folberg (ed.), *Joint custody and shared parenting,* pp. 3–10. Washington, D.C.: Bureau of National Affairs and the Association of Family and Conciliation Courts.

(ed.) (1984). *Joint custody and shared parenting.* Washington, D.C.: Bureau of National Affairs and the Association of Family and Conciliation Courts.

Føllesdal, D. (1982). The status of rationality assumptions in interpretation and in the explanation of action. *Dialectica* 36: 301–16.

Frank, R. (1985). *Choosing the right pond.* New York: Oxford University Press.

Frankfurt, H. G. (1971). Freedom of will and the concept of a person. *Journal of Philosophy* 68: 5–20.

Frazer, J. (1963). *The golden bough.* New York: Collier.

Freeman, J. R. and Snidal, D. (1982). Diffusion, development and democratization: Enfranchisement in Western Europe. *Canadian Journal of Political Science* 15, 299–329.

Freeman, M. A. (1983). *The rights and wrongs of children.* London: Pinter.

Freeman, R. B. and Medoff, J. L. (1984). *What do unions do?* New York: Basic Books.

Frey, R. G., ed. (1985). *Utility and rights.* Oxford: Blackwell Publisher.

Frohlich, N., Oppenheimer, J. and Eavey, C. (1987). Laboratory results on Rawls's distributive justice. *British Journal of Political Economy* 17: 1–21.

Galanter, M. (1981). Justice in many rooms: Private orderings and indigenous law. *Journal of Legal Pluralism* 19: 1–45.

Galasi, P. and Kertesi, G. (1987). The spread of bribery in a Soviet-type economy (unpublished manuscript).

Gardner, R. (1982). *Family evaluation in child custody litigation.* Cresskil, N.J.: Creative Therapeutics.

(1984). Joint custody is not for everyone. In J. Folberg (ed.), *Joint custody and shared parenting,* pp. 63–71. Washington, D.C.: Bureau of National Affairs and the Association of Family and Conciliation Courts.

Gataker, T. (1627). *On the nature and use of lots,* 2d ed. London.

Gauthier, D. (1986). *Morality by agreement.* New York: Oxford University Press.

Gibbard, A. (1973). Manipulation of voting schemes. *Econometrica* 41: 587–601.

(1977). Manipulation of voting schemes that mix voting with chance. *Econometrica* 45: 665–81.

222   *References*

Glover, J. (1977). *Causing deaths and saving lives*. Hardmondsworth: Penguin Books.
Goldstein, J., Freud, A. and Solnit, A. (1979a). *Beyond the best interests of the child*, new ed. New York: Free Press.
  (1979b). *Before the best interests of the child*. New York: Free Press.
Goldstein, J., Freud, A., Solnit, A. and Goldstein, S. (1986). *In the best interests of the child*. New York: Free Press.
Goldstine, H. (1972). *The computer from Pascal to von Neumann*. Princeton, N.J.: Princeton University Press.
Goldzband, M. G. (1982). *Consulting in child custody: An introduction to the ugliest litigation for mental-health professionals*. Lexington, Mass.: Lexington Books.
Goodwin, B. (1984). Justice and the lottery. *Political Studies* 32: 190–202.
Greely, H. (1977). The equality of allocation by lot. *Harvard Civil Rights–Civil Liberties Review* 12: 113–41.
Guggenheim, M. (1984). The right to be represented but not heard: Reflections on legal representation for children. *New York University Law Review* 59: 76–155.
Gullestad, S. and Tschudi, F. (1982). Labeling theories of mental illness. *Psychiatry and Social Sciences* 2: 213–26.
Gundersen, L. (1984). *Barneloven blir til*. Unpublished master's thesis in history, University of Bergen.
Gunn, C. (1984). *Workers' self-management in the United States*. Ithaca, N.Y.: Cornell University Press.
Habermas, J. (1982). *Zur Theorie des kommunikativen Handelns*. Frankfurt a.M.: Suhrkamp.
Hans, V. P. and Vidmar, N. (1986). *Judging the jury*. New York: Plenum Press.
Hansen, M. (1974). *The sovereignty of the people's court in Athens in the fourth century B.C. and the public action against unconstitutional proposals*. Odense University Press.
  (1979). *Embedsmændene*. Copenhagen: Museum Tusculanum.
  (1986). *The Athenian assembly*. Oxford: Blackwell Publisher.
Hapgood, F. (1975). Chances of a lifetime. *Working Papers for a New Society* 3: 37–42.
Harris, J. (1975). The survival lottery. *Philosophy* 50: 81–7.
Harris, R. J. and Joyce, M. A. (1980). What's fair? It depends on how you phrase the question. *Journal of Personality and Social Psychology* 80: 165–79.
Harsanyi, J. (1955). Cardinal welfare, individualistic ethics, and interpersonal comparisons of utility. *Journal of Political Economy* 63: 309–21.
  (1977a). *Rational behavior and bargaining equilibrium in games and social situations*. Cambridge University Press.
  (1977b). Rule utilitarianism and decision theory. *Erkenntnis* 11: 25–53.
Harvard Study Group (1967). On the draft. *Public Interest* 9: 93–9.
Hasofer, A. M. (1967). Random mechanisms in the Talmud. *Biometrika* 54: 316–21.
Haspel, A. (1985). Drilling for dollars: The federal oil-lease lottery program. *Regulation: American Enterprise Journal for Government and Society* 9 (July–August): 25–31.
Hayek, F. A. (1937). Economics and knowledge. *Economica* n.s. 13, 33–54.
  (1982). *Law, legislation and liberty*, vols. 1–3. London: Routledge & Kegan Paul.
Headlam, J. W. (1933). *Election by lot at Athens*. Cambridge University Press.

Heal, G. (1973). *The theory of economic planning*. Amsterdam: North-Holland.
Heiner, R. (1983). The origin of predictable behavior. *American Economic Review* 83: 560–95.
  (1988). The necessity of imperfect decision. *Journal of Economic Behavior and Organization* 10: 29–55.
Herrnstein, R. (1988). A behavioral alternative to utility maximization. In S. Maital (ed.), *Applied behavioral economics*, pp. 3–60. New York: New York University Press.
Herrnstein, R. and Vaughan, W. (1980). Melioration and behavioral allocation. In J. E. R. Staddon (ed.), *Limits to action: The allocation of individual behavior*, pp. 143–76. New York: Academic Press.
Herzfeld, M. (1980). Social tension and inheritance by lot in three Greek villages. *Anthropological Quarterly* 53: 91–100.
Hess, R. D. and Camara, K. A. (1979). Post-divorce family relationships as mediating factors in the consequences of divorce for children. *Journal of Social Issues* 35: 79–96.
Hey, J. D. (1981). Are optimal search rules reasonable? *Journal of Economic Behavior and Organization* 2: 47–70.
  (1982). Search for rules of search. *Journal of Economic Behavior and Organization* 3: 65–82.
Hoel, M. (1986). Employment and allocation effects of reducing the length of the workday. *Economica* 53: 75–85.
Hoffman, E. and Spitzer, M. (1985). Entitlements, rights and fairness: An experimental examination of subjects' concepts of distributive justice. *Journal of Legal Studies* 14: 159–97.
Hofstee, W. K. B. (1983). The case for compromise in educational selection and grading. In S. B. Anderson and J. S. Helmick (eds.), *On educational testing*, pp. 109–27. San Francisco: Jossey-Bass.
Hume, D. (1739). *A treatise of human nature*, ed. Selby-Bigge. New York: Oxford University Press 1960.
  (1963). *Essays: moral, political and literary*. New York: Oxford University Press.
Hylland, A. (forthcoming). Aggregation of interpersonal comparisons. In J. Elster and J. Roemer (eds.), *Interpersonal comparisons of welfare*.
Ireland, N. J. and Law, P. J. (1982). *The economics of labour-managed enterprises*. London: Croom Helm.
Janis, I. (1972). *Victims of group-think*. Boston: Houghton Mifflin.
Jay, P. (1980). The workers' cooperative economy. In A. Clayre (ed.), *The political economy of co-operation and participation*, pp. 9–45. New York: Oxford University Press.
Jensen, A. (1926). The representative method in practice. *Bulletin of the International Statistical Institute* 22: 381–439.
Johansen, L. (1977). *Lectures on macroeconomic planning*, vol. 1. Amsterdam: North-Holland.
  (1987). Queues (and 'rent-seeking') as non-cooperative games. In *Collected Works of Leif Johansen*, vol. 2, pp. 827–76. Amsterdam: North-Holland.
Jones, B. (1894). *Co-operative production*. Reprint, New York: Augustus Kelley (1968).
Kagan, J. (1984). *The nature of the child*. New York: Basic Books.
Kahneman, D., Knetsch, J. and Thaler, R. (1986). Fairness as a constraint on profit-seeking. *American Economic Review* 76: 728–41.

Kahneman, D. and Tversky, A. (1979). Prospect theory. *Econometrica* 47: 263–91.
 (1982a). Subjective probability: A judgment of representativeness. In D. Kahneman, P. Slovic and A. Tversky (eds.), *Judgment under uncertainty*, pp. 32–47. Cambridge University Press.
 (1982b). Variants of uncertainty. In D. Kahneman, P. Slovic, and A. Tversky (eds.), *Judgment under uncertainty*, pp. 509–20. Cambridge University Press.
 (1982c). The simulation heuristic. In D. Kahneman, P. Slovic, and A. Tversky (eds.), *Judgment under uncertainty*, pp. 201–8. Cambridge University Press.
Kahneman, D., Slovic, P. and Tversky, A. (eds.) (1982). *Judgment under uncertainty*. Cambridge University Press.
Kalai, E. (1985). Solutions to the bargaining problem. In L. Hurwicz, D. Schmeidler and H. Sonnenstein (eds.), *Social goals and social organization: Essays in memory of Elisha Pazner*, pp. 77–106. Cambridge University Press.
Katz, A. (1973). Process design for selection of hemodialysis and organ transplant recipients. *Buffalo Law Review* 22: 373–418.
Kay, J. A. (1986). The franchise factor in the rise of the English Labour Party. *English Historical Review* 91: 723–52.
Kesselman, J. R. (1978). Work relief programs in the great depression. In J. L. Palmer (ed.), *Creating jobs: Public employment programs and wage subsidies*, pp. 153–229. Washington, D.C.: Brookings Institution.
Keynes, J. M. (1936). *The general theory of employment, interest and money*. London: Macmillan Press.
Kilner, J. F. (1981). A moral allocation of scarce lifesaving medical resources. *Journal of Religious Ethics* 9: 245–71.
Kishlansky, M. (1986). *Parliamentary selection*. Cambridge University Press.
Kohlberg, L. (1981). *The philosophy of moral development*. New York: Harper & Row.
Kolm, S.-C. (1980). Psychanalyse et théorie des choix. *Social Science Information* 19: 269–340.
Krabbe, O. (1944). Om lodtrækning i fortid og nutid [On lotteries in past and present.] *Juristen* 157–75.
Krouse, R. and McPherson, M. (1986). A 'mixed' property regime: Equality and liberty in a market economy. *Ethics* 97: 119–38.
Laqueur, W. (1980). *The terrible secret*. Boston: Little, Brown.
Lea, H. C. (1973). *The ordeal*. University of Pennsylvania Press.
 (1974). *The duel and the oath*. University of Pennsylvania Press.
Leach, E. (1954). *Political systems of Highland Burma*. London: Bell.
Leibniz, G. W. F. (1875–90), *Die philosophische Schriften*, ed. C. J. Gerhard. Berlin.
Leiman, S. Z. (1983). Therapeutic homicide: A philosophic and halakhic critique of Harris's survival lottery. *Journal of Medicine and Philosophy* 8: 257–67.
Lerner, M. J. and Miller, D. T. (1978). Just world research and the attribution process. *Psychological Bulletin* 85: 1030–51.
Levi, I. (1974). On indeterminate probabilities. *Journal of Philosophy* 71: 391–418.
 (1982). Direct inference and randomization. *PSA* 2: 447–63.
 (1986). *Hard choices*. Cambridge University Press.
Lévi-Strauss, C. (1960). *La pensée sauvage*. Paris: Plon.
Lewinsohn, P., Mischel, W., Chaplin, W. and Barton, R. (1980). Social competence and depression: The role of illusory self-perception. *Journal of Abnormal Psychology* 89: 203–12.

Lewis, D. (1989). The punishment that leaves something to chance. *Philosophy and Public Affairs* 18: 53–67.

Lichtenstein, S., Fischhoff, B. and Phillips, L. D. (1982). Calibration of probabilities: The state of the art to 1980. In D. Kahneman, P. Slovic and A. Tversky (eds.), *Judgment under uncertainty*, pp. 306–34. Cambridge University Press.

Lindbeck, A. (1976). Stabilization policy in open economies with endogenous politicians. *American Economic Review: Papers and Preceedings* 66: 1–19.

Lindblom, J. (1964). Lot-casting in the Old Testament. *Vetus Testamentum* 12: 164–78.

Lipsey, R. G. and Lancaster, K. (1956). The general theory of the second best. *Review of Economic Studies* 24: 11–32.

Loevinger, J. (1976). *Ego development*. San Francisco: Jossey-Bass.

Loewenstein, G. (1987). Frames of mind in intertemporal choice. *Management Science* 34: 200–14.

Loomes, G. and Sugden, R. (1982). Regret theory. *Economic Journal* 92: 805–24.

Lopes, L. (1986). Doing the impossible: A note on the induction and experience of randomness. In H. R. Arles and K. R. Hammond (eds.), *Judgment and decision-making*, pp. 720–38. Cambridge University Press.

Löwy, I. (1986). Tissue groups and cadaver kidney-sharing. *International Journal of Technology Assessment in Health Care* 2: 195–218.

Luce, R. D. and Raiffa, H. (1957). *Games and decisions*. New York: Wiley.

MacDowell, D. M. (1978). *The law in classical Athens*. Ithaca, N.Y.: Cornell University Press.

Machina, M. (1983). Generalized expected utility analysis and the nature of observed violations of the independence axiom. In B. T. Stigum and F. Wenstøp (eds.), *Foundations of utility and risk theory with applications*, pp. 263–93. Dordrecht: Reidel.

(1987). Choice under uncertainty. *Journal of Economic Perspectives* 1(1): 121–54.

Maidment, S. (1984). *Child custody and divorce*. London: Croom Helm.

Marsily, G. de et al. (1977). Nuclear waste disposal: Can the geologist guarantee isolation? *Science* 197: 519–27.

Mashaw, J. L. (1977). The Supreme Court's due process calculus for administrative adjudication in *Mathews v. Eldridge:* Three factors in search of a theory. *University of Chicago Law Review* 44: 28–59.

(1985). *Due process in the administrative state*. New Haven, Conn.: Yale University Press.

Mavrodes, G. (1984). Choice and chance in the allocation of medical resources. *Journal of Religious Ethics* 12: 97–115.

McGovney, D. O. (1949). *The American suffrage medley*. University of Chicago Press.

Meade, J. E. (1964). *Efficiency, equality, and the ownership of property*. London: Allen & Unwin.

(1972). The theory of labour-managed firms and of profit-sharing. *Economic Journal* 82: 402–28.

(1980). Labour co-operatives, participation and value-added sharing. In A. Clayre (ed.), *The political economy of co-operation and participation*, pp. 89–108. New York: Oxford University Press.

Melton, G. B. and Saks, M. J. (1985). The law as an instrument of socialization and social structure. In G. B. Melton (ed.), *The law as a behavioral instrument:*

Nebraska symposium on motivation, pp. 237–79. Lincoln: University of Nebraska Press.

Menzel, P. T. (1983). *Medical costs, moral choices*. New Haven, Conn.: Yale University Press.

Messick, D. M. and Sentis, K. (1983). Fairness, preference, and fairness biases. In D. M. Messick and K. Cook (eds.), *Equity Theory*, pp. 61–94. New York: Praeger.

Middleton, E. (1986). Some testable implications of a preference for subjective novelty. *Kyklos* 39: 397–418.

Midgaard, K. (1980). On the significance of language and a richer concept of rationality. In L. Lewin and E. Vedung (eds.), *Politics as rational action*, pp. 83–97. Dordrecht: Reidel.

Miller, D. (1981). Market neutrality and the failure of co-operatives. *British Journal of Political Science* 11, 309–29.

Mnookin, R. (1973). Foster care – in whose best interest? *Harvard Educational Review* 43: 599–638.

  (1975). Child custody adjudication: Judicial functions in the face of indeterminacy. *Law and Contemporary Problems* 39: 226–93.

Mnookin, R. and Kornhauser, L. (1979). Bargaining in the shadow of the law. *Yale Law Journal* 88: 950–97.

Montmort, R. de (1713). *Essai d'analyse sur les jeux de hasard*, 2d ed. Paris.

Moore, O. K. (1957). Divination: A new perspective. *American Anthropologist* 59: 69–74.

Mueller, D. (1979). *Public choice*. Cambridge University Press.

Mulgan, R. G. (1984). Lot as a democratic device of selection. *Review of Politics* 46: 539–60.

Musante, L. (1985). The effects of type and favorability of verdict on perceptions of justice. *Journal of Applied Social Psychology* 14: 448–60.

Musetto, A. P. (1982). *Dilemmas in child custody*. Chicago: Nelson-Hall.

Nagel, T. (1979). *Mortal questions*. Cambridge University Press.

Najemy, J. (1982). *Corporatism and consensus in Florentine electoral politics, 1280–1400*. Chapel Hill: University of North Carolina Press.

Nakell, B. and Hardy, K. A. (1987). *The arbitrariness of the death penalty*. Philadelphia: Temple University Press.

Nanacakos, E. (1984). Joint custody as a fundamental right. In J. Folberg (ed.), *Joint custody and shared parenting*, pp. 223–34. Washington, D.C.: Bureau of National Affairs and the Association of Family and Conciliation Courts.

Neely, R. (1986). The hidden cost of divorce: Barter in the courts. *New Republic*, 10 February 1986.

Nelson, R. and Winter, S. (1982). *An evolutionary theory of economic change*. Cambridge, Mass.: Harvard University Press.

Neurath, O. (1913). Die verrirten des Cartesius und das Auxiliarmotiv: Zur Psychologie des Entschlusses. Cited after the translation in Otto Neurath, *Philosophical Papers, 1913–1946*, pp. 1–12, Dordrecht: Reidel (1983).

Nisbett, R. and Ross, L.(1981). *Human inference: Strategies and shortcomings of social judgment*. Englewood Cliffs, N.J.: Prentice Hall.

Nottarp, H. (1956). *Gottesurteilsstudien*. Munich: Kösel Verlag.

Nozick, R. (1974). *Anarchy, state and utopia*. New York: Basic Books.

Oliver, P., Marwell, G. and Teixeira, R. (1985). A theory of the critical mass. I.

Interdependence, group heterogeneity and the production of collective action. *American Journal of Sociology* 91: 522–56.

Ordeshook, P. (1986). *Game theory and political theory.* Cambridge University Press.

Owen, G. and Grofman, B. (1984). To vote or not to vote. *Public Choice* 42: 311–25.

Page, B. (1983). *Who gets what from government?* Berkeley and Los Angeles: University of California Press.

van Parijs, P. and van der Veen, R. (1986a). A capitalist road to communism. *Theory and Society* 15: 635–56.

(1986b). Reply to six critics. *Theory and Society* 15: 723–58.

Pateman, C. (1970). *Participation and democratic theory.* Cambridge University Press.

Polanyi, K. (1962). *Personal knowledge.* New York: Harper.

Pope, M. (forthcoming). *Democracy by random selection.*

Przeworski, A. (1988). Democracy as the contingent outcome of conflict. In J. Elster and R. Slagstad(eds.), *Constitutionalism and democracy*, pp. 59–80. Cambridge University Press.

Putterman, L. (1982). Some behavioral perspectives on the dominance of hierarchical over democratic forms of enterprise. *Journal of Economic Behavior and Organization* 3: 139–60.

Quattrone, G. and Tversky, A. (1986). Self-deception and the voter's illusion. In J. Elster(ed.), *The multiple self*, pp. 35–58. Cambridge University Press.

Rapoport, A. (1966). *Two-person game theory.* Ann Arbor: University of Michigan Press.

Rawls, J. (1971). *A theory of justice.* Cambridge, Mass.: Harvard University Press.

(1985). Justice as fairness: Political not metaphysical. *Philosophy and Public Affairs* 14:223–51.

Rescher, N. (1976). The allocation of exotic lifesaving therapy. In S. Gorowitz et al. (eds.), *Moral problems in medicine*, pp. 522–35. Englewood Cliffs, N.J.: Prentice Hall.

Riker, W. (1982). *Liberalism against populism.* San Francisco: Freeman.

Roemer, J. (1985). Equality of talent. *Economics and Philosophy* 2, 151–88.

(1988). Glimpses of China's economic reform (unpublished manuscript).

Rogowski, R. (1981). Representation in political theory and in law. *Ethics* 91: 395–430.

Rosenblatt, J. and Filliben, J. (1971). Randomization and the draft lottery. *Science* 171: 306–8.

Rosner, F. (1986). *Modern medicine and Jewish ethics.* New York: Yeshiva University Press.

Roth, A. (1979). *Axiomatic bargaining theory.* New York: Springer.

Rubin, S. and Pepau, A. (1973). Belief in a just world and reaction to another's lot: A study of the participants in the national draft lottery. *Journal of Social Issues* 29: 73–93.

Rubinstein, A. (1982). Perfect equilibrium in a bargaining model. *Econometrica* 50: 97–109.

Scarce medical resources. (1969). *Columbia Law Review* 69: 621–92.

Schelling, T. C. (1978). *Micromotives and macrobehavior.* New York: Norton.

(1984). *Choice and consequence.* Cambridge, Mass.: Harvard University Press.

Schlicht, E. (1984). Cognitive dissonance in economics. *Schriften des Vereins für*

Sozialpolitik, Gesellschaft für Wirtschafts- und Sozialwissenschaften, Neue Folge 141: 61–81.

Schulmann, J. and Pitt, V. (1984). Second thoughts on joint child custody. In J. Folberg (ed.), *Joint custody and shared parenting,* pp. 209–22. Washington, D.C.: Bureau of National Affairs and the Association of Family and Conciliation Courts.

Schumpeter, J. (1961). *Capitalism, socialism and democracy.* London: Allen & Unwin.

Sejersted, F. (1988). Democracy and the rule of law. In J. Elster and R. Slagstad (eds.), *Constitutionalism and democracy,* pp. 131–52. Cambridge University Press.

    (1982). *Choice, measurement and welfare.* Oxford: Blackwell Publisher.

Sen, A. and Williams, B. A. O. (1982). Introduction to A. Sen and B. A. O. Williams (eds.), *Utilitarianism and beyond,* pp. 1–22. Cambridge University Press.

Seymour, C. and Frary, D. O. (1918). *How the world votes,* vols. 1 and 2. Springfield, Mass.: Nichols.

Shepard, R. (1964). On subjectively optimum selection among multiattribute alternatives. In M. W. Shelley and G. L. Bryan (eds.), *Human judgment and optimality,* pp. 257–80. New York: Wiley.

Sher, G. (1980). What makes a lottery fair? *Nous* 14: 203–16.

    (1987). *Desert.* Princeton, N.J.: Princeton University Press.

Simpson, A. W. (1984). *Cannibalism and the common law.* University of Chicago Press.

Singer, P. (1977). Utility and the survival lottery. *Philosophy* 52: 218–22.

Skinner, G. W. (1977). Cities and the hierarchy of local systems. In G. W. Skinner (ed.), *The city in late imperial China,* pp. 275–352. Stanford, Calif.: Stanford University Press.

Smith, L. (1980). *Foreldremyndighet og barnerett.* Oslo: Universitetsforlaget.

Snidal, D. (1986). The game *theory* of international politics. In K. A. Oye (ed.), *Cooperation under anarchy,* pp. 25–57. Princeton University Press.

Staddon, J.E.R. (1983). *Adaptive behavior and learning.* Cambridge University Press.

    (1987). Optimality theory and behavior. In J. Dupré (ed.), *The latest on the best,* pp. 179–98. Cambridge, Mass.: MIT Press.

Staveley, E. S. (1972). *Greek and Roman voting and elections.* London: Thames & Hudson.

Steinman, S. (1984). Joint custody: What we know, what we have yet to learn, and the judicial and legislative implications. In J. Folberg (ed.), *Joint custody and shared parenting,* pp. 111–27. Washington, D.C.: Bureau of National Affairs and the Association of Family and Conciliation Courts.

Still, J. W. (1981). Political equality and election systems. *Ethics* 91: 375–94.

Stinchcombe, A. (1983). *Economic sociology.* New York: Academic Press.

Stouffer, S. et al. (1949). *The American soldier.* Princeton, N.J.: Princeton University Press.

Sturgill, G. (1975). Le tirage au sort de la milice en 1726 ou le début de la décadence de la royauté en France. *Revue Historique des Armées* 31: 26–38.

Summers, R. S. (1974). Evaluating and improving legal processes: A plea for process values. *Cornell Law Review* 60: 1–52.

Sunstein, C. (1986). Legal interference with private preferences. *University of Chicago Law Review* 53: 1129–74.

Suppes, P. (1984). *Probabilistic metaphysics.* Oxford: Blackwell Publisher.
Sutton, J. (1986). Non-cooperative bargaining theory: An introduction. *Review of Economic Studies* 53: 709–24.
Thaler, R. (1980). Towards a positive theory of consumer choice. *Journal of Economic Behavior and Organization* 1: 39–60.
  (1983). The mirages of public policy. *Public Interest* 73: 61–74.
Thibaut, J. and Walker, L. (1978). A theory of procedure. *California Law Review* 66: 541–66.
Thomas, K. (1973). *Religion and the decline of magic.* Harmondsworth: Penguin Books.
Thompson, E. P. (1968). *The making of the English working class.* Harmondsworth: Penguin Books.
Tocqueville, A. de (1952). *L'ancien regime et la révolution,* vol. 1. Paris: Gallimard (Edition des Oeuvres Complètes).
  (1953). *L'ancien regime et la révolution,* vol. 2. Paris: Gallimard (Edition des Oeuvres Complètes).
  (1969). *Democracy in America.* New York: Anchor Books.
Tversky, A. (1987). Conflict under decision (unpublished manuscript).
Tversky, A. and Kahneman, D. (1974). Judgment under uncertainty. *Science* 185: 1124–30.
  (1981). The framing of decisions and the psychology of choice. *Science* 211: 453–58.
  (1987). Rational choice and the framing of decisions. In R. M. Hogarth and M. W. Reder (eds.), *Rational choice,* pp. 67–94. University of Chicago Press.
Ullmann-Margalit, E. (1977). *The emergence of norms.* New York: Oxford University Press.
  (1983). On presumption. *Journal of Philosophy* 80: 143–63.
  (1985). Opting: The case of 'big' decisions (unpublished manuscript).
Ullmann-Margalit, E. and Morgenbesser, S. (1977). Picking and choosing. *Social Research* 44: 757–85.
Vaughan, W. and Herrnstein, R. (1987). Stability, melioration, and natural selection. In L. Green and J. Kagel (eds.), *Advances in behavioral economics,* vol. 1, pp. 185–215. Norwood, N.J.: Ablex.
Veyne, P. (1976). *Le pain et le cirque.* Paris: Editions du Seuil.
Wallerstein, J. (1985). The overburdened child: Some long-term consequences of divorce. *Columbia Journal of Law and Social Problems* 19: 165–83.
Wallerstein, J. S. and Kelly, J. (1980). *Surviving the breakup.* New York: Basic Books.
Weber, M. (1985). *The Protestant ethic and the spirit of capitalism.* New York: Scribner.
Weitzman, L. (1983). *The marriage contract.* New York: Free Press.
  (1985). *The divorce revolution.* New York: Free Press.
Weizsäcker, C. C. von (1971). Notes on endogenous change of tastes. *Journal of Economic Theory* 3: 345–72.
Wicklund, R. and Brehm, J. (1976). *Perspectives on cognitive dissonance.* Hillsdale, N.J.: Erlbaum.
Williams, B. A. O. (1973). Deciding to believe. In *Problems of the self,* pp. 136–41. Cambridge University Press.
  (1981). *Moral luck.* Cambridge University Press.
Williamson, C. (1960). *American suffrage from property to democracy, 1760–1860.* Princeton, N.J.: Princeton University Press.

Williamson, O. (1975). *Markets and hierarchies.* New York: Free Press.

Wilms, D. C. (1974). Georgia's land lottery of 1832. *Chronicles of Oklahoma* 52:52–60.

Winick, B. J. (1981). Legal limitations on correctional therapy and research. *Minnesota Law Review* 65: 331–42.

Winston, G. (1980). Addiction and backsliding: A theory of compulsive consumption. *Journal of Economic Behavior and Organization* 1: 295–324.

Wolfinger, R. E. and Rosenstone, S. J. (1980). *Who votes?* New Haven, Conn.: Yale University Press.

Yaari, M. and Bar-Hillel, M. (1984). On dividing justly. *Social Choice and Welfare* 1: 1–25.

Zabell, S. (1976). Review of N. L. Rabinovitch, Probability and statistical inference in ancient and medieval Jewish literature. *Journal of the American Statistical Association* 71: 996–8.

(1987). Symmetry and its discontents (unpublished manuscript).

Zeckhauser, R. (1969). Majority rules with lotteries on alternatives. *Quarterly Journal of Economics* 83: 696–703.

Zeisel, H. (1969). Dr. Spock and the case of the vanishing women jurors. *University of Chicago Law Review* 36: 1–18.

(1971). And then there were none. *University of Chicago Law Review* 38: 710–24.

INDEX

Aasness, J., 12
act versus rule, 26, 144
Ainslie, G., 18
Allen, F., 101
allocation of scarce resources, 2, 67–78
Aquinas, 51, 52
Augustine, 52

bargaining, 156, 164–70
Borges, J. L., 67, 90
Bowlby, J., 133
Broome, J. 114–15
Bruni, L., 85, 111

central planning, 178, 180, 199–200
Chambers, D., 153
child custody principles 123–74
  best interests of the child, 132, 134–50
  fault-based presumption, 130–1, 152
  joint custody, 128–9, 163
  maternal preference, 131–2, 159
  parental needs and rights, 139–43,
    154–5
  parental preference, 130
  primary-caregiver preference, 133, 152–
    3, 159–62
  random choice of custodial parent,
    163–72
  status quo presumption, 133, 153–4
Chinese economic reforms, 183, 192–4,
  197–200
Coons, J., 99, 102, 151–2
costs of decision making, 15–17, 26, 73,
  75, 107–8, 145–8

democratic politics, 177–8, 196, 211–12
  in Athens, 80
  in Florence, 81–5
Denning, Lord, 131, 139
Descartes, 116, 121–2
discrimination, 184–5

draft lottery, 42, 45–6, 56n, 64, 68
Dworkin, R., 49n, 141n, 176, 203, 210

excess of will, 19–20
expected utility theory, 23–4, 30–31
externalities, 186–7

fairness, 44, 113–15
feminism, 125, 132–3
framing, 23–4, 33
Freud, A., 126
Freud, S., 17–18
functional explanation, 56, 133n

Gataker, T., 36, 37–8, 44, 52, 64, 104, 115
Goldstein, J., 126
Greene, G., 67, 78

Habermas, J., 90n, 176
Harris, J., 112
Harsanyi, J., 9
Hayek, F., 175, 202
Herrnstein, R., 32
Hobbes, T., 71
Hume, D., 4
Hylland, A., 12, 42, 109n, 147n
hyperrationality, 11, 17, 25–6, 121–2

inadequacy, *see* rational-choice theory
incentive effects, 39, 69, 99, 110–13, 139,
  156–7, 212
indeterminacy, *see* rational-choice theory
irrationality
  of beliefs, 22–3, 24–6
  of desires, 20–2, 23–4
  of individual action, 17–18
  of political decisions, 194–202

Jackson, S., 66
Johansen, L., 61–2

231